across the tracks

MEXICAN-AMERICANS IN A TEXAS CITY

THE HOGG FOUNDATION RESEARCH SERIES

Wayne H. Holtzman, Editor

Tornadoes over Texas by Harry Estill Moore
Electrical Stimulation of the Brain edited by Daniel E. Sheer
Inkblot Perception and Personality by Wayne H. Holtzman, Joseph S. Thorpe, Jon D. Swartz, and E. Wayne Herron
Changing Parental Attitudes through Group Discussion by Carl F. Hereford
Tomorrow's Parents by Bernice Milburn Moore and Wayne H. Holtzman

Photo courtesy of John Avant.

A *chicano* family of Mexiquito.

across the tracks

MEXICAN-AMERICANS IN A TEXAS CITY

Arthur J. Rubel

Published for the Hogg Foundation for Mental Health
by the University of Texas Press, Austin & London

The warmth and understanding of my wife, Phyllis, contributed substantially to the success of field work in New Lots; she and I share many gratifying friendships with residents on both sides of its tracks. This work is dedicated to her and to our daughter, Laura.

FOREWORD

The great culture area of Latin America begins in the United States Southwest, including the state of Texas. Although an ethnic minority in this region, the Latin Americans form but one tiny segment of the largest and fastest growing population in the Western Hemisphere. The fact that they form only 15 percent of the Texas population is a product of the drawing of historical boundaries. Today they increasingly fill the cities as well as the rural regions.

It has been a repeated failing of many North Americans, especially those in the southwestern border states, to claim great interest in our neighbors to the south, but to studiously ignore the fact that some of those neighbors literally live next door and are citizens of the United States. Part of the reason surely lies in the fact that many of the Latin Americans are subjected to severe educational inequalities and consequent economic inferiority. They often speak with an accent and are set off socially and culturally from the Anglo population.

The author of this volume entered the neighborhood of Mexiquito with the tools of the antropologist. He lived there for two years, spending his time trying to observe, discuss, and participate enough so that he could begin to describe life as the Latin American population saw it. He wanted to describe their manner of living in a systematic way in order to better reveal the logic and coherence that exists within the life of the United States citizens of Mexican heritage. Professor Rubel is not a native Texan, although the state is now fortunate enough to count him among its residents. It is however, precisely the virtue of the anthropological approach that a person who is at the outset a total stranger, through diligent, skilled, and percepive work, can uncover the structure of a society.

It is hoped that this work by Professor Rubel will be but one in a growing series of studies that stem from work sponsored by The University of Texas in the problems that face this population. It can hardly be a matter of local pride that the descendants of the first

Europeans to conquer Texas are now to be counted among the state's most poorly educated, economically depressed citizens.

Professor William Madsen conceived the Hidalgo County Project, of which the present study is a major product; the Hogg Foundation for Mental Health had the vision to support the study; and Professor Rubel had the skill, imagination, sensitivity, and devotion to undertake this study and carry it through to a meaningful conclusion. It is, in a sense, now up to the reader, of whatever cultural heritage, to look seriously into the manner and structure of life of this most important sector of our population.

RICHARD N. ADAMS
Department of Anthropology, and
Institute of Latin American Studies
The University of Texas

PREFACE

(The *chicanos* of the lower Rio Grande Valley often tell on themselves the following narrative, and others similar to it.)

God formed the earth. And after He had rested for seven days He decided to place people on the earth.

God bent over to pick up some mud. He fashioned the mud into a ball and threw it to earth. When the ball of mud landed on earth, the Chinese people sprang up and began the planting of rice.

God formed another ball of mud, and this, also, He threw at earth. When the ball of mud hit earth, the French people sprang up and went about their business of planting grapes.

God formed another ball and threw it at the earth. When this landed on earth, the Americans sprang up and went about their business of making money. God formed all the people of earth in this fashion and then sat back to rest from His labors.

After He had rested for some time, He was approached by the Angel Gabriel. The Angel Gabriel said to God, "God, may I speak with you for a moment?" And God told the Angel Gabriel to speak. Then the Angel whispered into God's ear, "God, haven't you forgotten something?" God thought and thought, and finally He recalled that He had forgotten to form the Mexican people.

Then God bent over and picked up some mud which He formed into a ball. He threw the ball of mud to earth. When the ball of mud hit earth, the Mexicans jumped up with fists raised and cocked, dancing on one foot and then the other, they shouted belligerently, "Who pushed me? Who pushed me?"

ACKNOWLEDGMENTS

Research in New Lots was made possible by the financial generosity and the encouragement of the Hogg Foundation for Mental Health at The University of Texas. I am indebted to the Hogg Foundation for its support of field research and, later, for a Summer Research Fellowship, which permitted me to devote full time to final revisions of this volume. I am also indebted to the Research Fund of the University of North Carolina at Greensboro for assistance in the preparation of *Across the Tracks*.

Between 1957 and 1959 I participated as a research associate in the Hidalgo County Project, which was sponsored by the Hogg Foundation for Mental Health. I acknowledge with gratitude the encouragement of Professor William Madsen, who conceived and directed the Project. Without the assistance and continuous encouragement of the Hidalgo County Health Unit, under the direction of David M. Cowgill, M.D., this research would not have been possible.

Across the Tracks represents a revision of a doctoral dissertation directed by John J. Honigmann. This dissertation was prepared during the tenure of a Pre-Doctoral Research Fellowship from the National Institute of Mental Health (MF11, 816). Professor Honigmann's suggestions and thoughtful criticisms helped clarify many of the analyses on the following pages. I am indebted to him, also, for organizing a seminar on "The Atomistic Society," during which comments by the participants proved helpful in clarifying some of the arguments on these pages.

Richard N. Adams, Wayne Holtzman, Harriet J. Kupferer, William Madsen, Duane G. Metzger, Ralph C. Patrick, and Benjamin Paul have each patiently considered, commented on, and constructively criticized various drafts of this work. Needless to say, any remaining defects are solely the responsibility of the author.

Finally, the people of the small city of New Lots, particularly the neighborhood of Mexiquito, made possible this endeavor. To say that they cooperated in every possible way is not enough. Hopefully, this volume meets the wish expressed by residents of Mexiquito that someday someone would write an objective, yet sympathetic, account of their way of life. If these pages do satisfy their wish it will be but small repayment for the kind hospitality, assistance, and friendship the *chicanos* of Mexiquito extended to me and my family.

For permission to quote from works under copyright, acknowledgment and thanks are due the following publishers:

The Macmillan Company for quotations from *The Moral Basis of a Backward Society*, by Edward Banfield (copyright 1958 by The Free Press).

The University of Chicago Press for quotations from *The People of Aritama*, by Gerardo and Alicia Reichel-Dolmatoff (copyright 1961 by Gerardo and Alicia Reichel-Dolmatoff).

The University of Pennsylvania Press for quotations from *Culture and Experience*, by A. Irving Hallowell (copyright 1955 by University of Pennsylvania Press).

Further acknowledgment is made for permission to quote from the following journals and bulletins:

Agricultural History for "Agricultural Histoy of the Lower Rio Grande Valley Region," by Edwin J. Foscue (March, 1934).

American Anthropologist for "The Dyadic Contract: A Model for the Social Structure of a Mexican Peasant Village," by George M. Foster (December, 1961).

Texas Agricultural Experiment Station, Texas A&M University, *Bulletin 950* for *Incomes of Migratory Agricultural Workers*, by William H. Metzler and Frederick O. Sargent (March, 1960).

Appreciation is expressed to Professor LeRoy P. Graf for permission to quote from his unpublished doctoral dissertation, "The Economic History of the Lower Rio Grande Valley: 1820–1875," and to Jovita González Mireles for permission to quote from her unpublished masters thesis, "Social Life in Cameron, Starr, and Zapata Counties."

CONTENTS

LIST OF ILLUSTRATIONS

LIST OF TABLES

INTRODUCTION

This book is about the way of life followed by Americans of Mexican descent who live in a small city in the lower Rio Grande Valley of South Texas.[1] In this city, which I will call New Lots, almost the entire Mexican-American population lives in a discrete neighborhood, which they have named Mexiquito—little Mexico.[2] Because one cannot fully understand life in the Mexiquito neighborhood unless account is taken of the Anglo-Americans residing in this city's other neighborhood—across the tracks in "American town"—it will be necessary to make frequent reference to the Anglo mode of living.

The people of Mexiquito are not by any means untraveled. A great number of the residents of this Spanish-speaking neighborhood are recent immigrants from rural Mexico, while the remainder are descendants of the original Spanish and Mexican settlers, who began colonization of this region in the middle of the eighteenth century. Today these Mexican-Americans travel up and down the lower Rio Grande Valley, across the international border into northern Mexico, and as far away as North Dakota and Virginia. Mexiquito is home only between December and April for many of those who are agricultural migrant laborers and spend the remainder of the year working in northern crops. Nevertheless, despite a wide acquaintance with the United States and the northern reaches of Mexico, the people of Mexiquito consider this neighborhood their home and fully identify themselves with the society, economy, and

[1] Unless otherwise noted, the present refers to the period August, 1957–August, 1959.

[2] With the exception of Mexiquito, all places mentioned will be provided fictitious names to protect those who aided so willingly in this research endeavor.

history of the lower Rio Grande Valley. "The Valley," as it is popularly called, comprises the South Texas counties of Starr, Hidalgo, Cameron, and Willacy.

Goals of This Study

These pages were written with three goals in mind. The first was to provide an account of the way of life of Americans of Mexican descent who live in South Texas. Previous to the research on which this volume is based, there had been curiously little study of the people along the border.[3] It is true that there was a significant literature describing the Spanish-speaking Americans of Colorado and New Mexico, but the extent to which our understanding of those groups could be generalized to the Mexican-Americans of Texas was an open question, especially when one took into account the substantial contact which the Texans, unlike the others, maintained with their kinsmen and friends in northern Mexico. In many ways, the Mexican-Americans of South Texas were a mobile group. Here, as elsewhere in this nation and in other parts of the world, it was becoming increasingly evident that the movement of rural peoples to cities was a social phenomenon of considerable significance. Despite the acknowledged importance of this population movement, lamentably little was known about the manner in which those who left the country for the city adapted themselves to their new environment. One of the major purposes of this research, then, was to understand the social life of Mexican-Americans who had recently settled in a small city.

The second goal was to reveal the frame of reference used by Mexican-Americans as they coped with health problems. This interest was, in part, spurred by a request from Dr. David Cowgill, director of the Hidalgo County Health Department, for information on traditional beliefs and behavior which impeded Mexican-Americans in taking full advantage of professional health services. One of the more exciting consequences of this interest was discovering the extent to which problems of illness were intimately linked with

[3] A notable exception was the work of Ozzie Simmons "*Anglo-Americans and Mexican-Americans in South Texas,*" which was made available to me in a microfilm copy. An article based on these same data was subsequently published by Simmons in 1961: "The Mutual Images and Expectations of Anglo-Americans and Mexican-Americans," *Daedalus* (Spring, 1961), pp. 286–299.

other aspects of the social and belief systems of this group. A full discussion of beliefs and behavior associated with illness appears in Chapter 8.

After all the data had been gathered and the preliminary analysis begun, my curiosity was piqued by the readily apparent prominence of anxiety and disaffection associated with interpersonal relationships outside the immediate family. A parable, one of several which were circulating in Mexiquito, illustrates the last point.

Once, long ago in Mexico, a pastor was tending his sheep while he watched a pot in which he was boiling milk. He noted that the lid rose and fell, and surmised the connection between the movement of the lid and the steam inside. That is how the steam engine was first invented. But the pastor was quickly killed by his neighbors, who were envious of his discovery. Thus, Mexicans will always be poor and ignorant, and Americans will be educated and rich.

Neighbors are against one, it is asserted, and one's own good fortune only excites their envy and hostility. Those emotions are expressed by such recurrent statements as: "People don't want to see you get ahead, that's the way of *la raza*" (Mexican-Americans). Another frequently heard comment maintains that "Invidiousness is all around one; you can't improve your lot without *la gente* working against you." Also, "I don't know what it is about *la raza* but you can't work together with anyone." These and other similar citations from the everyday conversation of Mexican-Americans in Mexiquito describe the qualities which they, themselves, attribute to social relations. An effort to explain why anxiety and disaffection should be so salient in the lives of these people constitutes the third aim of this book.

To assist in the organization of the descriptive data and to help explain the prominence of anxiety and disaffection the concept of "social system" has been utilized. The social system is a network of relationships which attach members of a society to one another. It is a logical construct built upon observations of the patterns in which individuals and groups in a society interact with one another in a meaningful fashion. "Social system," in this book, then, refers to the network of relationships which attach the residents of Mexiquito to one another and to others of the lower Rio Grande Valley.[4]

[4] A. R. Radcliffe-Brown, *Structure and Function in Primitive Society*, p. 199.

Methods of Collecting Data

As a prerequisite to a discussion of Mexiquito and its people, some mention must be made of the manner in which these data were gathered. Three methods of field work were relied upon in Mexiquito, each complementing the other. They were participant observation, use of the key informant, and open-ended questionnaires.

Greatest reliance was placed on the technique of participant observation. In Mexiquito the close association between the observer and his subjects, the face-to-face personal relationship, proved to be a technique almost as valuable in this admittedly complex society as it is in simpler societies. Nevertheless, it quickly became quite clear that participant observation would have to be supplemented by other methods in order to insure an adequate representation of all segments of Mexiquito's populace.

My first ten days in New Lots were devoted to making acquaintanceships with the people of Mexiquito and, to a lesser extent, with those of the Anglo-American neighborhood. I walked along every street in the city and, on one pretext or another, entered every store. In the larger shops charge accounts were opened, while in the smaller establishments cash purchases were made. Each time I entered a store I purposely engaged in conversation with the proprietor, the clerk, or the other customers in order to provide as candid an explanation of my presence and of the ultimate goals of the research endeavor as was possible. In general, people found it difficult to believe that I was in New Lots for the reasons given them. On the other hand, the Mexican-Americans expressed concern that their people were not fairly presented in the pages of the current elementary and high-school texts and asked that I undertake to "set the record straight" as to the part played by *la raza* in the development of Texas. Because a historian's work was more meaningful to Mexiquito than that of an anthropologist, the historical aspects of this investigation were emphasized. However, I never refused a request by the inhabitants to discuss the other aims of this research. During the initial reconnaissance of New Lots I asked few direct questions, nor did I utilize pencil and notepad during conversations with citizens.

After the initial period I was regularly invited to social events, such as barbecues, dances, picnics, and political rallies, given by one or several young men, who constituted my *palomilla*; they considered me a peer and I began to interact with them with considerable frequency.

Participant observation within the peer group offered an unexcelled opportunity for noting real behavior instead of the ideal behavior verbalized by informants. However, it later became important to assert my independence from the peer group in order to widen the sample of Mexican-Americans from whom data were elicited. Participation in social activities with young men, none of whom were engaged in field labor, did not provide the representative sample of the population sorely needed for a study of this kind. Consequently, I tried to establish contact with families occupied as seasonal agricultural laborers, making acquaintance with three families consisting of young adults and their children, and with four families in which the adults were many years my senior. Still later, I spent one month in Laredo, Texas, where I administered questionnaires to more than fifty migrant labor families. Those questions pertained to social life, organization of work crews, and concepts of health and disease.[5]

Several factors contributed to my relationships with these impoverished families, which proved to be quite different from those enjoyed with my peer group. The migrant families could speak only Spanish, and none of the adults could either read or write. Three of the families were engaged in intensive efforts to legalize their presence in this country, and my aid in this matter was constantly solicited. I was also requested by these families to grant small loans and to write letters to prospective employers. Such requests I always granted. Another reason for the distinctive relations with this group was the fact that the older members either were too ill or were too tired after a day's work to seek recreation outside of the home. Furthermore, it was considered unseemly for an older man to engage in recreational activities with a younger man. Thus, my participation in the social life of the economically depressed families was formal and confined to open-ended interviews.

During two years of field work sixteen key informants were utilized. These were acute and articulate observers of their own culture; those who controlled areas of special knowledge. Five of the key in-

[5] Research in Laredo was supported by the Migrant Health Branch, United States Public Health Service, to which I am grateful.

formants were women, three were old men, and the remainder were young men. Interviews were focused on a single topic, but were open-ended and probing rather than restricted.

With the eight young male key informants my interaction extended well beyond the interview situation, as I participated with them in such activities as barbecues, hunting trips, and visits to prominent healers in the region. The same cannot be said about interaction with the remainder of the key informants.

Finally, to conclude this section of the discussion of field methods, pencil and paper were usually, but not always, used in the presence of key informants. The objections of some to the writing of notes during an interview was a problem that was never successfully resolved in Mexiquito. To offset that difficulty, I typed notes immediately after each interview; during the last few months of field work, my use of a tape recorder made possible the immediate dictation of what had been learned during an interview or as a result of participant observations.

After one year of experience in Mexiquito it was apparent that participant observation was not a useful technique for gathering information about women in this society. Furthermore, I learned that men tended not to volunteer information about their wives or mothers during the course of informal interaction or unrestricted interviews. I found also that male key informants either were unaware of the activities and attitudes of their womenfolk or did not wish to discuss them. To elicit information about the women of Mexiquito a different technique was called for. Therefore, an open-ended questionnaire was designed to obtain information about concepts of health and illness, sectors of life in which the women were specialized.

In order to administer this instrument, I made arrangements with the personnel of the Well-Baby Clinic in Mexiquito permitting me to become a part of their clinical procedures. In customary fashion, the staff very graciously acceded to that request. Briefly, the procedure was to subject the children to three examinations on Fridays. First, the child was weighed and measured, following which the mother was questioned by a nurse about the child's recent medical history. Mothers then attended a lecture given by one of the nurses on a subject related to personal hygiene. Lastly, the babies were examined by a physician in another of the rooms of the clinic. Interviews about health attitudes were administered by me to fifty-four mothers between the time of the nurse's lecture and the physician's examination.

Summary

This book endeavors to achieve three aims: to provide an account of the social life of Mexican-Americans in South Texas, to consider those characteristics of their social and belief systems which impede full utilization of available professional health services, and to develop an explanation for the prominence of anxiety and disaffection in Mexiquito. The concept of "social system" is utilized to assist in the organization of the descriptive material and to help explain the prominence and disaffection. Social system refers to the network of relationships which attach the inhabitants of Mexiquito to one another, to the Anglos across the tracks, and to other residents of the lower Rio Grande Valley.

Three methods were used for collecting the primary material. Most important was the technique of participant observation, which was complemented by elicitations from key informants and administration of an open-ended questionnaire to economically impoverished mothers.

Part I

THE CITY OF NEW LOTS

1. TWO SIDES OF THE TRACKS

New Lots is a city bisected by the railway of the Missouri Pacific. In 1921, the town's first year, the north side of the tracks was allocated by municipal ordinance to the residences and business establishments of Mexican-Americans, and to industrial complexes. Mexican-Americans refer to the north side of the tracks as Mexiquito, *el pueblo mexicano, nuestro lado;* even the traffic light north of the tracks is referred to as *la luz mexicana.* The other side of the tracks is spoken of as *el lado americano, el pueblo americano,* and other similar terms. Those who live south of the tracks also distinguish the two sides: "this side" and "the other side," "our side," and "their side," and "Mexican town" are all descriptive terms heard in the city of New Lots.

The north and south sides of the railway are far more than geographical zones useful for purposes of description. Each side of the tracks is a society with its own characteristics; each has a peculiar rhythm. Each side acts on the basis of understandings that were founded on separate traditions. Finally, each side of the tracks reacts to its social universe in terms of a distinctive framework of experience.

The parental generation of New Lots attempts to bring up the children with a sense of right and wrong, one of which is rewarded, the other punished. The right and wrong of one side of the tracks,

however, may conflict, and often does, with the sense of propriety
of those of the other side.

Until 1946 all of those who lived south of the tracks were subsumed under the term Anglo-Americans, while those residing north
of the railway were known as Mexican-Americans. The terms and
their equivalents perpetuated the concept that the city was divided
into two mutually exclusive zones—this side and the other side, *el
pueblo mexicano* and *el pueblo americano*. (Exceptions to the general nature of the north-side population were provided by about
twelve Negro families, who existed as an encapsulated community
with its own elementary school and a small church. Furthermore,
several Anglo-Americans married to Mexican-American spouses
lived surrounded by the Mexican-American community.)

On the south side of the railway the descriptive "Mexican" or
"Mexican-American" may often be used pejoratively, but such is
not always the case. These terms may simply be used to help describe some presumed or actual general characteristic of the group
to which the person referred to belongs; it lends context to the remark. For example, "That Mexican boy who works for me" may
simply refer to the only bilingual employee of a business firm. Of
course, it may also be meant in a derogatory way, pointing out some
characteristic which that employee presumably shares with others
of the Mexican-American group, a characteristic not possessed by
Anglo-Americans. The critical feature of the utterance, therefore,
is not the word "Mexican," but the relative stress which the speaker
places on that word. If he stresses the word "Mexican," thus differentiating it from the rest of the statement, it can with a great deal
of justice be considered an aspersive remark. On the other hand, if
"Mexican" is accorded the same relative stress as the other words,
we may rest assured that it is meant as a specifier, not as a deprecia-
tive. In any case, the person to whom reference is made will almost
surely consider the remark pejorative because of the use of the word
"Mexican," however it may be stressed. Such is the manner in
which the nuances of language keep alive antagonism and mutual
hostilities between the two ethnic groups.

In New Lots, Mexican-Americans almost always attach an ex-
planatory preface to a description of the actions of someone else of
the city. This preface places into a larger context the actions of the
individual mentioned by intimating that so-and-so performed this
action in such a manner *because* that is the way in which the ge-

neric Anglo-American does things, or because that is the fashion of the Mexican-American.

A number of other descriptives are used to imply a different way of life as perceived from one side of the tracks about the other. The north side of the railway is spoken of as Mexiquito—Little Mexico— or Mexican-town. *That* side is contrasted with *this* side, and *their* side with *our* side. When an Anglo-American speaks of the Mexican-American segment of the population, he says "they," "them," "the Mexicans," or, more politely, "the Latins." Use of any one of those terms encompasses all those residents of New Lots whose background contains some Mexican or Spanish ancestry. The terms are therefore inclusive of a varied group of individuals, for its members are by no means genetically homogeneous, nor possessed of a common citizenship status. A Mexican-American of New Lots may be a tall person of slender stature with blue eyes, blonde hair, and a nose structure either long and slender or snubbed and slender. The term will also subsume those whose pigmentation is dark, whose stature is short and stout, and whose features include brown eyes, straight black hair, a wide nose, and a trace of epicanthic fold over the eye.

A large proportion of the 9,000 Mexican-Americans have either immigrated to the city from the Republic of Mexico in recent years, or are the children of immigrants. Many of the north-siders, however, are individuals from families which have lived for the past two hundred years on the Texas side of the international boundary. Nevertheless the terms used by Anglo-Americans to describe the Mexican-Americans of New Lots refer to citizen and noncitizen alike; to recent immigrant and native-born American; and to those who speak only Spanish, those who are bilingual, and the small number who speak only English. In New Lots the most common denominator of those recognized as Mexican-Americans is the possession of a progenitor of Mexican or Spanish descent.

Today's Anglo-American group of New Lots also represents a variety of distinctive social, religious, and racial backgrounds. The term Anglo-American is umbrellalike and covers a variety of hyphenated Americans: German-Americans; Swedish-Americans; English-, Irish-, and Scotch-Americans; Italian-Americans; and even Japanese-Americans. Persons in these categories are *never* spoken of in terms of their subgrouping, and the subject comes up only during discussions of parental and grandparental backgrounds.

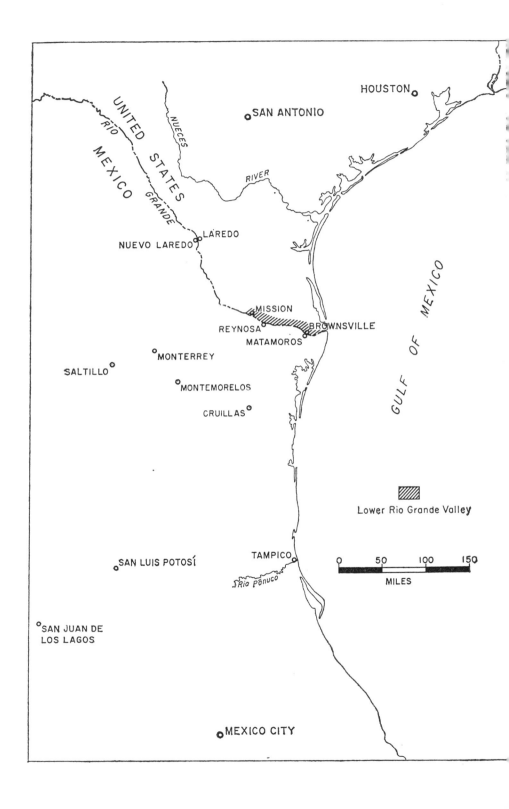

By contrast, those with one or more Spanish or Mexican ancestors are *always* designated by Mexican-American, Latin American, or a similar term.

The approximately 6,000 Anglo-Americans in New Lots belong to a number of different religious persuasions. Some are Catholics, but they are relatively few, as the overwhelming majority are Protestants. The churches with the largest memberships are the Baptists and the Methodists, but there are also strong representations of Presbyterians, Christians, Episcopalians, and Seventh-Day Adventists. The Reorganized Church of Latter-Day Saints and a number of Pentecostal groups, supplemented by a small Christian Science institution, complete the roster.

Although the founding stratum of Anglo-American society in New Lots was composed of well-to-do emigrants from small towns of the north-central and north-eastern states of this nation, as well as from Canada, they were joined by a later influx of poor Southerners from East Texas, Louisiana, Mississippi, and Georgia. Each segment contributed its mores to the Anglo-American society of this city. But the alternative ways of behavior of the many strands in the south-side Anglo society tend to be minimized, and the more universal aspects of the "Anglo way of life" are maximized in the face of the numerically more important Mexican-American segment of the town. From the commencement of social life in New Lots the Anglo-American group has striven to protect its mode of living from Mexican-American influences, while assuming at the same time that the Mexican-American way of life should and would be changed.

Today in New Lots, Mexican-Americans speak of the others as *anglos, angloamericanos, bolillos, gavachos,* and *gringos.* When speaking of themselves, the Mexican-Americans speak of the *chicanos* or *la raza*; they also employ two other terms, the *mexicanos* and the *latinos,* or *latinoamericanos.* The last two are utilized only in the presence of a *bolillo* with whom one is not acquainted. *La raza* groups together all those in the world who speak Spanish; it implies both a mystical bond uniting Spanish-speaking people and a separation of them from all others.

The manner in which a Mexican-American attacks a problem, or the way in which an individual chicano conceptualizes a problem, is generalized to indicate that that particular coping behavior or conceptualization is peculiarly chicano. Mexican-Americans are wont to speak of generic attitudes or behaviors uniquely chicano. Quite often the contrast between a presumed Mexican-American solution to a problem and that which an Anglo-American would elect is set forth in the form of a self-turned witticism. For example, Mexican air-conditioning is described as the emptying of a sack of dry ice in the rear seat of an automobile. The self-turned witticism takes other forms as well. At times when the very popular tune "Mexico! No hay dos" blares from the jukebox, a wit exclaims "Gracias a Dios!" (There is but one Mexico! Thank God!)

The numerous stories and the often-quoted witticisms expressive of ambivalence and inconsistency—supposedly inherent traits of the Mexican-American—are tokens of the cultural and social fact that the Mexiquito Mexican-Americans are across the tracks from the Anglo-Americans, and across the frontier from the wellsprings of their traditional culture. Neither fish nor fowl, they are at home with neither of the groups that are significant to them. A young man who is a native-born citizen of the United States, as are his wife and children, posed the poignant problem of identity: "The other day my boy came home from school and asked me, 'Daddy, am I an American citizen?'"

As one walks across the tracks along the main thoroughfare of the city, he leaves one kind of scene and enters another. North of the tracks the whirring sounds of the mechanical belts, which bring the crates of packed vegetables and fruits from packing shed to motor truck and railroad car, are heard throughout the day and often until midnight. Interspersed with this north-side sound is the raucousness of the *ranchero* tunes from the juke boxes of the thirteen *cantinas* of that side of the tracks. These bars along the thoroughfare form the most popular type of commercial enterprise owned by Mexican-Americans, with the exception of food markets. Ten grocery stores front on the Boulevard on the north side, and more than fifty small neighborhood grocery stores are distributed in the residential areas. Although they are conveniently located, their stock is small; most of the smaller groceries cannot sell either fresh meat or milk products, for example, because they lack refrigerating facilities. Consequently, here the forgetful housewife purchases an onion, a single tomato, or a loaf of bread. The major family shopping is done in one of the larger grocery stores, where beans, flour, and rice may be purchased in sacks weighing twenty or fifty pounds. On Friday and Saturday nights the sidewalks in front of the three largest groceries north of the railway are thronged with shoppers; with boxes of groceries and sacks of staples, the families await the truck or station wagon provided by the store to carry them home to the peripheries of the north side, or to the vegetable farms where their cabins are located.

Three of the largest stores fronting on the main street sell work clothing. Prominently displayed in the show windows are high rubber boots, so useful for those who must work in the irrigation canals; denim and gabardine shirts and trousers; and the character- istic wide-brimmed straw hats, which deflect the rays of the sun from the face of the agricultural wage laborer. Two of the large clothing stores on the north side are owned and managed by Euro- pean Jewish immigrants who escaped from the Polish *pogroms;* the other is the property of a Catholic chicano, who is so devout that he is called Jesusito—Little Jesus.

Four of the shops along the north Boulevard specialize in lending money to Mexican-Americans at usurious interest rates: 50 per cent of the principal for short-term, small loans. A number of retail out- lets sell used furniture and household appliances. In fact, more stores sell used articles of clothing and furniture than sell those goods new. Although one of the three drug stores of the north side boasts a licensed pharmacist, all three are heavily stocked with well-advertised patent medicines, which are supplemented by an inventory of brightly packaged *medicinas caseras*—home cures. Mostly balms made from herbs, barks, roots, and oils, these are wrapped in the colorful emblems of Don Pedrito or La Palma, the two wholesale distributors, whose traditional *remedios* are sold throughout South Texas. These remedies are retailed in New Lots at two other shops on the north side as well, both of which also sell Spanish-language periodicals and books. *Policía,* the Spanish equiva- lent of the Police Gazette, rests between volumes on how to learn English in just a few weeks and a book of instructions in the art of bewitching and beguiling by means of charm and incantation. In addition, traditional remedies are sold in several of the ten grocery stores along the Boulevard.

The remaining frontage on North Boulevard is occupied by a movie house dedicated to the showing of Spanish-language films, by seven restaurants, seven gasoline service stations, three bakeries, a tortilla factory, two photographic studios, a window-glass shop, a shoe repair store, a beauty shop, and a dry-cleaning establishment.

All of the restaurants and bars are licensed for the sale of beer, a prodigious amount of which is consumed during the oppressively hot, humid months between April and October.

In Mexiquito, New Lots' north side, is a total of five elementary schools. One is attended exclusively by Negro children; another is a Catholic parochial institution attended by 575 students, of whom 25 are Anglos. The remainder of the grade schools are attended exclusively by Mexican-Americans. It is estimated that the Mexican-American students in the elementary grades total 3,100, but the number of registrants varies markedly according to the migratory work cycle. For example, in the 1957–1958 school year 400 more children were registered in the eighth week of the term than in the first week. During that same year there were 40 more registrants in the tenth week than in the eighth.

Of course, the growth cycle of the fruits, vegetables, and cotton, on which most of Mexiquito's families are dependent for a livelihood, varies from year to year, and school registrations reflect those variations in crop cycles. For example, there were 133 fewer registrants in the eighth week of the 1958–1959 term than in the previous year, and 10 fewer in the tenth week.

In Mexiquito, where most of the students do not continue in school beyond the primary grades, officials estimate a drop-out rate of 75 per cent at the sixth-grade level. Because relatively few of those who attain a sixth-grade level ever participate in activities of the senior high school, the administration has originated a special certificate of achievement to be awarded those who discontinue their studies at this time.

There are a number of factors which mitigate against continuance of studies in senior or even junior high school for the bulk of the Mexican-American youngsters. Undoubtedly, the most important single problem is that posed by financial hardship in the families dependent on wage labor in agriculture and other unskilled employment. Furthermore, it is unquestionably true that many of the children are simply not motivated to continue studies past the sixth-grade level, as is true of many others who are not Mexican-Americans. But there are factors which are peculiarly applicable to the bicultural circumstances found in New Lots, factors which discourage students from Mexiquito.

Teachers and administrators of the city school system place an extraordinary emphasis on what might best be thought of as "civic responsibilities" and "personal hygiene," or "citizenship," if you will. This emphasis is apparent in all grades of the school system, but its intensity is exaggerated at the junior- and senior-high-school levels. The New Lots school system is organized to make of its students mirror-images of contemporary Anglo society, a type of society in which one's primary orientations, even if only on the surface, are toward responsibilities to civic and religious groups in which one holds membership. Later sections of this volume will point out that such orientations contrast with the basic values of the Mexican-American society. In many instances it seemed that the personnel of the school system were intent on developing Anglo-Americans out of young Mexican-Americans as a primary goal, and paid far less attention to their academic achievements. For example, an administrator commented as follows about the admission procedures with regard to the transfer of Mexican-American children from the elementary school in Mexiquito to the junior high school located south of the tracks.

We try to get kids' hair cut, get 'em to look like the rest; cut off the *pachuco* style, and the bowl-type haircut. You've been down to Old Mexico where they go around with their shirts unbuttoned all the way down to the navel, and then they tie it around their waist. They think it makes them look sexy. We can't have that here.

Another said:

I don't know what you think about it, but we screen our kids before they are admitted to the school. If a kid wants to stay he has to get a good haircut, cut off the sideburns; we don't allow any mustaches in this school, once the subject has begun to shave.

Despite such hazards a growing number of Mexican-American youngsters enter and graduate from junior and senior high school. Education has assumed major importance as a criterion of achieved social status among young people of Mexiquito. They are quite aware that education, in particular English-language skills, is a prerequisite for attainment of improved occupation and income in the New Lots society. Increased income gained from steady, "clean" employment is the prize won by those who have gained fluency in English.

During the Second World War and the conflict in Korea a number of chicano servicemen received training as clerical workers,

mechanics, and technicians. After the wars many returning servicemen took advantage of veterans' benefits to continue their education. Today's work force in Mexiquito, unlike that of former years,
contains a significant proportion of laborers engaged in occupations
other than "stoop" or "dirty" work. Some chicanos are engaged as
physicians, teachers, nurses, pharmacists, and ministers of religion.
Many others are salesclerks, and most clerical positions in New
Lots—north and south side—are filled by qualified chicano men
and women. Furthermore, several retail businessmen today com-
pete successfully with their Anglo counterparts.

These chicanos aspire toward life goals which include social equality with Anglos. Some distinguishing features of this aggregation
of mobile Mexican-Americans are its aspirations toward such status
symbols as regular income derived from "clean," that is, nonagricultural, employment, English-language skills, high-school and college education, and possession of such other status markers as automobiles, refrigerators, television sets, and barbecue "pits." Among
chicanos the status marker which excites the most comment is the
type of house in which an individual resides, and the neighborhood
in which it is located, that is, whether it is found in *el pueblo mexicano* or *el pueblo americano*.

Within Mexiquito one fails to discover neighborhoods marked by
distinctive life styles indicative of social-class differentials. If one
strays from the main Boulevard the dust of the unpaved side streets
clings to face, hands, and clothing during the hot, humid spring and
summer months. In autumn and winter the passage of pedestrian
or automobile along these side streets is made difficult, or sometimes,
impossible by mud and standing water. Homes are generally impoverished and unpainted, with here and there a brightly painted building surrounded by a high wire fence. The residences of the north
side range from one-room shacks, consisting of corrugated paper
stretched around four posts and covered by a roof of planks, to multi-
room structures of wood or plaster, handsomely maintained and
painted in bright colors of blue, green, orange, pink, or white. In
these, a visitor finds the appurtenances of middle-class life: a bright
new refrigerator, a large gas stove and oven, an electric mixer for
cooking, an electric washing machine, a suite of well-padded furniture, and, sometimes, a cocktail bar. Homes such as these are scattered throughout Mexiquito's neighborhoods, where they house

teachers, pharmacists, salesclerks, successful businessmen, commercial truckers, and supervisory employees in the packing sheds.

The buildings just described, and the material goods which they contain, are in marked contrast to most of the homes in any Mexiquito neighborhood. Most households north of the tracks clearly show the effect of a prevailing wage of fifty cents an hour; that is, when work is available. Most of the populace of Mexiquito are dependent on seasonal work as agricultural laborers. As a consequence, incomes in Mexiquito tend to be low, seasonal, and undependable.

In this neighborhood, as in South Texas generally, most Mexican-Americans are occupied as agricultural wage laborers. Approximately two thirds of the residents of the north side are employed as field laborers, most of whom are forced by dire necessity to migrate between March and December of every year in search of employment. A study of the earnings of wage laborers residing in South Texas shows that the average daily earnings of a farm worker were as low as $4.02, and that the daily wages earned by seasonal workers while employed in nonagricultural tasks averaged $5.03. These estimates are based on a sample of 594 chicano workers.[1] During late

Table 1

EARNINGS OF MIGRATORY FARMWORKERS AT THE
HOME BASE, SOUTH TEXAS, 1956

Home-base City	Total Workers Reporting	Average Earnings Per Worker at Home Base		
			Per Day	
		Per Year	At Nonfarm Jobs	At Farm Jobs
All cities	594	$448	$5.03	$4.79
San Antonio	114	664	6.07	4.69
Crystal City	124	521	6.99	5.48
Eagle Pass	104	312	3.20	4.11
Laredo	45	294	2.73	4.02
Weslaco	118	460	4.33	5.01
Robstown	89	436	6.84	5.40

Adapted from Metzler and Sargent, *Incomes*, p. 6.

[1] William H. Metzler and Frederic P. O. Sargent, *Incomes of Migratory Agricultural Workers, Bulletin 950*, p. 2.

Table 2

TYPES OF WORK DONE BY MIGRATORY FARMWORKERS IN SOUTH
TEXAS, 1956 WITH DAYS OF EMPLOYMENT AND EARNINGS

Type of Work	Average Days Worked	Average Earnings per Worker	Average Earnings per Worker per Day
Farmwork	63	$288	$4.59
Cotton			
Chopping	44	243	5.25
Picking	46	247	5.37
Onions	58	222	3.83
Spinach	58	260	4.48
Carrots	78	259	3.32
Other vegetables	57	199	3.49
Other crops	65	282	4.34
Truck or tractor driver	84	564	6.71
Other farmwork	73	311	4.26
Nonfarmwork	74	448	6.01
Construction	84	682	8.12
Service	79	319	4.04
Cannery	70	488	6.97
Packinghouse	83	490	5.90
Ice or storage plant	84	376	4.48
Sawmill	29	135	4.66
Other factory	71	633	8.92
Professional services	62	336	5.42
Transportation	85	452	5.32
Other nonfarmwork	90	564	6.27

Adapted from Metzler and Sargent, *Incomes*, p. 7.

fall and early winter, when agricultural workers reside in this region, the average daily earnings amounted to $4.91.[2] Tables 1, 2,
and 3 provide earnings of chicanos while they were at their home
base in South Texas and while they were migrating. The wage
scales which reign here rank among the very lowest in the nation.[3]

Independent calculations made in Mexiquito during the course
of the present study fully support the reports by Metzler and Sargent. According to our figures, seasonal workers seldom earn more
than $4.50 for a full day's work in the fields around Mexiquito, and

[2] *Ibid.*
[3] Willis Weatherford, *Geographical Differentials of Agricultural Wages in
the United States.*

Table 3

EARNINGS AND NONFARM EMPLOYMENT OF MIGRATORY
FARMWORKERS WHILE OUTSIDE TEXAS, 1956, BY
STATE AND TYPE OF WORK

Location and Type of Work	Average No. Days Worked	Average Earnings per Year	Average Earnings per Day
California			
Canning	105	$1,348.40	$12.84
Illinois			
Packinghouse	200	2,600.00	13.00
Other factory	82	692.00	8.44
Indiana			
Packinghouse	49	288.00	5.88
Michigan			
Packinghouse	85	650.00	7.65
Cannery	72	500.00	6.94
Railroad	96	1,152.00	12.00
Minnesota			
Cannery	17	117.00	6.88
Other factory	12	150.00	12.50
Oregon			
Cannery	70	840.00	12.00
Utah			
Cannery	63	500.00	7.94
Washington			
Cannery	34	256.00	7.53
Domestic service	134	854.00	6.37
Other service	100	482.00	4.82
Wisconsin			
Packinghouse	124	1,356.00	10.94
Cannery	39	322.00	8.26
Other factory	80	578.00	7.22

Adapted from Metzler and Sargent, *Incomes*, p. 9.

even those who are employed as delivery truck drivers, package-boys in grocery stores, and other work of that ilk, earn between $3.50 and $4.00 for a full day's employment. Moreover, those who have been able to secure "clean," nonagricultural, jobs consider themselves peculiarly fortunate because of the regularity of the employment. The low wage scale is not the only serious problem which seasonal workers confront while at home base; as has already been implied, *under*employment in Mexiquito is at least as important!

During the period in which they are not migrating in the northern states, chicano agricultural laborers are insured employment only three out of six work days in any single week. The study by Metzler and Sargent found underemployment of laborers to be a problem of utmost gravity throughout the south of Texas.[4]

As a consequence of the underemployment and depressed wage scale, which characterize the Valley economy, almost all residents of Mexiquito who are employed as farm laborers must migrate periodically to other sectors of the nation to augment their income. In 1958 a total of 7,637 migrants left New Lots and a nearby smaller town in search of work during the spring, summer, and fall months of the year.[5] That sum represented approximately 90 per cent of the total of interstate migrants, and 60 per cent of those who migrated within the boundaries of Texas. In 1956 an incomplete tabulation reported that 4,005 migrants had left the city in search of work elsewhere in the nation. Based on a sample of thirty Mexiquito households, the average earnings per migrant household amount to $2,400 in a prosperous year (1957).

The depressed wage scale which characterizes agricultural employment in Mexiquito affects the wage scale of nonagricultural employees as well. Only those employers of New Lots who are engaged in interstate commerce offer employment which pays laborers one dollar an hour, the minimum federal wage. Most of the work available to the unskilled and semiskilled workers of Mexiquito pays between forty and seventy-five cents per hour. Despite the comparatively low wages, steady, nonagricultural employment in New Lots is at a premium. Those who earn as much as $40.00 per week comment that "We're never going to be millionaires but we've come a long ways," while a young family head who earns $27.00 for a sixty-six–hour work week recalls that when he received his first pay check, "I thought I was rich."

There are some Mexican-Americans in Mexiquito who earn well above $30.00 and $40.00 per week, but not many. Among them are one physician, thirty school teachers, approximately twenty successful merchants, some commission-salesmen, and ten municipal employees other than teachers. Those chicanos who do not regularly migrate from Mexiquito regard themselves as a fortunate few, and

---

[4] Metzler and Sargent, *Incomes*, p. 1.
[5] Personal communication from the Texas Employment Commission.

are so regarded by others. Although their wages are by no means high when compared with wages elsewhere in the nation, their employment is steady and not dependent upon the vagaries of the weather.

Several reasons are advanced by employers for the low wage scale which prevails in the city. Some assert that their trade will not permit an increase in the wages of those whom they employ, and others claim that they do not raise wages of their employees for moral reasons. "Some of those who know the Mexicans best tell us that if we *have* to raise their wages, to do it slowly because their moral fiber can't stand too much money all at one time," according to one Anglo employer.

There are, however, more compelling factors which contribute to the unusually low rate of pay in this city. New Lots' location, just across the international boundary with Mexico, makes it very attractive to illegal immigrants. Inasmuch as the dollar is worth more than twelve times the Mexican peso, wages in dollars seem incredibly high to the "wetback." One young, native-born citizen of the United States described the economic situation succinctly.

The bad thing about New Lots is that people are always wanting to work for less than you are and take your job. Jobs are hard to get; suppose Mr. Smith went up to a boy on the street, one who spoke English, and said to him: "Do you want a job in a store?" "Sure!" he would say. "You bet!" Maybe he wouldn't even ask what the pay was, but if they offered him $18.00 or $20.00 and I'm getting $35.00 he would take it like that!

Then Mr. Smith would come over to me and say: "Well Telésforo, things are slow at the store, and I'm afraid that we're going to have to let you go." That's the trouble with the Mexican people; we need the money so bad, we have to feed our kids, we have to get frijoles into the house. Any job is good; we need the money real bad, and we'll work for anything!

Take that Señora Filomena, she works for any money. One of us— people who were born here in this country—will be working for an Anglo as a maid and getting $8.00 a week, ironing. She'll work from eight in the morning until two in the afternoon. But when someone like Señora Filomena comes around from Mexico she won't even ask what the Anglos will pay her. She'll work from seven until seven and when they hand her $3.00 at the end of the week there's nothing she can say about it. All she wanted was work so that she could get some food in the house. You see, that's the trouble—we don't even have any way to be sure that we have a job. Our people will work for anything, they'll take your job away from you.

Between 1946 and 1957 some, but not all, status-conscious and upwardly mobile young veterans of the Second World War moved across the tracks to the Anglo side. In 1957 a census counted 150 such mobile families. During 1958 four intimate acquaintances of mine made inquiries of realtors about property located on the Anglo side, and so the trend continues. Some of those chicanos now living south of the tracks reside in elaborate two-storied homes, or in more recently constructed ranch-type houses. These tend to cost a sum which amounts to more than $10,000. On the other hand, some who have moved across the tracks now reside in square, weathered, board buildings. In any case, the monetary value of the residence is of far less importance than is the fact that it is located in *"el pueblo americano."*

Some generalizations may be advanced about those chicanos who have elected to move south of the tracks. They are less than fifty years old; the rarely encountered oldsters prove to be widowed parents residing with a married son or daughter. The great majority of those who have moved from the north side are veterans of either the Second World War or the Korean conflict. Those who cross the tracks take advantage of federal veterans' legislation to facilitate the purchase of their house lot, and the construction or remodeling of their homes. The young men are all bilingual, but some of their wives speak only Spanish. None of these south-side chicanos work as "stoop" laborers in agricultural season labor, and their annual income ranges from $2,400 to $20,000. However, the *sum* of the income is of far less significance than its dependability. All chicanos living across the tracks today are either salaried or self-employed. In many families both husband and wife work; their unvarying income, regardless of its total worth, permits them to engage extensively in credit buying. It is a generally acknowledged fact that one need not possess a handsome income in order to make expensive purchases. Chicanos who move to the Anglo side of town represent an aggregation of upwardly mobile young people with steady incomes.

Those who move south of the tracks and others who seriously contemplate the action share significant objective indicators of social-class status. They have completed elementary or high school, are employed in "clean" occupations, and boast dependable incomes; they also share corollary indices of class position, for example, substantial homes, relatively new automobiles, and such indoor appurtenances as television sets, refrigerators, ovens and stoves, and indoor plumbing.

Not all those who possess these material and cultural goods elect to move to the Anglo side of the tracks. Some decide to erect new homes and bring up their children in one of Mexiquito's neighborhoods, while others leave the city entirely. Whether it is appropriate to move across the tracks and be associated with the *bolillos* is a debate which stirs strong sentiments among chicanos whose acquisition of the aforementioned prerequisites of status mobility makes such a move attractive. Those electing to leave Mexiquito contend that one's obligations are restricted to himself and his family, and that a move to the other side will show Anglos that chicanos are as good as they are. Those who remain in Mexiquito, on the other hand, express the point of view that the more successful chicanos have an obligation to show or demonstrate to the less motivated how to achieve a "better" mode of life. However, from information garnered in private conversations, it appears that those who elect not to leave Mexiquito, although financially capable of doing so, feel less adequate and more timid about moving into *el pueblo americano*. In some cases a wife or coresident mother speaks little or no English, or one of the parents fears that his children's darker pigmentation will invite open hostility from the new neighbors. Hostilities are not, however, unidirectional, for some of the aspiring Mexican-Americans give as their reasons for not moving across the tracks the undesirability of living next door to "white hilly-billies," or to "white trash."

The apprehensions of those chicanos whose aspirations for enhanced social status urge them to leave Mexiquito, but who elect instead to remain, are nurtured by the evident unhappiness and disillusionment of those who preceded them across the tracks. Today, Anglos continue to lump together as "Mexicans" or "Latins," or "Latin Americans," all those with a Spanish or Mexican ancestor, regardless of the side of town on which they reside. The entire *chicanazgo*—laborer and professional alike—is lumped together by Anglos into a subordinate group based on ascribed characteristics. Those chicanos who move across the tracks prove unsuccessful in their attempts to engage Anglo neighbors in fruitful personal rela-

tionships. To an objective observer the discouraging response is less a
failure by Anglos to validate the newly achieved status of the aspirant than a reflection of the manner by which Anglos organize social
life.[6] Among Anglos, friendships derive from consociation in formal
corporate groups, such as Lions Club, Rotary, Optimists, Volunteer
Fire Department, Chamber of Commerce, Beef Trust, Bible-Study
Class, and others too numerous to mention here. By contrast, chicanos incorporate formal groups on foundations of informal associations with acquaintances or *palomillas*. Inability to engage Anglo
peers in friendship relations is bitterly galling to upwardly striving
chicanos. They interpret the "rebuff" as discriminatory and liken it
to the rejection of Negroes by whites. Although there is no doubt that
a number of fraternal clubs and church organizations are closed to
chicanos, others do cultivate their participation, where as they do
not cultivate that of the Negro. When the Mexican-Americans fail to
join the organizations open to them, or to participate actively in
them, reluctance is interpreted by the Anglos as unfriendliness, and
is considered diagnostic of a lack of civic responsibility. In the final
analysis, whatever may be the objective reason why chicanos do
not participate with their Anglo neighbors in activities both formal
and informal, the chicanos conclude that a ceiling has been placed
on their access to higher social status.

As one consequence of the assumed "rebuff," chicanos who reside
in Anglo neighborhoods do not cut their ties with Mexiquito; they
continue to interact with Mexiquito-based *palomillas* with the same
frequency and intensity as before they moved across the tracks. The
high frequency of interaction between those on the south side and
those who remain in Mexiquito deters crystallization of social-class
sentiments in the Mexican-American society. One young couple,
who recently moved to the other side of the tracks, offer a representative example of the feelings of insecurity felt and voiced by the
mobile young chicanos of New Lots. Both man and wife speak per-
fect English as well as Spanish and each is a high-school graduate.
The young husband manages a retail store, and his wife is employed
as a salesclerk elsewhere. The wife is bitterly disappointed with life
"over there." "What's the matter with our people?" she asks. "No-

[6] *Cf.* Leonard Broom and John I. Kitsuse, "The Validation of Acculturation:
A Condition to Ethnic Assimilation," *American Anthropologist*, LVII (February,
1955), pp. 44–49.

body comes to visit us, and we haven't made any friends over there."
The disenchantment of this young couple with life across the tracks
is brought forth by other young chicanos as ammunition to support
their position that the more affluent and better educated chicanos
should remain with "our own people."

The ethnographic evidence reveals the lack of clearly defined social classes among chicanos. Distinctions between ranked categories
are at best tenuous and ill-defined, but such concepts are not totally
absent from the chicanos' frame of reference.[7] Furthermore, those
sentiments seem to be increasing in significance. More explicitly,
chicanos on the south side have not developed a sense of solidarity
which excludes those who elect to remain in Mexiquito. Mexican-
Americans motivated toward upward mobility do not conceive of
themselves as filling a unique status vis-à-vis Anglos. One *never*
hears south-side chicanos speak of "we," "us," "our," or similar
terms to distinguish them from residents of the north side of the
tracks.

Two terms, "high Mexicans" and "low Mexicans," were invented
by the editor of a neighborhood news sheets to refer to those who
move to the south side and to those who remain north-siders, respectively. The former term is being utilized in opprobrium, for a person mentioned in the newssheet as a "high Mexican" is one considered to have "turned his back" on the chicano way of life, though
he need not be a person of either affluence or prestige. A "low Mexican," on the other hand, is one who remains a resident of Mexiquito,
regardless of income and influence. Neither of the two terms has
gained any currency among the chicanos, and their usage appears
to be confined to the editor of the newssheet and his family.

Once a very acculturated chicano described as a "bracket" some
men whom he planned to invite to an exclusive social function, but
I never again heard the term. Similarly, those who perform lowpaid "stoop" labor in agriculture are sometimes derogated by the
adjective *tomateros* (literally, those who work with tomatoes). However, in a search for verbal symbols of social distinctions, although

---

[7] Compare Lin's emphatic denial of clear or crystallized social-class differentials recognized by Mexican-Americans in Kansas City. "There are *no* differential terms in use in Greater Kansas City to designate a distinctive group as a
class, such as *los medianos* used in some colonies in California" (Paul Ming-
Chang Lin, "Voluntary Kinship and Voluntary Association in a Mexican-American Community," p. 61).

it proved possible to elicit the term from informants, I never heard *tomateros* used in conversation with others, or in discussions that were overheard.

New Lots today reveals two kinds of stratification, one of which is based on ascribed features, the other on achievement. In the first place, Anglos interact with Anglos, chicanos with other chicanos. For example, employees of a retail establishment, Anglo and chicano alike, may banter, bet on the outcome of sports contests, and discuss world affairs in animated fashion. But, at the coffee break or the lunch hour, members of one cultural group separate from fellow employees of the other group, whether or not English is a means of communication commonly shared. Little League baseball games draw enthusiasts throughout the season. The stands are not segregated (nor are any other publicly owned facilities) and chicanos sit right next to Anglo rooters, but an incredible lack of communication between chicanos and Anglos is evident although they may occupy adjoining seats throughout the season. These are several examples of chicano-Anglo relations, but the list is too extensive to include all observations here. In New Lots one continues to be an Anglo or a Latin, a chicano or an *americano*. The society is stratified on the basis of ascribed characteristics into two cultural groups, Anglo and chicano.

Within the chicano group are present more subtle stratifications, based mainly on the kind of occupation in which one engages. Those employed as agricultural field laborers do not interact with others not so occupied, nor do members of each of the occupational groups attend public dances in the plaza on the same evening. Observations of behavior in Mexiquito indicate that the schism between agricultural laborers and others is widening, but further status distinctions within the Mexican-American society have been slower to emerge.

An emergent sentiment of class identification by status seekers who share certain symbols, in particular, type of employment and English-language skills, heralds a new phase in the history of group relations in New Lots. Upwardly mobile chicanos aspire to a life goal of equality with Anglos, whose status symbols they have acquired. If aspiring chicanos continue to feel "rebuffed" by dominant Anglos, and if they continue to feel their aspirations are capped by status ceilings, either of two results may be foreseen. Either the socially ambitious will leave the city in an attempt to resolve the perceived status inconsistency or else the qualities of alienation and anxiety, which figure so prominently in their attitudes, will increase in intensity. However, if upwardly mobile chicanos find that ceilings on their status aspirations have been removed, they will channel their energies to achievement of the social status which they seek.

Summary

From its very inception the city of New Lots has been divided into two clearly demarcated neighborhoods. The north side of the railway was assigned to industrial plants and the residences of Spanish-speaking families, while the south side was allocated to English-speaking families. Over the course of the years each side of the tracks became clearly identified as either the Mexican or the Anglo side, *el pueblo mexicano* and *el pueblo americano*, this side and the other side. The lives of those on one side of the tracks were different from those on the other side; each of the neighborhoods preserved its own linguistic, educational, social, and dietary habits.

Today, as one crosses the tracks from one neighborhood to the other, a considerable change is evident from what is reported to have prevailed in the 1920's; yet each side remains distinctive. In part, the differences to be found today are due to the traditional cultures which guide the lives of those who live north and south of the tracks, respectively, but, also, the differences reflect the low income characteristic of Mexiquito families in contrast to the relatively high income of those living in *el pueblo americano*. Furthermore, the level of income is clearly associated with the amount of formal education one has achieved.

In Mexiquito there are five elementary schools, of which three are attended exclusively by Mexican-American youngsters, another exclusively by Negroes, and, finally, the fifth, a Catholic parochial school is attended by 575 children from Mexiquito and by 25 others from across the tracks. Beyond the sixth grade the relatively few children from Mexiquito (approximately 25%) who continue their education converge with their Anglo peers on the junior and senior high school, both located south of the tracks. Over the years, and especially since 1946, increasingly large numbers of Mexican-American children have attended high school. The manifest goals of these highly motivated youngsters are English-language competence and "clean," steady employment, which is its correlate.

Moreover, beginning in 1946 the south-side bars on Mexican-American residents were lifted, and one now encounters approximately 150 such families in what was formerly an exclusively Anglo neighborhood. Characteristically, the adults of these newcomer families are young, are competent in both Spanish and English, possess a high-school or college education, and are engaged in occupations other than agricultural field labor.

Despite the differences in income, level of education, occupation, and bilingual skills, which set apart those chicanos now living south of the tracks from their counterparts in Mexiquito, no sense of solidarity binds together those on one side and excludes chicano residents of the other side. The failure of such a sense of solidarity to develop may be traced to two factors, of which the most important is that many chicanos, who are high-school and college graduates, who are employed in regular clean jobs, and who control English as well as Spanish-language skills, choose *not* to leave Mexiquito for the other side of the tracks. Secondly, those who have so elected to cross from the north to the south side have not yet been assimilated into the Anglo way of life. In New Lots, cultural differences continue to divide Anglo-American from Mexican-American, no matter on which side of the tracks a family resides.

2. NEW LOTS IN HISTORICAL CONTEXT

The contemporary relations which exist between Anglo-Americans and Mexican-Americans in New Lots have evolved over the course of many years. The nature of the present social relationships may best be understood when they are provided an historical setting. It is useful to think of the evolution of those relationships in terms of a sequence of several phases. The first began when the lower Rio Grande Valley was populated by a homogeneous group of Spanish-speaking residents, most of whom were ranchers. The second phase of the sequence was inaugurated by the arrival of merchants, engineers, and soldiery from the United States and Western Europe. Those aliens interacted with the Spanish-speaking ranchers on egalitarian terms, and marriage between natives and aliens was a frequent occurrence. The third phase of the historical sequence saw the arrival of farmers from the central and northern plains of the United States and Canada. Their relations with the Spanish-speaking ranchers were those of superiors to subordinates, quite different from antecedent intergroup relations.

The First Phase (1746–1848)

Until 1848 the population of the lower Rio Grande Valley was homogeneous and isolated from alien influences. Those who lived in the Valley were dependent on livestock and simple horticulture for their livelihood.

In 1746 efforts were initiated to colonize the lower Rio Grande

Valley in order to protect the wealthy mining and agricultural settlements of central Mexico from marauding Apache Indians, and
to prevent encroachment on New Spain from New France. In order
to establish Spanish dominion over the lower Rio Grande Valley, a
royal commission was bestowed on José de Escandón. The commission

. . . provided for the conquest and settlement of a district more than
one hundred leagues from north to south, and sixty or eighty leagues
from east to west; it extended from Pánuco, Villa de Valles, and Sierra
Gordo on the south, to the Medina and San Antonio rivers on the north,
and from Guadalcazar, Las Charcas, Venado, Cadereyta and Cerralvo
on the west, to the Gulf of Mexico on the east.[1]

The new province was given the name of Colonia del Nueva Santander.

The recruitment of settlers by Escandón was assisted handsomely
by inducements offered by the Crown to new colonizers in the un-
charted areas of Nueva Santander. The enticements included the
granting of free lands, and an exemption from taxation of both the
land and its produce. Also, a sum of cash was offered to defray the
traveling expenses of the parties as they moved to the new sites, as
well as the outlay of money incidental to the first year of occupation.[2]

Among the colonizers, the Falcón party arrived with an enormous
quantity of livestock, including 13,000 sheep. The economic dependence upon livestock by the Spanish-speaking population of the
region was destined to continue until the beginning of the present
century. For example, in 1750, at the settlement known as Guerrero,

. . . there were forty-three families with thousands of goats, sheep, and
horses pastured over the surrounding country. . . . At Comargo there
were sixty-five families numbering seven hundred persons, and these
settlers owned 30,000 head of stock including horses, mules, cattle,
sheep, and goats.

At Reynosa there were forty-three families which owned approximately 6,000 head of stock.[3]

[1] Herbert Eugene Bolton, *Texas in the Middle Eighteenth Century: Studies in
Spanish Colonial History and Administration*, p. 292.
[2] Florence Johnson Scott, *Historical Heritage of the Lower Rio Grande*, pp. 18,
23.
[3] *Ibid.*, p. 33.

Another of the region's historians gave the following estimate of the ratio of livestock to human population in that early epoch (Table 4). Originally, the figures were contained in the first official census of the lower Valley area.[4]

Table 4

RATIO OF LIVESTOCK TO HUMAN POPULATION

Settlement	Inhabitants	Indians	Livestock
Reynosa	289	200	16,000
Comargo	637	243	81,000
Mier	195	150	44,000
Revilla	357	0	50,000
Dolores	115	2	8,000
Laredo	85	0	10,000

But, although the raising of livestock was the most important aspect of the early economy, agriculture was not unimportant. All earlier travelers and chroniclers in the region report a dependence of the early settlements on irrigation or flood-plain farming to supplement the meat from the herds.

The most common practice was to plant small crops on the delta immediately next to the channel of a stream. After the annual flood this delta land proved itself particularly rich garden land. The other method was to plant crops in the channel of the stream during the dry season. Around Laredo the floods reportedly carried off the crops every year because of the peasants' practice of planting in damp spots immediately adjacent to the channel edge. A similar practice was reported from the Mier settlement in 1828, and Luther Giddings reported the same technique at a ranch bordering the Rio Grande.[5] Sánchez, the draftsman for the Mier and Terán expedition, noted that in Laredo "Food is extremely scarce; the little corn which is cultivated by the inhabitants is planted near the city in tracts

[4] Edwin J. Foscue, "Agricultural History of the Lower Rio Grande Valley Region," Agricultural History, VIII (March, 1934), 124–138.

[5] Luis Berlandier and Rafael Chovell, Diario de Viaje de la Comisión de Límites que Puso el Gobierno de la República, pp. 92, 94, 135; Luther Giddings, Sketches of the Campaign in Northern Mexico in Eighteen Hundred Forty Six and Seven, p. 52.

which are over-flooded by the river in time of high water because
the scarcity of rain does not permit planting it in other places."[6]

In the middle of the nineteenth century an American woman by
name of Mrs. Vielé described what she saw of ranch life during a
brief stopover along the Rio Grande. She disembarked from a river
steamer and followed "a road that led from the river's bank in a
winding direction through the chaparral . . . a beaten footpath led
us on . . . each side overrun with briers . . . we soon emerged from
the tangled brush-wood of the chaparral and came to a cleared spot
of some acres in extent." In the cleared area she saw:

Half-a-dozen mud huts neatly thatched with straw and open sheds
attached for culinary purposes, where the kettle hung suspended over
a wood fire . . .

The Mexican peasant of the Rio Grande is a character peculiar to
that region of country, possessing within himself all the elements of a
social existence. He is his own shoe maker and tailor, the leather of
his garments and of his sandals is made from the skins of the animals
he has himself killed.

He makes his own carts, hewing the wheels out of the solid wood.
He makes the plow he uses, which is a sharp-pointed log with a pole
at one end by which it is guided, and one at the other by which it is
drawn. To it a pair of oxen are strapped by the horns; sometimes a
mule and a cow are yoked together to drag it! His harrow is made of
the branch of a tree. The corn is put into the ground and then left to
providence to either ripen or dry up, of which there is an even chance.[7]

Another chronicler wrote that the houses of the poorer *rancheros*
were "constructed of the most flimsy materials, and utterly devoid
of taste or comfort. Along the river we saw some formed of hides,
fastened to a light framework, and many of reeds placed upright in
the ground, and interwoven and thatched with leaves or grass."[8]

The poorer homes belonged to the *peóns* and *medieros*, those who
worked as servants and herders for the gentry, as well as those who
share-cropped the lands. The landed-gentry—*los agraciados*—are
reported to have lived in larger homes built of adobe and masonry;
some Mexican-Americans of Mexiquito remember having been told
of the fine furniture and silver which adorned the homes of *los agra-*

      [6] José María Sánchez, "A Trip to Texas in 1828," *The Southwestern Historical
Quarterly*, XXIX (April, 1926), 249–289, translated by Carlos R. Castañeda.
      [7] Mrs. [Egbert L.] Vielé, *Following the Drum: A Glimpse of Frontier Life*,
pp. 125, 128.
      [8] Giddings, *Sketches of the Campaign*, p. 52.

ciados in the last century. Strangely, the pages of history contain little about the gentry of the lower Rio Grande Valley.

The landowner had certain duties toward his servants, and they in turn had specific obligations to perform. He was the protector in time of danger, the adviser and counselor, and not seldom the judge who tried the case as well as inflicted the punishment. Besides his moral duties, the master had material obligations toward his workers and their families. He furnished them their living quarters and a small quantity of money amounting to six reales, or approximately seventy-five cents, in Mexican currency. Indeed, in some parts of the Valley the system of "four bits and meals, or six reales and furnish your own" continued until 1914.[9]

It is unfortunate that travelers in the lower Valley region before 1850 made so few observations and comments on social life of the Spanish-speaking ranchers. We know only that there were two classes of persons, *los agraciados* and those who worked for them. Despite the differences in status the most important social unit in each of the segments of the population was the small family. Other than that we know very little.

The Second Phase (1848–1900)

The year 1848 began an era of diminishing isolation in the region. Previously visitors to the isolated ranches and towns had been few and far between. The fact that parties of travelers were comprised of explorers, surveyors, and naturalists testifies to the unsettled character of that northeastern corner of Mexico. In the second half of the century, however, the area was visited by increasing numbers of aliens, many of whom settled permanently among the ranchers and townspeople. During this era the nature of the social life changed. Before we discuss those changes a description of some of the people instrumental in effecting the changing way of life is in order.

The international boundary between Mexico and the United States offered a golden opportunity to mercantilists, and by the middle of the nineteenth century most of the large-scale commerce in the region was in the hands of non-Mexicans. Also, the absence of ministers of religion in the forbidding area of northeastern Mexico

[9] Jovita González Mireles, "Social Life in Cameron, Starr and Zapata Counties," pp. 48–49.

caused the concern of clerics of several faiths. Catholic orders and
Protestant sects hastened to fill the vacuum. Another cause of
change was the so-called Mexican War, which drew to the frontier
many thousands of United States troops and members of ancillary
forces.

The aliens congregated in conveniently placed crossing points located at the mouth of the Rio Grande or along its banks, and also at
well-established warehousing locations. For example, the small town
of Roma, located on the south bank of the Rio Grande, offered an
enticing opportunity to the enterprising merchant. It is estimated
that by winter of 1849 approximately 160 inhabitants, of whom
nearly half were from the United States, were living in Roma.[10]
Throughout the frontier region non-Mexicans conducted most of
the mercantile operations; Americans, British, Germans, and French
were represented in important numbers.[11]

Attracted by cheap lands and freedom from taxation increasing
numbers of American and European colonists arrived in the delta
lands of the lower Rio Grande. Hardly had they arrived than they
clamored for independence from Mexico. Quickly and easily Texas
wrested its independence from the mother country and declared its
sovereignty in 1836; but the new Republic did not seek to establish
its jurisdiction over the Rio Grande settlements, largely because of
the lack of sympathy for the young Republic manifested by the
Spanish-speaking majority of the borderland.

The diminishing isolation of the delta lands of the Rio Grande and
the provinces of Tamaulipas and Texas as a whole, brought their
residents more and more to the attention of the world. Clerics and
other representatives of religious orders voiced concern about the
virtual absence of ministers of religion in the area. Jesuits cared for
the spiritual needs of the populace in and around the city of Monterrey, but proved unable to extend their services to the people of the
Rio Grande settlements or ranches because of the great distances involved.

So forbidding was the semidesert area to the religious that the Oblates of Mary Immaculate, a group notable for its preference for
work in the most inhospitable environments, undertook missionary

[10] Leroy P. Graf, "The Economic History of the Lower Rio Grande Valley:
1820–1875," pp. 437–438.
[11] *Ibid.*, p. 719.

labors in the area between the Rio Grande and San Antonio, Texas.[12] However, the plans of the order to establish itself in the region met with some opposition from other orders of Catholic missionaries whose areas of responsibility extended to the delta. One of the earliest of the Oblates in the lower Valley wrote disparagingly of those few priests who had preceded the Oblates to the frontier. He wrote that, almost to a man, the religious of the other orders detested the Mexican ranchers, and that "few priests take any interest in them."[13]

The chronicler just quoted arrived in the lower Valley in 1849, the first of his order to minister to the ranchers. It was his assignment to reactivate the faith of those who, it was claimed, had been without religious instruction since the departure of the Franciscan brothers a century before. At the half century the newly appointed Oblate bishop received special permission from the ordinary of Monterrey to make a pastoral visit on both sides of the Rio Grande, the first such visit in forty-five years. From Laredo to Brownsville and Matamoros he confirmed 11,000 people on that pastoral journey.[14]

Despite the fact that the Oblates were Catholic, as were all the Spanish speakers in the Valley, the priests were from lands other than Mexico and Spain and could not speak Spanish. Only through great effort were the Oblates able to establish themselves in the region, but succeed they did. The priests encountered not only problems of communication with their parishioners and objections from other Catholic orders already established in the region, but opposition from Protestant missionary organizations as well.

To Protestant evangelists the people of the Rio Grande delta offered a golden opportunity for demonstration of a nearly true pathway to righteousness and eternity than any they had previously known. Melinda Rankin, a zealous Presbyterian, was the first to appear on the scene for the cause of Protestantism. Commencing her labors in 1852, she immediately opened a school in Brownsville, where she taught the English language and Presbyterian interpretations of Christianity to the children of Mexican families on both sides of the international frontier.[15] During her first several years

[12] For a good description of the Oblates in this region: Bernard Doyon, O.M.I., *The Cavalry of Christ on the Rio Grande.*

[13] *Ibid.*, p. 133.

[14] *Ibid.*, p. 26.

[15] Melinda Rankin, *Twenty Years among the Mexicans: A Narrative of Missionary Labor*, p. 38.

of travail along the border Miss Rankin was confined to the north side, although people from south of the border were converted and attended her school.

Unwilling to remain confined to the American side Miss Rankin impatiently awaited permission to enter Mexico. As a consequence of the Reform Movement, led by the renowned Benito Juárez, Mexico's laws were liberalized and the climate for Protestantism became less hostile. Miss Rankin left as soon as possible for Monterrey to establish her mission, where she sought to "grapple with the prince of darkness on his throne, by establishing the truth in the very heart of his dominions."[16] In Monterrey, Miss Rankin succeeded in converting rural Mexicans and they, in turn, traveled about northern Mexico converting others to Protestantism.[17] From 1852 onward, the Spanish-speaking Catholics of the delta lands north and south of the Rio Grande were beset by American missionary representatives of the Methodist, Baptist, and Quaker religions, as well as by the zealous Miss Rankin.

In addition to missionary activities fostered by newly arrived Protestants, native religious movements also were disturbing the countrypeople. These were probably a reflection of the instability of the era, a period during which unfamiliar dogmas were being introduced to the populace. Father Parisot, a perceptive Oblate, describes one such native movement well:

It occurred in 1860. The rumor had been current for some time that a Saint had appeared in the mountains of Nuevo León, Mexico, and that he was working astounding miracles, healing all kinds of diseases which man is heir to, and fortelling future events. Men, women, and children were seen on the roads leaving their homes and their occupations in order to pay their respects to the Saint, or to be cured of some disease. Many came to consult me before undertaking the journey. My answer was, "The hand of God is not shortened. What has been seen so often may be repeated for the edification of the faithful, and the conversion of sinners."[18]

Parisot, moved by curiosity, decided to meet the mystic Saint to whom so many of the local populace were making pilgrimages.

I saw crowds of pilgrims on their way to visit Tatita. I also saw invalids carried to him, in vehicles of every description. I reached Mier

16 *Ibid.*, p. 121.
17 *Ibid.*, pp. 145–146.
18 P. F. Parisot, O.M.I., *The Reminiscences of a Texas Missionary*, p. 43.

at 8 P.M. The streets were crowded with strangers, and the principal plaza of the city was packed with human beings, all on their knees, reciting the Rosary with this singular personage, who was looked upon as a Saint. He appeared to be about 60 years old with stolid features. His hair and beard seemed unacquainted with comb and brush. He wore a kind of Franciscan garment reaching to a little below the knees, and a long cord knotted at the end, hung down by his side as far as his feet.

A Rosary with large beads hung from his neck, and he wore sandals on his feet. He was kneeling before 100 lighted candles, which were stuck in the ground in the form of a cross. These candles he extinguished himself and gave as a reason for so doing, that any one else attempting to extinguish them would drop dead on the spot. Close by was a coarse, wooden cross, about five feet long, which he used to carry on his shoulders during his wanderings, which were constantly performed on foot. But here is the most curious part of the farce. He stood up and began to preach and this is a compendium of his doctrine, which I heard distinctly: "My brethren! The new religion which I am sent to deliver to you was revealed to me by Almighty God Himself, for the Mexican nation. It consists exclusively in three things: To adore the Eternal Father and the Holy Cross, and to say the Rosary. Confession, Mass, and all other religious practices are abolished. Follow me, adore the cross, and you shall be saved." This nonsense did not surprise me very much, but I was pained to see such a mulitude paying the most respectful attention to his false declarations.[19]

The Reverend Parisot decided to unmask the pretender and began to conspire with the pastor of the Mier parish. However, the latter was obviously overawed by the charismatic Tatita, and replied:

My whole parish has abandoned me to follow this charlatan, this diabolical hypocrite. Last Sunday I had only six women at Mass. The imposter has 300 *Hermanos* [Brothers] armed to the teeth, who draw their share of the profits. An American is the manager of the whole thing. This man, it is true, has performed some wonderful cures, but all within the province of nature. His medicines are pure water, mescal, herbs, and roots. He is quite successful in treating ordinary diseases, and he makes the people believe that all his cures are performed through supernatural agencies.[20]

Despite the fears of his colleague, Parisot went to visit with the

[19] *Ibid.*
[20] *Ibid.*, p. 46.

Saint. "He received me kindly, and brought me to an altar, in the centre of which was a large cross. He then lit two candles and invited me to say the Rosary with him." When Father Parisot refused the invitation and unceremoniously blew out the candles, the watching crowd demonstrated increased hostility toward him. Tatita then addressed the multitude and asked that they avenge the insult. They moved toward the platform in menacing fashion, but Parisot was saved by the intervention of the Mayor of Mier, who escorted the good Father out through a rear exit and away from the town. After being so ungraciously delivered to the town limits, Parisot returned to the United States. He heard on the following day that the Saint and a follower had been assassinated by a "young man from a neighboring village [who] gathered a certain number of comrades and resolved to go and meet Tatita on the road and kill him because, he said, such a man as that would bring shame and dishonour on religion and our country. Viva México!"[21]

The foregoing paragraphs have discussed the slow decline of the isolation in which the peasantry of the lower Rio Grande Valley lived. By the middle of the nineteenth century that region witnessed the increasingly important influence of aliens, who brought with them rival systems of belief. Such novelties as Catholic missionary priests and teaching orders of nuns, both groups from western Europe, were introduced.[22] Furthermore, by 1870 fourteen missionaries representing a variety of Protestant churches were ministering to the local Spanish-speaking population.

During the period 1848 to 1900 the lower Rio Grande Valley played host to a relatively small number of highly skilled technicians from the United States and western Europe. Between 1880 and 1904 a continued effort was expended by American citizens to sever the historic dependence of the Valley on Monterrey and old Mexico. Capital and technological know-how were sought to bring the Valley into the orbit of Corpus Christi and San Antonio, Texas, and St. Louis in Missouri. As late as 1903 a railroad surveying party:

. . . found a region practically cut off from the rest of the world. Commercial activity was limited to a few small ships and the mail stage. Without transportation or irrigation, agriculture could contribute very

[21] *Ibid.*, p. 49.
[22] Doyon, *Cavalry of Christ*, p. 238; González, *"Social Life,"* p. 76.

little; and the cattle industy was carried on under tremendous handicaps. Brownsville had a population of 7,000 most of whom had come from south of the border; Corpus Christi could count but 4,500 citizens. The only telegraph service was over a military line from Fort McIntosh, at Laredo, to Fort Brown.[23]

To aliens the most attractive feature of the lower Valley was land with which one might speculate. So cheap were these otherwise undesirable lands that purchase appealed only to those of a gambling nature. Capitalized land companies then purchased the riverside tracts, improved them, and broke up large tracts into smaller lots.

Most of the large tracts of land purchased by Anglo-American speculators fronted on the Rio Grande; each of the speculative companies laid out a small town on its tract. In the Valley the history of land purchases is also the history of group relations. Two methods of purchase predominated.

In many cases when Americans sought to buy these lands the Mexican owners were more than delighted to receive even a small sum for their rights. . . . For his part, the American who purchases [sic] was anxious for the opportunity to speculate on the future development of the valley, especially when his speculation cost him so little.[24]

In turn, those who bought from the speculative land company were not interested in cultivating the land, but in reselling the lot at a profit. Each purchaser depended on the continued tendency of the land values to rise to assist him in paying for his purchase.[25]

Another of the favorite techniques by which to acquire land was the sheriff's sale, an occasion when lands appropriated by a county sheriff to cover back taxes were sold at auction. Land thus sold was bought for so ridiculously low a sum that contemporary Mexican-Americans of the lower Valley contend that their ancestors were swindled of their holdings.[26] The contention is nursed as a sore grievance, and contributes greatly to present-day tensions between the two groups.

The history of the land on which stands the present city of New

[23] J. Lee Stambaugh and Lillian J. Stambaugh, *The Lower Rio Grande Valley of Texas*, p. 169.

[24] Graf, "Economic History," pp. 256–257.

[25] *Ibid.*, pp. 235–236.

[26] Ozzie Simmons, "The Mutual Images and Expectations of Anglo-Americans and Mexican-Americans," *Daedalus* (Spring, 1961), p. 287.

Lots, Texas, is typical of the history of the entire Valley east of Mission. New Lots rests on a grant of land originally bestowed by the Spanish Crown on Juan José Hinajosa, who had petitioned the land from the King. At the time that the petition was awarded the grant bordered the Rio Grande for eleven and one-half miles and extended north from the river for a distance of fifteen miles. The land was owned by the descendants of the grantees, although it was divided into several lots between then and the mid-nineteenth century. Between 1848 and 1877 portions of the original grant changed hands several times, but it was not until 1877 that a non-Spanish surname figured in the transactions. In June of that year the sheriff of Hidalgo County sold 3,027 acres of the grant for a total cash price of $15.00 in order to cover tax arrears. Then in May of the following year the Hidalgo County sheriff sold 4,000 additional acres of delta land from the original grant, receiving a total price of $17.75 for the 4,000 acres. In both transactions the purchasers of the lands were persons with non-Spanish surnames.

The history of land transactions in the lower Valley may be divided into three periods, each of which was important to the social history of the border region. The three periods may be represented in the following manner:

Period	*Characteristics of Transactions*
1746–1848	All land transactions recorded took place between individuals or families with Spanish surnames.
1848–1900	All transactions recorded transpired between individuals with Spanish surnames and others with non-Spanish surnames. Lands, in all cases, passed from Spanish surnames to non-Spanish surnames.
1900–present	All transactions recorded took place between individuals with non-Spanish surnames or their corporate representatives.

Each of the land developers improved the tract he had purchased. The large tracts were irrigated and then divided into smaller lots intended to be sold to vegetable farmers. As further inducement to the potential purchaser, the seeds were sometimes planted previous to the lots' sale. The stage was set. It was time to lure prospective buyers to the lower Valley.

Before describing what happened to the lower Valley when it was settled by many thousands of farmers and townsmen from other states of the nation, I shall sum up the characteristic nature of the relationships between the two groups, Mexican-American and Anglo-American, during the second phase of the historical sequence.

Fortunately firsthand accounts in the form of recollections of some of those who took part in those relationships are available. The reminiscences garnered by González in 1929 all came from individuals of advanced age who had been youths when the related events transpired.

The Garzas, the original owners of the land, have many descendants living in Starr County. Many of the Garzas married Texans [Anglos]. One of the Garza girls married Henry Clay Davis, a Kentuckian. . . . After the marriage in Camargo, Davis came to Texas, and on property inherited by his wife built the first cabin which was to be the nucleus for the present city of Rio Grande.[27]

During the fifties the Americans and foreigners who came were all single men. But they did not remain so for long; they married the daughters of the leading Spanish-Mexican families and made of Rio Grande city a cosmopolitan little town.

Such names as Lacaze, Laborde, Lafargue, Decker, Marx, Block, Monroe, Nix, Stuard and Ellert among families who claim the Spanish language as their own show the mixture of races in the native element of the town.[28]

Society was different in those days to what it is now. The men were more gentlemanly, the ladies more gentile [sic]. The dances were held in what is now the old court house. The officers from Fort Ringgold and their wives were the honor guests. There were neither racial nor social distinctions between Americans and Mexicans, we were just one family. This was due to the fact that so many of us of that generation had a Mexican mother and an American or European father.[29]

We, Texas-Mexicans of the border . . . although we hold on to our traditions, and are proud of our race, are loyal to the United States, in spite of the treatment we receive by some of the new Americans. Before their arrival, there were no racial or social distinctions between us. Their children married ours, ours married theirs, and both were glad and proud of the fact. But since the coming of the "white trash" from the north and middle west we felt the change. They made us feel for the first time that we were Mexicans and that they considered themselves our superiors.[30]

[27] Mireles, "Social Life," p. 26.
[28] Ibid., p. 27.
[29] Ibid.   [30] Ibid., p. 28 (italics added).

Although I was not so fortunate as to interview persons who were alive in the 1850's, the reports of older informants recollecting what *their* parents had told them of life in the mid-nineteenth century fully support those garnered by González more than thirty years ago.

The lower Rio Grande Valley underwent a transformation between 1850 and 1915. No longer a land isolated from the main currents of Mexican or United States national life, it was swept up by a changing continent. The native Mexican was exposed to a number of different religious philosophies advanced by missionaries from Protestant and Catholic orders. Concurrently, the quiet, bucolic scene of subsistence pastoralism and gardening was rent by the clangor of steamships, railroads, and irrigation steam pumps. These noisy machines were introduced by technicians from other lands, who brought to the lower Valley new elements of culture by which man might adapt himself to the environment.

The newcomers and the natives lived side by side. Each stood to the other in a mutually recognized relationship of superiority and inferiority, but with no factor of actual social or political dominance involved. With rare exceptions, the Spanish-speaking peasants felt themselves the intellectual and economic inferiors of the more recently arrived Americans and Europeans. Socially, there were two classes of Mexicans. One class subsumed those who owned large tracts of land—*los agraciados*. The second class—*los peones*—included those who herded the livestock, weeded the gardens, or worked as the servants for *los agraciados*. Both groups eagerly borrowed new technological ways brought by the aliens. They reasoned— incorrectly, as it turned out—that as quickly as technological and educational equality was achieved, social equality would follow. Conversely, the newcomer, so confident of his superiority in the face of the low technological standard of the Mexican, could afford to learn the Spanish language and adopt the ways of the native to some extent. Native herbal cures, ranch clothing specially adapted to the thornbrush forests of the region, and Mexican foods were utilized by the newcomers. The more impecunious of them found it well worth while to marry members of rich, landed Mexican families. In this second phase of the history of social relations in the lower Valley, Mexican-Americans and Anglo-Americans each sought to adopt some of the characteristic modes of life of the other.

The Third Phase (1900–Present)

In the first two decades of the twentieth century intergroup relations changed for the worse. The English-speaking people who purchased the lands from speculating development companies represented middle-class, Anglo-American culture, a life style quite incompatible with that of the Mexican-American ranchers. The newcomers who flocked to the Valley included businessmen and professional people, as well as a number of successful commercial farmers.

According to an account by one of the land salesmen, a man who traveled throughout the United States east of the Rockies in his attempts to induce the well-off to invest their savings in the newly developed frontier:

We went looking for people who were already successful as doctors and lawyers, successful in business, people who could recognize a good thing when they saw it. We wouldn't touch anyone who didn't have money. Most of those people had stocks and bonds; land down here was a self-evident business with citrus as a crop.[31]

Another former land salesman recalled to me that those who purchased land during the boom years:

. . . were not wealthy, but they were fairly well-off; they had some money. A great deal of the land was sold to northerners after it had been improved by the development companies. The land was bought just as you would buy stock in General Motors. Some of those investors expected to be made rich on their investment; others expected a steady money-maker out of the project.

For the most part, the homeseekers made the trip to New Lots on specially scheduled excursion trains of the Southern Pacific and Union Pacific Railways. In order to facilitate the transportation of potential buyers of Valley land, special discount rates were arranged by the land companies. For example, the usual round-trip rate between Kansas City and Lyford, Texas, southernmost terminal of the Union Pacific, was ninety dollars. However, the land-development companies arranged with the railroads to cut the rate from ninety to fifty dollars. Upon their arrival in Lyford, the potential buyer and his family received an openhanded welcome.

[31] Personal communication. In actual fact citrus was of little commercial importance in the lower Valley until the middle of the 1920's.

Representatives of each land company drove their clients to company developments, and then the prospects were entertained by the land agents at barbecues, picnics, and other festivities, during which they were wooed by the blandishments of the salesmen. Unpleasant sights of the countryside were avoided whenever possible. Some of those who were homeseekers recall that when they were in the company of a salesman and passed a sinkhole or impenetrable patch of scrub forest, all aboard were invited to "bow your heads in prayer."

The land companies spared no effort to portray the Rio Grande Valley as an area in which, given the proper attitudes of pioneering and plenty of hard work, a great return would be made on every investment. Advertising campaigns were conducted by means of mass media and handbills in many of the northern states and Canada. They were supplemented, moreover, by personal visits from salesmen, who traveled throughout the continent east of the Rockies.

The new Anglo settlers came to the valley as pioneers. What struck them upon their arrival may be summed up in the pithy statement of an early homeseeker: "When we came here there was nothing but rats, cactus, mesquite, and Mexicans." With vigor characteristic of pioneers, the Anglos set about to change what they found. The modern history of the lower Valley may be written in terms of the effort by Anglo-Americans to change the conditions which they encountered, and the reaction of the Mexican-Americans to those efforts.

To the newcomers the Mexican-Americans represented a group subject to vast improvements, although they would first have to be shown the way. The new frontiersmen extolled the values of the old frontier, on which they had been raised. The new Valley society was to be open, not closed, and social mobility was open to all. It was a basic assumption of the new society that, once guided along the way, the Mexican-Americans would evidence strong desires to emulate the life style of the Anglo-Americans. In the new open-class society the natives were urged to exhibit industry, perseverance, and sobriety if they aspired to equality with the Anglo-American middle-class settlers. In the Anglo-American conception of the new society the values of individualism, self-achievement, and social equality were prized above all. Social equality with the Anglo-Americans was the premium offered for the acquirement of a new life style by the Mexican-Americans. Given such values as building blocks for the new society envisioned by the Anglo-Americans, the stratification system they created was not cast into a mold characterized by rigidity, but was kept open and variable. Social differentiation was held to be dependent upon the achievements of the individual, himself, rather than upon ascribed characteristics.

It became a self-imposed task of the Anglo-Americans to offer to the Mexican-Americans an opportunity to emulate their better-educated, better-employed, and more community-conscious neighbors. The fact that Anglo-Americans conceived of the lower Valley and the city of New Lots as an open- rather than a closed-class system is crucial to an understanding of present intergroup relationships and misunderstandings. At the turn of the century, when the mass immigration to the Valley from the northlands began, the area was sparsely settled by native Spanish-speaking families. The extensive construction of towns, irrigation facilities, railroads, and warehouses during the early decades of the present century attracted large numbers of Spanish-speaking laborers from the Republic of Mexico. Who were they, and from where did they come? Probably, those who labored in the construction of the ditches, the causeways, the towns, and the warehouses represented all sectors of the Republic of Mexico as well as the hamlets and villages of southeastern Texas. If we may infer the distribution of the points of origin of the population on the basis of the Spanish-speaking population which remained in Mexiquito after the boom years, the great majority came from northeast Mexico and southeast Texas (see accompanying map). Proportionately fewer will have come from the central plateau of Mexico, and almost none from the south of that Republic. There are few published materials on the points of origin of the Spanish-speaking population of Texas, much less on the people of Hidalgo County.[32] Today's Mexican-Americans of New

---

[32] In a summary of the demographic materials Lyle Saunders discussed some of the problems which the data pose: ("The Spanish-Speaking Population of Texas," *Inter-American Education, Occasional Papers*, No. 5). Also note the absence of material referring to points of origin in the exhaustive bibliography by Charles C. Cumberland ("The United States-Mexican Border: A Selective Guide to the Literature of the Region," Supplement to *Rural Sociology*, XXV [June, 1960], 90–102); see also Paul S. Taylor, "Note on Streams of Mexican Migration," *American Journal of Sociology*, XXXVI (September, 1930), 287–288. The most current discussion of demographic characteristics of the Mexican-American populace of Texas is that of Harley L. Browning and S. Dale McLemore (*A Statistical Profile of the Spanish-Surname Population of Texas*).

Lots maintain close ties to the northeasternmost corner of the Republic of Mexico. Although their religious pilgrimages take them to San Juan de Los Lagos, seldom, if ever, do their visits to relatives take them south of Saltillo. The Spanish-speaking people of New Lots retain their ties to the motherland through visits to northern religious shrines, through contacts with kinfolk who are *norteños,* and through enjoyment of music and foods considered to be uniquely northern. Mexican-Americans of New Lots were all born within a remarkably small transect encompassing sectors of the United States and Mexico.

Mrs. Ramírez, a woman now in her sixties, recalls that she and her husband came to the new nation with ambitions of giving their children the things that they had never been able to have for themselves.

My husband worked for the La Purísima hacienda near Montemorelos in Mexico. Even though we had managed to raise a couple of cows for ourselves, the conditions there were so bad that we decided to come to this country in 1916. My husband started digging irrigation ditches, but then, after a couple of years, we were able to buy a couple of shacks from the water company and we started renting these out to other families.

A young man, Epifanio, said that his father, who had come to this country earlier than most of the immigrants, came from a ranch near the small town of Cruillas, northeast Mexico.

My father came over here and did wage work clearing the land of mesquite around Mercedes, Texas. After a while he got himself a couple of wooden barrels and a horse, and started carrying water from the river to sell to the housewives. He transported water like this until 1908, and then opened a small grocery store in Mercedes. When construction began in New Lots many of the Mexicans moved from Mercedes to the new town. My father was among them.

A woman in her middle sixties, Mrs. Gavilán, described how:

. . . times were hard in those days, and my husband was working all of the time. We finally got enough money together to buy a car, and my husband used it for a taxi. We used to bring the people from their shacks on the outside of town to the grocery store and back on Saturday nights. For myself, I always had my hand in some kind of selling. Sometimes I was selling fruit from a street stand, and sometimes it was peanuts.

An older man, now past his sixtieth birthday, furrowed his brow as he attempted to recall the details of his arrival in this country. As with many people who are unable to either read or write, dates and names have become permanently etched in his memory.

My father had been a soldier with the government forces, but he was killed in a battle with revolutionaries near Puebla. My two uncles had been working on a ranch on this side near Brownsville, and they sent word for my mother, my sister, and myself to join them working for Americans. I was fourteen years old then, and I can remember that we crossed the bridge at Brownsville in May of 1919. We all lived together in a shack on a ranch. I think the ranch was called Los Cuates. We worked in the fields, uprooting the mesquite brush from the earth. When I first saw the site on which New Lots was to be, it was known as Rancho Resaca, and there was nothing but mesquite on it.

Old Rogélio, now the sexton of the church in Mexiquito, claims to be one of the first to reside in New Lots, having come to this country in 1912. Between that year and 1917 he worked as foreman of a labor crew, clearing the delta lands of brush and trees. Rogélio recalls that at times he had eighty men working under his direction. The crew represented all shades of political opinion: "Villistas, Carrancistas, Governistas, Zapatistas, tenía todos. Mucha gente decía que yo tenía mucho valor trabajar con estos matones, tantos revolucionários." (Followers of Villa, of Carranza, as well as supporters of the government and even of Zapata, everybody. Many people commented that I was very brave to work with all these killers, so many revolutionaries.)

In the lower Valley, homes and processing plants for the harvests were constructed as quickly as the brush could be cleared. With the exception of several petty merchandising ventures all Mexican-Americans in the new city of New Lots were employed as unskilled and semiskilled laborers, whereas Anglo-Americans were engaged in commerce, in the professions, and in managerial roles of the commercial farms and processing plants.

Almost as quickly as the new city was incorporated all Spanish-speaking residents were segregated from those of English speech. In an editorial written one year after the beginning of the construction of the townsite, the New Lots newspaper commented on the already emergent segregation of one group from the other.

One year ago the townsite was an entanglement of brush. One year ago the first town lot was sold. Today a flourishing town is established where the wilderness prevailed 365 days ago. Beautiful homes dot its streets, business blocks re-echo to the sound of continuous tramping of pedestrian and the honk of the auto. A school building such as one would expect to find in a ten-year-old town is being completed—well, what's the use. We could go on and on and not be able to tell it all. However, the writer was amazed upon making a count of the residences to find there are seventy families occupying homes on the south side of the track. Counting five houses to the block it would make fourteen blocks, almost a solid mile of houses. There are almost as many families in the *Mexican section* [italics added].

"They didn't want Mexicans to live in New Lots," a reflective resident of today's north side recalled. Indeed, the local newspaper commented:

That part of the townsite north of the M.P. Railway has been given over to our Mexican Neighbors and to industrial institutions. They have their own Chamber of Commerce, and work in conjunction with the New Lots Chamber of Commerce.

In another editorial of the era, the newspaper commented: "The building for the Mexican school has been placed in Mexiquito and will be opened to Mexican children in the near future."

As soon as the construction of a school system began, pupils were assigned either to a "Mexican" school or to an "Anglo" school. All teaching in the north-side schools was to be in English. Indeed, to-day, officials and teachers of the unified school system perceive the teaching of English to be the primary goal of the north-side institutions. Conversely, Spanish was not taught in the elementary schools south of the tracks, nor is it today. Spanish *is* taught as one of the foreign languages in the high school, however, occupying a position in the curriculum similar to the other foreign languages, French and German.

In the earlier days of the city some traffic passed across the tracks from one social entity to the other. Most of that traffic consisted of Mexican-Americans going to and from work in Anglo homes and businesses. Such movement across the tracks came to a halt after dusk, for a Mexican-American who was found south of the railway after dark aroused suspicion. He was questioned immediately by the police and hustled across the line, either by the officer, or, less graciously, by the more rowdy of the south-siders. One middle-aged north-sider remembers the time that he attended an afternoon movie on the south side, only to emerge during the evening hours; he was kicked and punched by the young men he encountered until he had successfully made his way across the line. Today, a young married Anglo recalls such experiences and says: "I guess we did it just for meanness."

Early in the life of the city, two groups were recognized and labeled "Mexicans" and "Anglos," or *mexicanos* and *americanos*. All individuals descended from one or more ancestors of Mexican background were arbitrarily aggregated in the social group known by the rubric "Mexican." Some of those individuals were freckled and red-haired, while others were blonde with blue eyes and very light skin. Most, however, were dark-skinned, with black hair, brown eyes, and short stature. All persons in this category spoke Spanish, though some were bilingual.

The "Mexican" group included former *peones* and goatherds, descendants of the *agraciados*, and others formerly engaged in small commercial ventures. Some were native-born American citizens, while others had just crossed the border from Mexico. The great majority of the individuals of this group had little schooling and were functionally illiterate. Consequently, most of them were engaged in pursuits which required little skill or training. Differences between persons subsumed by the term "Mexican" were completely overshadowed by the subordination of all of them as a group to the Anglos. Illustrative of the leveling influence that that subordination to the Anglos had is shown by the fact that those formerly spoken of as *los agraciados* were now *los tuvos*: Those who once had.

During and after the First World War, American troops were sent to the border to provide protection against bandits and irregulars, who caused mischief in the small settlements. After the troops were withdrawn, a series of punitive actions against local Mexican-Americans were undertaken by the ascendant Anglo society. Many stories are told in the Valley about the hostilities between Anglos and Mexican-Americans during that era. The tale which is most often recounted and which generates the strongest sentiments is that of the infamous lynching of a young Mexican who came to live in New Lots. Trained as a telegrapher, the young man opened a school in which he taught telegraphy and radio-repair work. Anglo-American as well as Mexican-American young men came for training, and the young man earned a great deal of respect from the Spanish-speaking folk of the city, although the same people attribute to the Anglo-Americans a great deal of envy of the young man, "They thought that he was making good too early."

The young telegrapher also worked as a construction laborer in order to supplement his income, and on one building-trades job a young Anglo came up to the telegrapher and insulted him, according to the story. The insulted man retorted that the other could not speak to him like that with impunity, "Soy puro mexicano!" In other words: "You can't insult a Mexican like that!" The young telegrapher then hit the other and knocked him out the window. Although hurt, the young Anglo was not seriously injured.

The young Mexican was arrested and taken to the local jail. So tense was the relationship between the two groups of the city that the Mexican-American community mounted an around-the-clock guard at the jail. For three days and three nights the Mexican-American men took turns watching the cell. Then one night, when the guard had departed without having been properly relieved, the prisoner was removed by persons unknown. (The kidnapping probably occurred in September, because those who narrate the story recall that the booths for the celebration of the 16th of September, the day of Mexican national independence, were already constructed in the north-side plaza, and all were awaiting the Mexican consul as the major speaker for the occasion.)

Three days after the kidnapping a search party discovered the corpse. Its condition may best be described as gruesome. It showed evidence of having been tortured and mutilated. So badly did the Spanish-speaking population feel that the Independence Day celebration was called off, the booths in the plaza dismantled. However, the Mexican consul *did* speak; he told the gathering that the telegrapher was killed because he was a Mexican.

Although the death of the telegrapher brought the strongest sentiments to the fore, the event was representative of an era of intergroup hostilities. From the point of view of the Mexican-Americans, the most reprehensible agents of the ascending Anglo society during the third phase of the historical sequence were the Texas Rangers, *los rinches*. The Mexican-Americans perceive *los rinches* as a force which was *designed* to curb and crush any sign of progress or independent action by members of the Mexican-American sociocultural group. They are depicted as dastardly agents of the anti-Mexican attitude fostered by the new Anglo-Americans during the 1920's and 1930's. Some representative tales about the Texas Rangers follow.

A usually placid older man of New Lots' north side recalled that the Rangers would ask a person only "Where are you from?" If the answer was "Mexico," the respondent was told to board the Rangers' truck. Then, a short distance from town those aboard would be shot. On the other hand, the narrator recalled, "If a Mexican had very good references, he would not be shot or picked up." The older man recalled with some pleasure an incident in which he was involved with the Rangers during that period. It occurred while he was working on the ranch of an Anglo. One day when he was driving the boss' young child to town and back in a buckboard, some Rangers came upon the couple and asked the man where he was from. The answer was "Mexico." The Rangers then ordered him to drive the child and buckboard back to the ranch while they followed. When all arrived at the ranch the Rangers told the rancher that they were taking "his Mexican." But the rancher told them that he would shoot the first man who touched his employee, and with that he picked up his rifle. In the face of the threat the Rangers allowed the narrator to remain where he was.

A woman recalls that, when she was a timid young bride, she opened the door of her home to step into the street. In a neighboring doorway she noted what she thought were bundles of old, discarded clothes. When she called her husband he told her to come back into the house, for the bundles were not discarded clothing but human bodies. His answer to her tearful question was simply a shrug of his shoulders and the comment: "*Los rinches* don't like Mexicans."

Such stories are common in New Lots among the Mexican-American populace. But these stories are not confined to New Lots; others, equally frightening, are told throughout the lower Rio Grande Valley. Their interest for us is that they depict a phase characteristic of open tension and hostility between members of the Anglo-American and Mexican-American groups. It should be noted in contrast that such stories are not told about the earlier phase of culture contact.

The Anglo-Americans were not the only ones who made efforts to attend to the problems inherent in a situation of such cultural conflict. Two formal organizations were formed in Mexiquito to help resolve some of the problems faced by the Mexican-Americans in adapting themselves to a new environment. The Sociedad de

Beneficéncia General Ignácio Zaragoza and the Sociedad Mutualista Amigos del Pueblo had much in common, but each was short-lived and, according to all reports, meetings of both mutual societies were scenes of bitter, rancorous argument.

Today in Mexiquito none of the civic groups is oriented toward the maintenance of the bonds between the residents and the Republic to the south. On the contrary, those few committees which exist in Mexiquito have as goals attainment of a satisfactory life for the membership in the United States, although the way in which the goals are to be achieved differ from group to group. A fuller discussion of the few civic groups found in Mexiquito will appear in Chapter 6. However, the present absence of organized groups fostering sentimental ties to Mexico is not a true indication of the pulse of Mexiquito in this regard. Among the oldsters there is considerable feeling that for one born in Mexico to acquire United States citizenship is like "spitting on the [Mexican] flag," or "being a traitor." There are others who find American citizenship unacceptable because they do not feel wanted in this country. On the other hand, the children of those adamant oldsters continually urge them to acquire citizenship. None of the middle-aged or younger residents express a desire to establish closer ties with Mexico, or a preference to keep their Mexican citizenship rather than acquiring citizenship in the United States. But such unanimity of opinion with regard to citizenship does not preclude the fact that there exists a difference of opinion among the young adults of Mexiquito as to the extent to which they should identify with the culture of the Anglo-Americans. That difference of opinion also will be discussed later.

In 1930 the Anglo-American society formed by the newly arrived townsmen and farmers of the lower Valley had assured themselves an impregnable, superior position technologically, economically, and socially. But one source of strength remained with the Mexican social group: local politics. The county Democratic Party and its offices rested upon a foundation of the Spanish-speaking voters controlled by a party machine built on the basis of traditional reciprocity between the power-holder and those to whom he dispensed favors. Weeks described the relationship as characteristically feudal:

In becoming masters they [Anglos] were forced to adjust themselves to the Mexican inhabitant. They learned Spanish and acquainted themselves with the Mexican's psychology, traditions, and habits. In the process they were themselves in a measure Mexicanized. The whole relationship was natural and was not necessarily resented by those who submitted to it; most of them had never been used to anything else, either in Texas or Mexico.[33]

One of the greatest of the political "bosses" in the lower Valley at that time was James Wells, but, with the arrival of the new masses of Anglo settlers, Wells and other old-style politicians were defeated. The old political system was destroyed and Wells and others were subjected to state and federal investigations on charges of corruption. The old-style political system was summed up nicely by Wells, himself, when he testified before an investigation committee of the Texas Senate.

So far as I being a boss, if I exercise any influence among these people because in the 41 years I have lived among them I have tried to so conduct myself as to show them I was their friend and they could trust me, I take no advantage of them or their ignorance. I buried many a one of them with my money and married many a one of them, it wasn't two or three days before the election, but through the years around, and they have always been true to me and if it earned me the title of boss, every effort and all my money went for the benefit of the Democratic ticket from President to constable.[34]

Their friendship is individual. For instance you have a great many friends among them, and they would follow your name and your fortunes and that is the way it is.[35]

Then, again, Mexicans under their race, under Spanish rule, go to their leader. I suppose in twenty or thirty days I would see 100 of them; they would just drop in town and come up and ask me what ticket I thought they ought to vote, and so with the heads of the ranches; a Mexican would go ask his major domo, as they call him, like padrone, very few of them own their own farms.[36]

The political system represented by James Wells was congruent with the society of the lower Valley prior to 1913, a society in which personal relationships were of great importance. Such a

[33] O. Douglas Weeks, "The Texas-Mexican and the Politics of South Texas," *American Political Science Review*, XLII (August, 1930), 610.

[34] *Glasscock* vs. *Parr*, Supplement to Texas Senate Journal, 36th Session (1919), pp. 846–851.

[35] *Ibid.*

[36] *Ibid.*

political system was incongruent with the new society and did not reflect the new balance of power.

This struggle of power between the two points of view culminated in the "reform movement" of the 1930's. In 1930 the Anglos organized the Good Government League, whose avowed purpose was to wrest control of the Democratic Party in the Valley and to "clean up" local politics. The Good Government League nominated and elected delegates from many precincts represented by opposition delegates from New Lots and its Spanish-speaking neighborhood, Mexiquito. In spite of the fact that some of the Valley delegates to the Good Government League possessed Spanish surnames, none of those who represented the two precincts in New Lots had a Spanish surname.

So potent a force was the newly organized reform movement in the lower Valley that the Good Government League swept away all opposition in all elections in 1930. In general the proportion of ballots cast for the League compared with those cast for the regular Democratic machine was in the ratio of six to four. But the votes cast in favor of the League from New Lots' south-side (i.e., Anglo) precinct were in the ratio of five to one. On the contrary, the vote from north New Lots (the Mexiquito precinct) was in favor of the county Democratic candidates in a ratio of five to one.

The victory of the Good Government League at the polls was strengthened by the trial and conviction of the political boss of the regular Democratic organization, as well as others powerful in the county or regional system of Democratic Party politics, for example, James Wells. By the end of 1930 the Anglo society was assured unassailable superiority in all spheres of activity over the subordinated Mexican-Americans.

Summary

Culture contact between an Anglo social group and a native Mexican-American social group began in the lower Rio Grande Valley during the middle of the nineteenth century. The phase of intergroup relations between that time and 1915 was characterized by mutual toleration and esteem by members of one group for the way of life of the other. The members of each of the social groups valued and adopted certain elements of the other's culture, and marriage across group lines met with approbation. Although participants in the two contrasting ways of life shared the same environmental niche, neither assumed a role of social or political dominance over the other.

In 1915 many thousands of immigrants from the northern sectors of the continent arrived in the lower Valley. They were commercial farmers and merchants, in contrast to the peripatetic surveyors, sailors, and naturalists by whom they were preceded. Their perception of themselves was as pioneers on a new frontier; consequently, rather than adapting themselves to an already existent way of life, such as that of the Mexican-Americans, the pioneers conceived as their role the modification of the physical and social environment of the Valley. The environment was to be changed in order to fulfill the needs and expectations of the newcomers.

The intergroup relations characteristic of this era were quite distinct from those of the first and second phases of the historical sequence. Phase Three had begun. In this third phase of the sequence, the adoption of Mexican cultural elements by members of the Anglo group was disapproved. Moreover, the use of the Spanish language by Anglos met with strong social sanction, while marriage between an Anglo and a Mexican-American meant the removal of the Anglo spouse from his or her social group. All persons married to a Mexican-American, or their children, were relegated to a neighborhood actually and symbolically inferior. Finally, severely punitive activities were engaged in by representatives of the new Anglo society against Mexican-Americans *as* Mexican-Americans. Many of the activities and attitudes of today's Mexican-Americans of New Lots are colored by the nature of the relationship between the two groups during an earlier era.

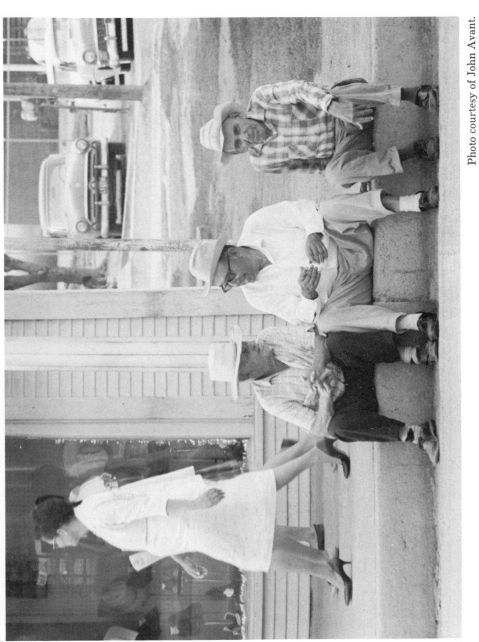

1. Chatting in front of Jesuito's store.

2. A neighborhood grocery.

3.   A North Boulevard store.

4. The Roman Catholic Church.

5. The Church of Christ.

6. The Assembly of God Church.

Photo courtesy of John Avant.

7. One of the Pentecostal churches.

8. A home of seasonal migrant laborers.

Part II

SOCIAL RELATIONS

3. THE FAMILY

Contact between the two ethnic groupings of New Lots has given rise to changes in the traditional patterns of behavior which characterized the Mexican-American family. The contemporary society of Mexiquito is comprised of a number of bilaterally oriented small families, to which individuals acknowledge their only binding allegiance. The strength with which a person is bound to his family so overshadows all other bonds in importance that it contributes to the atomistic nature of the neighborhood. Socially, if not spatially, each household stands alone, separated from others.[1]

Any study of the contemporary society of Mexican-Americans in New Lots leads to the familial socialization within an extensive kindred. The nuclear family stands out in sharp relief from the rest of kin, and it is characterized by denotative kinship terminology, which contrasts with the generally classificatory usage of the system. An individual's essential social unit is comprised of his parents and his parents' brothers and sisters. Particularly important to an individual are his mother's sisters. In the second ascending generation—that of an individual's grandparents—both sets of grandparents are revered, but not the siblings of the grandparents. In the individual's generation his own siblings (*hermano, hermana*) are conceptually separated from others, as are also his first cousins

[1] Cf., Paul Ming-Chang Lin, "Voluntary Kinship and Voluntary Association in a Mexican-American Community," p. 73.

(*primos hermanos*), who are separated from other, farther removed cousins (*primos*). In all contexts a reference to a first cousin on either side pointedly distinguishes that class from other classes of relatives.[2] *Primos hermanos* are said to be somewhat like one's sisters and brothers. One is expected to have especially affective relations with them; this is particularly true between female first cousins. One night while I was standing on the sidewalk talking with a young man his niece approached us holding hands with a younger girl. When they departed I mentioned to him in a joking fashion that "They look cute, walking hand in hand." He responded heartily: "Si, hombre! Son primas hermanas, ellas!" (Indeed! They're first cousins.)

Another time, several young men were discussing the relationship between two others, known to us all. The young men under discussion were first cousins, one of whom was a physician who was said to have expressed the desire to send his first cousin through medical school. One of the discussants expressed doubt that the physician would come through with his promise, but another rejoined: "Sure he'll pay for it, they're cousins!" Another interjected: "Cousins *hell!* They're *first* cousins!"

Once a young man was regaling his friends with accounts of a dance he had recently attended in Mexico. The dance was held in celebration of the fifteenth birthday of his very lovely girl cousin. After he showed snapshots of the girl to the rest of us one of the others present asked him for an introduction, which, he intimated, the lucky man could effect, since he and the girl were cousins. Another of the young men suggested that there was a strong probability that the introduction could be brought about because the two were not only *primos* but *primos hermanos!*

In the first descending generation, in which are found one's own offspring, the terminology differentiates between one's own children (*hijos, hijas*) and others. All other kinsmen of that generation are spoken of as *sobrinos* and *sobrinas*. Note that the distinction observed between first cousins and all other degrees of cousinship in one's own generation is lost in the generation of the cousins' children.

In Mexiquito a domestic group comprised of a nuclear family is

---

[2] In Lin's data from Kansas City, the distinction between first and other cousins is absent (*Ibid*, p. 77).

not only the unit most commonly found but, also, serves as an ideal. Mrs. de la Garza, who feels strongly about that, says:

A couple never gets along with the husband's mother, so you are better off living far away from her. That's because when the wife and her mother-in-law are angry with one another, the poor man is caught in-between. If he sides with his wife, his mother will slap him, and if he sides with his mother, the girl will leave him.

Baldemar, a young man, was questioned about the arrangements he had made to set up his household after his marriage. While his own parents lived in Mexiquito, his parents-in-law resided in the nearby town of Graciela. Baldemar states that since he had a steady job in New Lots at the time, it seemed wise to reside here.

. . . though my wife's parents lived in Graciela, I settled where I made my living. But if I didn't have my job here, I might move to Graciela, for that's where my wife's folks are. Right now I live in my folks' house. We live here so as to help them out with the rent. We may as well pay it here as to someone else. I know some fellows who live with their wife's parents because of the free rent, but they're not happy there.[3]

On another occasion a young college student volunteered the information that:

If I had to choose, I'd live near-by my wife's folks. The trouble with the Latins is that the mother favors the son; she knows what his likes and dislikes are.

If you live near your mother, then its hard on the wife. She would always be interfering. I know my mother! It's easier on the girl to live near her mother. If you live near her mother, then she'll see that the girl works hard for you. But the best thing of all, if you had the chance, would be to live away from both parents.

The trouble with the Latins is that they stay around the family too much. That's why you see those people who go to California but don't stay there. They always come back here at the end of six months. They pay taxes out there and they pay them here, but still they come back because their family is here. That's why so few kids go out of the Valley to college.

A young chicano veteran married a German woman, a widow with one child. He had made up his mind to request an army discharge in Germany, and to remain there with his new family in

---

[3] Although the house in which Baldemar lives is owned by his parents, they do not reside in it.

order to attend college. When he wrote his parents about his plans, "they replied that they hadn't seen me in a long time, and so it would be best for me to come home and be with my family."

As a result, the young veteran returned to the Valley with his wife and child. He lived there with his own parents while commencing classwork in a local college; however, those living arrangements aroused such tensions between his parents and his wife that he moved to another, but nearby, town. He now lives ten miles from New Lots. He described his parents' reactions:

> You should have heard my folks, then. My mother kept crying; my father accused me of all kinds of things because I was moving away. I wasn't going any further than Spire and they lived in New Lots, yet they accused me of leaving them. This is what I call Latin-American relations. Your parents don't let you go. They don't give you a chance to make something of yourself. There is hardly a week goes by that I don't visit with them, either going to New Lots or they coming to Spire. Yet they think I have left them.

The above theme is repeated incessantly by Mexiquito's younger married set.

One young woman was most candid about the difficulties considered to inhere in the relationship between a wife and her husband's mother. In her own case she and her husband married while he was still in the armed forces, and after their marriage she went to the home of her parents-in-law. When her husband was released from the army, they continued to reside with his parents until they could find a home of their own. Those first years were not blissful. She recalls that when her husband returned home during leaves of absence, he would take her and his mother on outings in the family automobile. "Imagine! There I was, the bride, in the back seat of the car while my mother-in-law sat in front!" After several such excursions the informant, Mrs. Gálvez, complained to her husband. She requested him to place his mother in the back seat and her by his side. After some hesitation Mr. Gálvez brought the matter to the attention of his mother who retorted that *she* was not a lap dog (*perra fina*) to sit in the back seat of an automobile. On subsequent outings the wife remained in the back seat, and the mother beside her son.

Peevishly, Mrs. Gálvez continued her story. While residing with her in-laws she became pregnant, yet her mother-in-law commanded her to wash windows and to hand-wax the floors. The young woman felt that her husband's mother was expressing aggression against her in this way, and she refused to submit. In that instance she was supported by one of her husband's brothers and by her father-in-law, who took pains to assure her that the floors had never yet been waxed and that there was no good reason to begin now.

Mrs. Gálvez went on to say that even today her mother-in-law invites her three sons to dinner, but not their wives. Then she voiced a complaint often heard in Mexiquito: Her mother-in-law insists that it is the duty of the sons (El deber de los hijos) to support their elderly parents, even though the sons are married. Mrs. Gálvez believes such an expectation is not "right," for married sons have their own families to support. "I wish I was like my sister-in-law," she said in an envious tone:

My sister-in-law is always fighting with my mother-in-law, and she always tells the mother-in-law where to get off. She's terrible that way. You should hear some of the scenes! I can't do that, although I wish I could. I've always taken everything from my mother-in-law because mother brought us up to always respect our elders. In the fourteen years that I have been married, I have never said anything wrong to my mother-in-law. I don't know whether that is such a good thing to respect your elders to such an extent, though. They take advantage of you a lot of the time.

The respect for one's elders is a major organizing principle of the Mexican-American family. When coupled with the principle of male dominance, the pattern of ideal relations within the family is produced. As a young wife pithily summed it up: "In la raza, the older order the younger, and the men the women." It is difficult to establish with certitude the extent to which the respect of younger for older was practiced in years gone by, but certainly such behavior is presently extolled, while, at the same time, it is almost universally agreed to be a thing of the past.

Mrs. Gongória said that her father had always admonished his younger sons to respect their older brothers. The father advised the older brothers to slap the younger with the back of their hands, or with a stick, if the former showed disrespect or were playful with their elder siblings.

Another woman, now in her forties, advised that she never could bring herself to smoke in front of her mother or older brothers (her father had died when she was a child). It was only a few years ago that her mother told her to smoke in her presence instead of leaving the house each time that she wanted to "sneak" a smoke. She said that things are indeed very different from the times of her girlhood. Today, for instance, a girl will go out with the full knowledge of her parents and her older brothers, and none of them will say anything about her activities. The whole attitude of the humility which was expected, but which no longer is present, may be summed up in the statement: Things aren't what they used to be!

However, there are vestiges of that attitude which remain. There are those who point to "old-fashioned" members of their family who will neither drink nor smoke in front of their parents or older brothers. One informant says that his aunt "won't touch a drop if her older brother is around, and she's fifty years old."

On the Christmas Eve which preceded my arrival in New Lots, the following incident was said to have occurred. A young man had invited a number of couples to his home after midnight Mass was celebrated. However, one friend of the host arrived earlier in the evening from out-of-town. The guest was a young schoolteacher employed in the school system of one of Texas' larger cities. At any rate, when the guests arrived from church they found the young teacher in the house with a drink in his hand. After an exchange of pleasantries the early arrival announced to his host that he was leaving. The host and his wife attempted to prevail on the teacher to remain, but the latter was adamant; he had others to visit. Those who related this story were in agreement that the real reason behind the young man's departure was his discomfiture at finding himself drinking at a party in the presence of his elder brother, one of the later arrivals from the church. The narrators expressed surprise at the occurrence, but not because of the younger brother's attitude toward his elder sibling. Rather, they were surprised that such attitudes had remained so firmly a part of the character of the young man in spite of his long absence from Mexiquito, a period in which he had lived in the more cosmopolitan atmosphere of a large city.

Men of the Family

A household is the residence and center of activity of a nuclear family, over which a husband and father is expected to dominate.

With very few exceptions those who pay social calls to a household are persons whose range of conduct is quite circumscribed. They are either close kin—parents or siblings of the residents—or else are related by virtue of ritual kinship. Whosoever is permitted to visit in a household is expected to behave in decorous and deferential manner toward the residents. A man's home is his castle; the home is a sanctified locality, within which one's womenfolk are safe. At the head of the household is the father or, in the event of his death or absence, the oldest son. "In my home," says a sixty-year-old, "I am judge, jury, and policeman."

An accurate depiction of the ideal relationship which is said to exist between a father and others of his domestic grouping is found in the following account.

My mother is quiet and seldom laughs or tells jokes. I never tell jokes to my mother because I have respect for her; but my younger sister is the clown of the family. She likes to kid around. When I'm with my younger sister, she tells jokes to my mother, and we laugh. Sometimes I, too, will tell jokes to my mother, when we're with my younger sister. I *never* tell jokes to my father! We [the children] don't even talk with him! If we are laughing in his presence, he right away wants to know what we are laughing about. He thinks that maybe we are laughing about something that he did.

The husband and father of a family is expected to be firm but just, he is the *jefe de la casa* (boss of the house). Abel remembers that one winter, when he was a youngster of ten, he and his brother were taken by their father to the river. Bade by the stern parent to undress and enter the chilling waters they swam about until almost numbed by the cold. This was to make men of them, they were advised. When commanded to emerge from their swim they could hardly stand on the river bank, and wished only to approach the fire their father had been careful to prepare. However, before he would permit them to dress, the old man insisted on rubbing down each of his sons "so that we might not catch cold." Whether this story is apocryphal is of little importance. It sketches the *jefe de la casa* as gruff and firm, yet neither capricious nor tyrannous. That portrait is painted by other informants.

Mrs. de la Garza volunteered that her sisters and brothers were very obedient to her father's mandates. In those days, she said, no one would question what the father said or what he did. The father would tell the child only once what to do, and so it would be. He managed all the social affairs engaged in by members of the family, as well as all financial matters. Her father always told his daughters, "We are your best friends," meaning the family. At this point her daughter-in-law interjected: "You know, some of that old stuff still goes on here in New Lots among the more ignorant people." Indeed, one young key informant continues to distinguish one of his older brothers by the affectionate term *el oso* (the bear) precisely "*because* he played with us even though we were younger"; he displayed the affectionate side of his nature to his younger siblings as well as acting in the sterner role of an older brother.

Ignácio, a man nearing fifty years of age and a father of five children, asserted proudly that he began to smoke in the presence of his own father only three years ago. His brothers too showed the same respect toward their father. When they were growing up only two of his brothers ever did things together; the others interacted with their own peers, apart from their brothers.

The following account illustrates the concept that the chicanos hold of the structure of the domestic group. In response to a direct question about courting customs, Ignacio said:

In earlier days a man would have an intermediary request the hand of his girl, just as many people still do today. I don't think that's a good custom. I believe that the young man should confront the girl's father directly [*pecho a pecho*]. That way the father can see for himself the kind of man that wishes to marry his daughter.

If a young man confronts the girl's father in a direct manner, and if the couple elopes because her father rejects the proposal of marriage, then the law can't punish the young people. The police can search for the couple, but they can't punish them. They can't punish them because the boy came directly to her father with his proposal. The father is the prosecuting attorney and judge [*fiscal y juez*] of his own household. It was the father that rejected the suit, even though it was presented in a correct manner. The fault of the matter rests with his *incorrect* judgment! On the other hand, if the boy did not make the proposal directly to her father, the police quite properly search for, find, and punish the boy if he takes away his sweetheart.

A middle-aged woman of the neighborhood offered the following opinion.

In those days there was no one else but the father who gave the word on family actions. He would say what had to be said just once; there was

never any second time! His word was an order. But now things have
changed. It is still true that the man's word is carried out, but it is not
so strict as it once was. My father was a very proper [*recto*] man!
Nowadays a man and his wife may talk things out; they might try to
put the things of the two minds together to solve something which both-
ers them. In those days there was only one word. It is a good thing that
the wife is able to say what is on her mind now.

In Mexiquito no failure is more likely to bring in its wake divine
retribution than inappropriate behavior between members of the
close family. Telésforo was requested to provide *any* hypothetical
circumstances that came to his mind which would be expected to
elicit divine retribution. Rejecting myriad possibilities, his thoughts
went immediately to misconduct between members of a household.
He said:

Well—if you were to hit your father or your mother. Or, if you said
something real bad to your mother or to your father; or, if you were to
have a *real* fight with one of your brothers. For example, if you have a
fight with someone, just anyone, everybody sees it and they begin talking about so-and-so drinking and fighting with such-and-such a person.
There would not be divine retribution [*castigo de Dios*] there, because
everyone knew about it. But if you were to get into a real fight, with
your fists or with a knife, with your own brother, you wouldn't talk
about it; but God would be watching and you would suffer from a
castigo sooner or later.

Maybe the next day, maybe in a week, or in a couple of months, you
can't tell when it will happen, something bad will happen to you. Maybe you will be hit by a car, or maybe you will burn up in a fire, maybe
you will break an arm or a leg. Then you will know that it was a *castigo
de Dios*.

A curious observed incident illuminates the relationship between
father and son. It occurred when lack of respect shown by one close
friend (*amigo de confianza*) to the father of the other almost
brought the two chums to blows. This is what happened. At the
annual Fourth of July barbecue sponsored by the League of United
Latin American Citizens, each member was allocated a specific responsibility. Accordingly, the two *amigos de confianza* were obliged
to keep the fire supplied with wood.

During the latter part of the outing, one member of the pair approached his best friend and constant companion to advise him that
the pit fire was burning alarmingly low. He blamed the almost ex-

tinguished fire on his friend, who had failed to meet his obligation;
but most galling was his accusation that his best friend never did
anything but sit around, guzzle beer, and chase skirts. The remark
was so inflammatory that the accused challenged the other to battle.
Although a fight did not result, the accused did not speak to the
other for weeks, nor would he appear at the same public functions as
did his former friend. The vexed youth candidly explained to all
who would listen that the accusations, when taken by themselves,
were not unusually riling. However, his friend had "stupidly" made
those accusations in front of the speaker's father! Wittingly or not,
by extension, his best friend had intimated that his father had not
brought him up in an adequate fashion. What had probably been
meant as a *mosca* (tart jest) became an insult, which would somehow have to be repaid.

The same young woman who had so succinctly summed up the
Mexican-American family organization in the words "In *la raza*
the older order the younger, and the men the women," provided
some of her own familial background, too. During her courtship
days:

I would stand behind the olive tree in the yard watering the lawn,
but really I was hiding so that nobody could see me standing there with
my husband, even though he was on the other side of the fence.

I got married when I was thirteen years and eleven months old, in
June. I quit school when I was in the seventh. My brothers used to tease
me a lot in school, and they would run after me because they were
jealous. They used to tell me that one of the boys had said he would
murder me.

Then one day one of my brothers went home and told my father that
one of the boys in school had said that he was going to marry me. My
father called me in to ask me if this was so; but I told him that it wasn't.
I think that my father just wanted a motive, because he said, "If you're
going to be a flirt in school, I might as well take you out." I told him,
"Papá (We never called my father Daddy, we always called him
Papá. My father was the kind of man who always kept his distance from
the children, and my mother was my best friend.), if you want me to
quit school, I won't go tomorrow."

Then the next morning instead of going to school I ran little errands
around the house, and helped in the store. My father asked me what I
was doing at home, and I told him that he had said he might take me
out of school, so I hadn't gone. Then my father said, "You shouldn't

leave school until I tell you to!" That was in December, and I got married in June.

A father, as *jefe de la casa* or *jefe de la familia*, represents his household to the world outside; it is he who mediates between the domestic group and outside agencies. Correspondingly, the conduct of each of the members of his family reflects on the *jefe de la familia*.

Although on earlier pages it was suggested that the father represents a gruff and correct (*muy recto*) figure to the others of the household, his actions appear to be motivated neither by caprice nor arbitrariness. Nevertheless, young people speak of their fathers *as if* they acted in a capricious and arbitrary fashion. That perception is particularly true of young men, who, almost to a man, describe their fathers so. A young man was asked whether he was not happy to be back in the city after his tour of duty with the army. He answered: "Yeh, here you have only *one* father, in the army you have too many!"

When Joaquín, another of Mexiquito's young men, was a small boy his mother died. Joaquín's father brought him up, but the boy spent a great amount of his time in the home of his mother's two sisters. As soon as Joaquín and his brother had attained a marriageable age, their father sought a second wife. Joaquín's best friend (*amigo de confianza*) described Joaquín's reaction to his father's plans to marry an attractive widow:

Joaquín certainly hates this city! When he came back here in May, he said to me that he wished that an atom bomb landed right in the middle of it. If he's mad at just one person here, he doesn't have to hate the whole community. He's mad at his father for remarrying. That's just natural for a man to want companionship. The widow's husband's family didn't object; all of her kids are ready for marriage, that's why! They're the ones you would expect to object! If her husband's family didn't object, then no one else should! [The fact of the matter is that very strong objections were reported to have been voiced by the eldest brother of the deceased husband.]

Joaquín's *amigo de confianza* then expressed the opinion that Joaquín was at fault in the matter:

I'm a very good friend of his, and many times have meant to ask him what was the trouble, but each time I hold back. Someday when

I'm good and drunk I'm going to ask him right out. I'll probably lose a friend that way, but I sure do want to talk to him about it. No matter what my parents did to me, I wouldn't speak about them the way Joaquín is speaking about his father.

The chicanos, especially the young men, carry an image of their fathers as stern, gruff, and domineering personages. When young men speak of their fathers, their attitude tends to have a resentful note, albeit respectful. Some, but not many, opportunities were presented for making observations of the actual interaction which occurs between fathers and children within the confines of the home. Such observations of actual behavior serve to modify an expectation that the father acts in an overweaningly powerful manner in relation to his very young children. Without exception, direct observations note the warmth and affection exhibited by fathers with their young sons and daughters, children under ten years of age. In several instances the field notes comment that the father was, in fact, far more gentle with his children than was their mother. On other occasions it was noted that fathers were observed feeding children from bottles while holding them in their arms. On still another occasion there appears a comment that a father told his young son of nine several times to go to bed, but without success. When his wife entered the room the father pointed to his son's reddened eyes and suggested to her that the lad was sleepy and should be put to bed. His wife simply claimed that the reddened eyes were symptomatic of illness, not sleepiness. The boy did not retire for another hour, despite his father's repeated insistence that he do so.

In another home it was observed that "the informant sits alternately on the armchair and on the bed, taking care of the child [a two-year-old] while his wife talks with the interviewer. He appears very patient and indulgent with the child, at times raising his voice a little, and putting a note of authority into it." In a separate notation in the field diary appears a comment on another father, as follows: ". . . once again it must be stated that the father at all times treated the child most gently, embraced it, cooed to it, held it in his arms, and kept making remarks about what a grand person he [boy] was going to prove himself to be."

The above observations of real behavior of fathers with their young children represent the homes of both agricultural field laborers and white-collar workers.

In the case of a household in which the father is deceased or ab-

sent, the oldest son becomes his surrogate. Ideal behavior between
an older and younger brother is in many ways similar to that which
is expected between fathers and sons.

When Pilo was asked to characterize the relationship between
brothers, he said:

Well, I don't know about the other races, but I know for our race that
brothers don't play together. We just never did. . . . [But] just wait until
a brother gets hurt by someone or gets into a fight, that's when he knows
that he has a brother! When you're in trouble and need someone, then
your brother lets you know that he's there!

Others, also, stress the fact that brothers tend not to engage in frivolity together. On the basis of participant observations of young
men's cliques—*palomillas*—one must reach the noteworthy conclusion that in the less serious day-to-day activities brothers participate together in minimal degree. Playful interaction is never con-
ducive to respect of one another.

One of the means elected to avoid the ever-present threat of insult, intentional or otherwise, is to avoid those situations in which
one encounters brothers to whom decorous behavior is prescribed.
The previously mentioned incident in which a younger brother left
the scene of a party in order to avoid a possibility that he might act
in such a way as to embarrass his older brother is an example of this
artifice. The case of the barbecue in which one *amigo de confianza*
was accused of having insulted the father of another is an example
of the danger inherent in having fathers and sons interact in an
atmosphere of frivolity. The best and easiest manner in which to
prevent abrasive relationships is for fathers and sons, and older
and younger brothers to go their separate ways.

Women of the Family

In contrast with the husband-father of a household group, or his
surrogate, the oldest brother, a wife and mother is, ideally, submis-
sive, unworldly, and chaste. She is interested primarily in the welfare of her husband and children, and secondarily in her own requirements. Both the mother and father of a household are accorded
extraordinary respect by their children, but the restraint shown in
relation to each is derived from different sources. The father must be
respected because of his authoritative position at the head of the
household, whereas the mother is respected because she minimizes

her own necessities in order to better provide for those of her family. She devotes herself to her family, and the consistent idealized portrait one receives of Mexican-American mothers is that of a suffering (*padeciendo*)woman.

Mrs. Cruz responded in the following manner to the question: "Is it a good thing that girls be discouraged from attending school?"

Yes, I think that that's a good way. If a girl goes through school, then she may get to know more than the man. She'll boss the man, and he won't feel that he's working for her and the family. Only one of my sisters and myself have changed from the way that my mother was. My mother was married at the age of fourteen, and had a number of children. She could never get out of the house. My father would never even take her for a ride in the car. She has been in the house for thirty years now. [Mrs. Cruz has evidently made up her mind that the same thing will not happen to her.]

I don't know why it should be that way, but we're the only two who have changed. My sister went to nursing school, although she doesn't have a degree . . . I think she is what they call a practical nurse now. She can earn more than her husband can. She tells him, "If you don't like it, you can leave. I can get along without you, and make more money than you can, too!" She's not working now, but she will soon begin to work with a doctor in La Laguna. Her husband is an electrician and makes about fifty dollars. She can take care of herself and her kids too, because she has an education. I don't think that that is a good thing. It makes a man feel inferior to his wife.

The relationship between a daughter and her mother is of great importance to women of all ages, and it perdures throughout a woman's married life. Speaking of the closeness which characterized the relationship between herself and her mother, Mrs. Ramírez said:

If I only had two children, a son and a daughter, I would probably object to one of them marrying. That's all there were in *our* family. I used to be invited out to dances all the time, but I always wanted to get home to be with mother when I was out, instead of enjoying myself at the dances.

In New Lots one finds that couples who had moved from the lower Valley to live in such far-off places as San Antonio, Houston, Chicago, and Los Angeles returned as often as possible. When asked the purpose of the visit, they usually phrased their response to indicate a desire to be with the mother or the sisters of the wife. In those cases when neither of the parents was alive, the trip was occasioned by a desire of the woman to visit with a sister. The husband's reasons tended to be of far less significance; he came simply because his wife wished to visit with her sister. Many persons also leave the Valley on visits to places far removed from Mexiquito, and those journeys, too, are often undertaken for the purpose of a meeting between sisters or between a mother and daughter. The strength of the bond between sisters is such that sisters' husbands are separated from all other relatives-in-law of the same generation. They are considered as being in a special kind of bond and are spoken of as *concuños*. The self-reciprocal *concuño* relationship is separated from all other in-laws of the same generation (*cuñado, cuñada*). However, there is no similar usage of the feminine equivalent, *concuña*; the term is never used and almost unknown in Mexiquito. Informants agree that such a term exists in the vocabulary, but that it is never used. I never heard it used.[4]

A typical illustration of the closeness of sisters was offered by an informant named Melindo. His wife was ill, and, although the doctor ordered complete rest, the regimen was interrupted in the following manner, described by Melindo himself:

> My *concuño* and his family came yesterday. After they were here a couple of hours, he wanted to leave because the kids were making such a racket that my wife couldn't rest. My wife *wanted* to rest, but *it's her sister*, she wanted to talk with *her*. They stayed awake talking until two this morning! [Emphasis his]

At this point in our conversation the sick woman's father joined us and smiled with satisfaction as he remarked that the two sisters had talked together so long that they had greeted the dawn (*madrugaron*).

Informants readily supplied other incidents to demonstrate the validity of their assertions that sisters of whatever age and marital status were closely knit in their affections. For example, when Roberto was asked about the relationship between sisters he described his observations of the interaction between his own wife and her sisters. Roberto's wife has six sisters and four brothers. But, "I

---

[4] Compare the *concuñada* in Argentine *criollo* society as described by Arnold Strickon ("Class and Kinship in Argentina," *Ethnology*, I, No. 4 [October, 1962], 500–515). There is no evidence from Mexiquito that people extend the *concuño* relationship to the same extent as the Argentinian *criollos*.

have never seen those sisters say one bad word to one another, or about one another. María's elder sister sees her almost every day, they grew up together, and when she comes over to visit they'll sit and talk as if they hadn't seen each other for ten years."

Orphans

Unlike Anglo-American usage, the Mexican-Americans description of an orphan indicates a child who has lost either one or both of his parents. The lot of the orphaned child is universally averred to be incalculably difficult. Not only is the orphan to be pitied, but his lot scarcely improves as a consequence of his surviving parent's re-marriage, or of his own adoption by relatives or strangers. (For despite the often quoted adage, "A falta de padres, padrinos,"[5] there is no record of the adoption of orphaned children by their godparents.) Instead orphans are appended to the families of relatives.

Telésforo recalls well the bitterness of an orphaned childhood. His father died while the boy was still a youngster. The entire family at that time was living on a small ranch in central Texas, but somehow or other the poverty-stricken widow found the means by which she could bring her eight young children to Mexiquito, where she had relatives. Then she remarried.

The relations between the stepfather and his wife's children were chronically bitter and often openly hostile; one by one Telésforo's older siblings moved from the household to strike out for themselves. When one of Telésforo's older sisters married, the relationship between the step-relations had reached so low an ebb that the newly-married sister took with her the two brothers who still were under the care of their mother. The bride, her new husband, and her two youngest brothers then lived in the house of the husband's mother, where all shared a life of poverty.

In time, relations between the mother-in-law and the daughter-in-law, as well as the latter's young brothers, became so strained that in spite of the absence of financial resources the four young people moved to another section of the city. After a while the young husband found it impossible to provide for both the household of his mother and his own. "So we all moved back again." After their return to the old lady:

. . . there never was enough room to eat, so my brother-in-law and his brother were always served first by their mother. They were told to eat

[5] When parents are lacking, then godparents.

as much as they wanted. When they had finished eating, my brother, myself, and my sister were allowed to sit down to eat. My sister's mother-in-law always told us that we were sitting down "only to taste, but not to fill ourselves."

When I lived at the old lady's house I used to fill up by eating breakfast in the house of my *padrino* [a man he regularly addresses as "*Papá*"]. Then later in the day I used to eat beans in the home of my friend, Abrám.

Still later the relationship between the two families sharing the household became so strained that Telésforo's sister, her husband, and the two youngsters, once more moved to a home of their own.

An old lady nearing her seventieth birthday told a story perhaps apocryphal, perhaps not. When she was a bride she traveled from ranch to ranch with her husband, who was an itinerant carpenter and mechanic. On a ranch to which the husband had been called to repair a machine, she had noted the following.

The ranch was occupied by its owner, his only son, and the second wife of the former, the boy's stepmother. As is true for all step-relationships, according to the narrator, the boy and his stepmother did not get along at all well. During the time that the narrator's husband was occupied with his repair work, the owner of the ranch was slaughtering a sheep, aided by, among others, his son. During the course of the morning the stepmother called for the boy to come and perform some chore or another for her. However, the boy's father called out that the lad was busy and would not be able to help her.

After the sheep had been slaughtered and dressed, the stepmother cut up the baked head into small pieces and served it to the men. When a piece of sheep bone lodged in the throat of the unfortunate stepson a doctor was called. The lad died while the doctor was performing an operation. Those present more or less accused the stepmother of having deliberately caused her stepson's death. She, on the other hand, retorted that the boy was too greedy, and had not been careful to guard himself against the presence of bones in his meat. Whoever was at fault, the teller of the story concluded that the dead boy had eaten greedily *because* he was a stepchild and stepchildren are always hungry!

Courtship and Marriage

Informants in Mexiquito took pains to emphasize the extent to which a girl is confined to the home of her parents until she is married, and then is restricted to the household of her husband. Oftentimes a married woman advises that until she married her husband she had not looked him in the eyes, much less gone out with another man. Such statements present a highly idealized version of real behavior; they are the moral norms of conduct, which are more or less adhered to by women of Mexiquito.

Social norms prescribe the circumscription of courtship by highly ritualized behavior. Ideally, the young man is expected to communicate with the parents of the girl when he wishes to announce his intentions of matrimony, for example, and a kiss or other bodily contact is forbidden between the courting couple. The girl is expected to become acquainted with her suitor by means of a protracted exchange of correspondence, either in the form of letters or by utilization of carefully chosen intermediaries. Persons highly respected in Mexiquito's social system are much in demand as intermediaries in marriage arrangements, for the more exalted the status of the intermediary (*portador*), the more weighty his brief for the suitor. Therefore the more revered the position of the *portador*, the more difficult it is for the girl's parents to refuse his petition pointblank. The *portador* thus invests something of his own personal prestige in winning a spouse for a client.

One young teacher in Mexiquito's school system recalls that he was once asked by a youth to act as a *portador*. (Schoolteachers occupy positions at the apex of the occupational system. They share that status with the physician and the priest, the latter being most exalted of all as *portador*). The teacher accepted the responsibility and subsequently went to visit the home of the girl, but the girl's parents received him coldly and left him unattended in the front room of the home. Meanwhile, they went to another room, ostensibly to ask their daughter her wishes in the matter. However, the *portador* overheard the couple berating their daughter and even thought he could discern the sound of blows. When the parents returned to the front room, they told him to return later for his answer. Eventually, the *portador* heard that the daughter was berated, cuffed, and otherwise ill-treated for many days by her mother. When the girl next encountered her suitor, she fulminated against him for not having had the good sense to solicit the services of the Catholic priest. The implication was that if the priest had been the *portador*, her parents would not have dared to react to the suit as they did.

An old man answered the following question in a self-satisfied manner. "In those days did you have *portadores* to ask for a girl's hand in marriage?"

Well, you did if there seemed as though there might be trouble in getting the girl. I remember that my half brother asked my father to get me to request the hand of his girl-friend in marriage. He wasn't a very good talker, and so my father told me to do it. The first time that I went to the house of the girl, I was told that her father wasn't home and they had no idea when he would be home. They knew why I was there! I told them to tell the father that I would return at six the following afternoon, and that if he wasn't there at that time, I would be back with the law.

The next day I came back in the afternoon and the girl's father answered the door. He asked me to come inside and to have a seat, and that's what I did. I started off by asking him whether my visit was not causing him some pain [*moléstia*], but he answered that it wasn't. Then I asked whether my visit wasn't causing him just a little pain [*media moléstia*], but he told me that was no trouble at all.

Then the girl's father addressed me and said: "To make a long story shorter, I will now go in and investigate the girl." So her father went into the kitchen where the daughter was performing some task or another pretending that she didn't know what was taking place in other parts of the house. Her father asked her where she knew the boy from, and whether or not they had been seeing each other regularly. She responded by telling her father that she and the boy had simply passed one another several times, and that there hadn't been anything serious between them.

Then her father asked her whether or not she had plenty of good clothes, and lots to eat, and whether they hadn't sent her to the best galas, to which she answered that all that was true; but that there was something more that she wanted now in her life. Then her father hit her hard in the face and asked her whether it wasn't simply a male [*macho*] that she sought![6]

Then her father came out of the kitchen and told me to come back in fifteen or twenty days and I would have my answer. I spoke up and told him there was no need to use such language as *macho* with the girl, and that love was a capricious thing. I told him that if a girl allows a man to reach his hand up to here [pointing to his upper leg between the knee and the thigh] then there is nothing that anyone can do about it. Love is capricious. In fifteen days I returned to his house and he answered me in the affirmative.

[6] *Macho* as used in this sense refers to the male organ.

A brief smile flickered about old Antonio's lips as he thought of his success with the irate father of the girl.

Ruperto explained that a *portador* was a man well respected by the people, and that he was usually an older man whose task was to represent the boy and to extol his virtues to the parents of the girl. When the informant began to describe the manner in which he himself conversed with a girl's parents when acting in the role of *portador*, he reverted unwittingly to an antiquated form of Spanish. This was an archaism that was never heard again in any other context during field work.

Ruperto said that it was customary to have one or two *portadores*, and that any person chosen as *portador* was one who was "not seen fooling around in bars or with women." According to Ruperto, if the *portador* was told to return for his answer in eight days, then the request was to be considered rejected. However, if he was advised to return in fifteen days or one month, then he could consider his venture a success. (The meaning of the time periods varies from person to person.) If the time limit was set at one year, the petitioner was given to understand that the girl's father was planning to change her mind about the match.

When Ruperto, himself, wished to marry, he requested his uncle to carry the proposal to his sweetheart's parents, since his uncle commanded much respect in the region. The latter had asked for the hands of all of the local girls when their time for marriage had arrived. According to the old man, when a proposal was accepted the boy was not expected to serve a test period in the home of his fiancée's parents. In lieu of that service the youth was expected to send food or money to her parents—a custom called the *diario*. In order to demonstrate his ability to care for the girl, the boy sent food and clothing or money for a period of eight months between the acceptance of the proposal and the actual marriage. Then after the marriage the young couple lived with the parents of the girl. If the two couples proved compatible, the younger pair would build or rent a home next door to the home of the wife's parents.

Another elderly gentleman of Mexiquito recalled how things used to be in respect to courtship.

It used to be that when a boy's father went to the home of the girl to ask her father for his daughter's hand that the girl's father would say: "Well, I don't know. I'll tell you what. Send your boy over to my house for two months and we'll see how he works. We'll see what we can expect from that young man!" Then the father of the boy would agree to do this. But he would tell the father of the girl that he, also, wished to see how the girl behaved and what kind of a worker she was. He suggested that the girl come to his house for two months. That way there was an exchange [*intercambio*].

The girl would get up at three in the morning and see what kind of condition the *nixtamal* [*tortilla* dough] was in, and she would set the fire, bake the *tortillas*, and tidy up the place. At her family's home the boy would be working himself to death; he would be walking in from the fields with a load of sweet cane over one shoulder, and a load of corn on the other shoulder. People knew how to work and keep house then! After two months, when the parents had seen how well the children were able to work, they would give them permission to wed.

One of Mexiquito's professional men told what occurred when he had been asked to act as a *portador*. He went to the home of the girl's parents and was told to return for his answer in three weeks' time. Then the plans went awry. The thwarted emissary said:

Well, do you know what happened? He backed out of the deal. He decided that he didn't want to get married after all. I felt real bad and embarrassed about doing a thing like that, so I went out to her place and told her that I was very embarrassed. I told her that I was sorry to have done such a thing. She told me that she understood this, and that it wasn't my fault. He had known what he was doing, she told me. I don't know why parents give the girl hell when she's going to get married, I *guess they just want to get even.*[7]

An enterprising Catholic priest remarked that a high incidence of elopements (*robamientos*) existed in Mexiquito. He blamed the high rate on two causes, the first being the excessive cost of the wedding celebrations demanded by local customs. The priest pointed out that such celebrations were prescribed by what he called "local folklore"; they were by no means required by canon law. The second practice contributing to elopement was frequent disapproval of the match by the parents of the girl. The priest claimed that he had established channels of communication through which he was informed when a couple planned to elope. He then contacted one of the pair and usually suggested that they elope directly to his church. After he married them, he accepted as *his* responsibility notification of the irate parents. By such means he made certain that the young couple had been married in church, while they, in turn, were as-

[7] Italics added.

sured that no less prominent a personage than the priest would assuage the anger of the parents.

The importance of the system by which one uses a *portador* to represent his virtues to the parents of the girl is now in sharp decline. Nevertheless it continues to serve as a normative guide for courtship in Mexiquito. In many instances it continues to be the mechanism by which marriage is contracted.

For example, a veteran of the Second World War returned to Mexiquito, having decided while he was away that he wanted to marry the girl to whom he had become attached before entering military service. She, too, wished to marry, but not until she had reached her fifteen birthday (*quinceaños*). He said:

One Sunday we talked together and spoke about going off together and getting married. We call it *robando la nóvia*.

She wanted to go off with me, but I told her that I wanted to play it straight. I went and told my father that I wanted to get married and told him that I might *robar* my bride. But he told me: "No, son; you must play it straight. You must show that you have testicles." So that same week I got hold of two older men. I gave them each ten dollars, and told them where the girl's house was located. I drove them over to La Finca where she lived. They went to her house, and I went over to the Rincón bar to drink some beer. I was very nervous.

After a while they came over to the Rincón and sat down. Their faces were glum. I immediately ordered two more beers, and they began to tell me that it was little use for me to continue my interest in the girl. Her parents had opposed the marriage. But, then, by the time it took them to get half-way through the bottle of beer, they broke into smiles. They told me that everything was O.K. They said that they had only been pulling my leg. They said that the parents of the girl had told them to come back in eight days, and that's a sign that they approve of the marriage. If they had told them to come back in fifteen days for an answer, then it would have meant that they disapproved of the marriage.

I was very happy about the whole thing. In eight days I went over with my parents to make the first of the visits. While we were there, I told them that I was prepared to give her twenty dollars each week so that she could tell how I would support her. But she said, "No. Don't give me any money. Save the money and we'll go on a honeymoon instead." And that was all right with her parents; so when we got married we went to Monterrey and had a wonderful time!

So far, this account has focused upon the effect which courtship and marriage have upon the young people most directly concerned.

An exploration will now be made of the reasons why parents, especially the mother, confront the daughter with repression and confinement when she prepares to establish her own family. The difficult relationship between a marriageable girl and her parents is known as *the trouble* (*el problema*).

The Mexican-American society of Mexiquito is one in which the essential social unit is the household, which is composed mostly of the members of a nuclear family. At first glance it seems odd that the very moment for which a girl has been prepared throughout her life—marriage and motherhood—should be fraught with hard feelings and conflict. Why should a middle-aged woman recall that when *she* wished to marry, she had expected *the trouble* with her parents? What does the marriage of a daughter imply to her parents?

In some respects her marriage carries the same implications for her mother that it does for her father. The daughter is a representative of a closely knit social group headed by her father, who is *jefe de la casa, jefe de la familia*. The girl has been brought up in such a manner that she represents herself as a paragon of virtue, a woman fit to mother the children of a respectable male of *la raza*. Early in her life she was made aware that she represented her household group fully as much as she represented herself, an individual. In all instances her claims to enjoyment were made secondary to the claim of propriety. In other words, hers was a road carefully planned from girlhood to womanhood within the tight restraint of family discipline. Her comportment reflected the abilities of the parents as taskmasters of the children.

When properly undertaken, courtship and marriage are triumphant phases in the life of the domestic group. The passage of the girl from the home of her parents to that of her husband is accompanied by rites and fanfare, which make public the announcement that the girl *and* her parents have adequately met their obligations. The approaching wedding of a daughter is publicly announced at a dance sponsored by *her* parents, and there at the dance the parents of the girl are introduced to the gathering by the master of ceremonies. Their obligations toward her met, *they* are honored as well as she. The financial outlay for such an announcement is considerable, but, after all, it is a life's work to prepare a daughter to become a worthy wife and mother.

Given the nature of the social system of the Mexican-Americans of Mexiquito, however, a daughter's marriage also tends to provoke conflict, which, along with discontinuity, is built into the marriage of a daughter. Yet one discovers nothing incongruous between or among the congeries of values which guide the socialization of a daughter in Mexiquito. I look to another level of analysis to discover a reason for the trauma and conflict which are expected to accompany the time of a girl's courtship and marriage and which, in fact, often do appear. "The trouble" may be understood as arising from the conflict between the personal needs of individual members of the domestic group and the values which guide the bringing-up of a daughter.

Quotations on previous pages have demonstrated that to the people of Mexiquito, from a subjective point of view, the place of a woman is within the confines of the home. Her friends and confidants are restricted to her mother, her sisters, and her close female relatives; initiation of acquaintanceship beyond that very narrow group of kinswomen is deterred. The meaning and effect of the axiomatic expression *La sociedad para ti es la suciedad para mí* is the same as the parental admonition: We are your best friends or, as one young woman recalled her father telling her: In the home there is no place for little friends, we are they. The striking dependence of a Mexican-American woman on a minimal unit of female relatives is intensified by the enjoined aloofness between the woman and her close male relatives. Consequently the emotional needs of a woman in this society are funneled to a microcosmic group of other women. Given the little world of familiars upon whom an adult woman is forced to depend, each of the others in that group is of critical importance to her. Therefore, the marriage of a daughter threatens to fracture a group already overstrained by interdependency.

Although, strictly speaking, incongruities among those prescriptive values which chart the course by which parents bring up a daughter are not found, there is discerned a striking example of incompatibility between the emotional needs of the members of this society and the culture which has exacerbated those needs; moreover, this incompatibility is built-in.

Courtship and marriage are by no means blissful for the households concerned. Each family has too much at stake. Courtship itself is enveloped in a ritualistic behavior, whose delicate procedures are often carried on by emissaries in order to avoid direct confrontation of the parties. The contemporary custom of the *diario* and the

past customs of bride and groom service in the homes of the prospective in-laws are mechanisms best described as attempts by the
two families to accommodate themselves to impending change. The
same may be said of the euphemistic waiting-periods, during which
the suitor is made to await his answer, since the stipulation of one
period of time or another permits the families involved to avoid
direct acceptance or rejection of the suit. The relatively elaborate,
ritualized behavior and language in which courtship is enmeshed is
best understood as a means of cushioning the loss of a son or a daughter. But those cultural mechanisms are inadequate for the task.
Courtship and the early years of marriage are periods of stress to
those persons immediately involved.

For the past fifty years the chicanos of Mexiquito have been affected by two processes of change brought about by contact with
Anglo-Americans. The Mexican-Americans have been quite aware
that their patterns of courtship and married life differ from those
of the Anglos. It has been especially difficult for young chicanos to
understand patterns of dating whereby a girl will go out with a boy
on one night, another on the following night, and still another on the
third night. As one chicano youth asked: "What *is* this dating business, anyway?" The young women on the other hand find "serial
dating" attractive. Moreover, chicano youths of both sexes find the
close chaperoning of the girl irksome; Anglos of the same age move
about quite freely, and the young chicanos are beginning to emulate
them.

Another quality of Anglos courtship and marriage which young
Mexican-Americans find attractive is the autonomy allowed a ro-
mancing youngster in electing his or her own spouse. This conflicts
with the older pattern by which chicano parents arranged strategic
marriages for their children. Each of the newly introduced alternative techniques of courtship and marriage which are products of
processes of acculturation and urbanization, conflict sharply with
more traditional customs. Moreover, adoption of new courting techniques by some members of the society, but not others, has led to
conflict between expectations and values of one generation with another, as well as between those held by young men and young
women.

However, neither process of change—neither acculturation nor
urbanization—helps to explain "the trouble" which is associated
with the periods of courtship and early marriage of the chicanos of

Mexiquito. To consider *that* particular stress a product of some soci-ocultural change phenomenon proves fruitless. On the contrary, the more rigidly conservative the adherence of a parental couple to the normative values of the culture, the more stress is found associated with the marriage of their daughter. And, it seems likely that the smaller the number of females in a household the more disturbing to the household group the marriage of a daughter will be. Rather than a consequence of change, "the trouble" is a consequence of conflicts built into the indigenous social system.

Ritual Kinship

Although Mexiquito's social system contains built-in conflict, it also provides institutionalized means to contain it. One institution which chicanos utilize to confine conflict is ritual kinship (*compa-drazgo*).[8]

For instance, in the preceding section it was noted that formal courtship patterns place the parents of the boy in opposition to those of the girl. Marriage between the two young people exacerbates the antagonisms of each parental set vis-à-vis the other: Both older cou-ples will soon be requesting assistance from their married children, an expectation known as *el deber de los hijos*. Yet, when the young married couple gives assistance to one set of parents, the others think themselves deprived. On the other hand, the two older couples will also share equally in rights to their grandchildren. The ambivalence of their feelings toward one another—antagonism on the one hand, shared interest on the other—is resolved by the inauguration of ritual kinship, which permits the two couples to interact, albeit in a manner remarkable for its constraint.[9]

Another example of the way in which chicanos utilize ritual kin-ship as a means to restrain conflict occurs in the following: "Some-times when someone is afraid that you are going to sleep with his wife, he'll make you his compadre. That way you can't do it."

Compadrazgo lends itself so well to the containment of conflict

[8] For a general discussion of ritual kinship in Latin America, Benjamin D. Paul, "Ritual Kinship with Special Reference to Godparenthood in Middle Amer-ica;" Sidney Mintz and Eric R. Wolf, "An Analysis of Ritual Co-Parenthood (Compadrazgo)," *Southwestern Journal of Anthropology* 6, No. 4 (Winter, 1950), 341–369.

[9] Avoidance relations, of which this is but one instance, are discussed by A. R. Radcliffe-Brown (*Structure and Function in Primitive Society*, p. 2).

because chicanos expect that those so related will treat one another with respect and deference. Whether the expected punctilio of respect and deference is emphasized by the two parties depends to a great extent on the motivations which led them to contract their relationship. For by no means all such ritual bonds are contracted in order to constrain potential conflict and ambivalence. In many instances individuals seek to make a friendship more firm and lasting by contracting fictive kinship ties. However, so salient are the qualities of decorum which obtain in this relationship that whether one intended to increase or to diminish the ranges of his interaction with the other by means of a *compadre* bond, those who enter into such an alliance must maintain their distance. Of all the kinds of *compadre* relationships into which chicanos may enter, the one in which qualities of respect and deference are most demanding is initiated at the time a child is baptized.

A couple which sponsors a child at its baptismal ceremony thenceforth relates to that child as its *padrinos de pila* or *padrinos de bautismo*.[10] The child they sponsor becomes their *ahijado*. Furthermore, by virtue of that relationship, the sponsors and the biological parents become *compadres* (coparents).

Although an infant is linked to his baptismal sponsors *(ahijado-padrinos)* and they inaugurate a fictive kin relationship with the child's biological parents (compadres-compadres), their relationship does not under any condition extend to the infant's siblings. As Telésforo phrased it, "If the sponsor of my first child's baptism comes to pay us a visit, then my second child will come in to tell me: 'Your compadre is here.' But he won't say: 'Compadre is here.' In other words, 'He's your compadre, not mine'!"

It is possible, however, for an individual to sponsor more than one child from a single family. This multiple relationship is described as making the sign of the cross (*haciendo la cruz*) because those families which countenance multiple sponsorship insist that it be limited to three children. *Haciendo la cruz* does not in any way conflict with the finding that a tie between a child and his *padrinos* does

---

[10] The two terms are used interchangeably, each referring to the relationship between the child and its sponsors. *Compadres de pila* and *compadres de bautismo*, by the same token, refer equally to the bond between the child's sponsors and its biological parents.

not extend to his siblings because when parents do elect the same sponsor for several of their children, each child is independently linked to the sponsor.

In any case, the importance which chicanos attribute to the baptismal triad—*padrino-adhijado-compadre*—cannot be overemphasized.

When one gets up to heaven it is the *compadres de pila* that look after one, never the family (*parientes*).[11] That is the reason why one doesn't choose his compadres from among his own family. Those little angels greet their compadres when they arrive in heaven and they take away many of his sins. It's only the *padrinos* of your child that recognize you in heaven. No one else there pays you any attention! It's as if you were on a long journey and you had *someone* recognize you in heaven and welcome you. These are your compadres. *Parientes* never!

In accord with previously cited views about the nature of a relationship between compadres, the following narrative neatly sums up those expectations:

A compadre means a lot. It's something real, it means a lot. When you make a compadre you have to respect him and he has to respect you. Compadres help each other; you can't talk about him, and he can't talk about you. For example, if you tell someone that your compadre is drinking too much then he may go over and tell your compadre that you were talking about him. Then your compadre will come to you and ask why you are talking about him. Then you may get into an argument and maybe you won't talk to each other after that. You shouldn't run around with the girls in front of him because of respect. You should try to show off that you're a nice man, and that you were chosen because you are a nice man.

Like you take Francisco, for example. He's a good friend of mine, but he wouldn't be good for a compadre. What I mean is that he comes into the house and jokes with me and my wife, he cusses around us, he doesn't respect us. He wouldn't be good for a compadre, but he's a good friend. Someone like you [author] would be a good compadre because you respect my wife, and like when I come in here I watch my manners with your wife and I ask for you, and you don't cuss or anything.

When you choose a compadre, you have to call him *Sir* in a way. You say *Usted*. When you see him on the street, you can't go rushing up to him and yelling, "Hey, you—come here!" If you know him real well, you address him by Sir. For example, you never say, "Fíjate, está muy

---

[11] The term *parientes* has reference to relatives beyond the range of the nuclear family.

buena la pesca ahora!" No! You would say, "Fíjase, está muy buena la pesca ahora!" You always say Sir. Even if he is younger than you are, you address him nicely.[12]

Aside from acting toward one another in terms of respect and deference, ritual kinsmen are also expected to assist each other in a more material fashion. An infant's baptismal *padrinos*, for example, are obliged to furnish their godchild's ceremonial clothing, to defray the costs of the rite, and to commission a portrait of the child by a local photographer. In the case of a wedding, those who act as sponsors assist with the costs of the bridal outfit, and meet the cleric's fee. (Note that the ties established at the wedding between the newlyweds and their sponsors are clearly distinct from those which are initiated between the parents of the bride and groom.)

In another, quite different, context a *compadrazgo* bond reflects the gratitude which patients and their families hold for those who have provided assistance in times of health crises. For instance, an individual (usually female) whose long-term illness has failed to respond satisfactorily to healing treatments elects a woman to be her *madrina de hábito*. The *madrina* purchases for the patient a habit which replicates one worn by a selected religious image, for example, San Juan de los Lagos. The patient then wears the garment until her condition is remedied or is terminated by death. Another less formalized instance of the foregoing contraction of *compadrazgo* bonds in appreciation of special healing services rendered a patient appears in a later chapter on health and illness.

As has already been indicated, the flexibility of *compadrazgo* permits this institution to be utilized for a variety of purposes. But whatever are the original reasons for initiating such a relationship, those who are ritually allied to an individual, together with his nuclear family, constitute his security system.

Neighbors

No account of Mexican-American family life is complete unless it takes notice of the principal assumptions and expectations that the nuclear family holds of the neighborhood in which its home is set.

The Mexican-Americans conceive of their households as places

[12] In this fashion Telésforo indicates the respect relationship between compadres by proscribing the reflexive of the informal *Tu*, and substituting the reflexive of the more formal *Usted*; thus *se* instead of *te*.

of security, from which the residents look out on a hostile world. Good fortune is attained in spite of the malice and invidious sanctions which are directed by neighbors against one's family. One of the most important aspects of the ethos of Mexiquito is a gnawing fear of these invidious sanctions. The householders are convinced that a successful year in the fields, a season without sickness, a journey free from occurrence of serious accidents, all provoke the invidiousness of other Mexican-Americans. Whenever the serenity of the family is disrupted by unseasonable weather which interferes with the wage earner's gainful employment, or a family member is afflicted by illness, or someone is incapacitated by a serious accident, such disturbances may be assumed to be the projection of willful malice by neighbors. In this society it is human, not suprahuman, forces with which the householders must contend.

Visiting between households in the neighborhood is discouraged. If a male not included in a category of relationship in which respectful behavior is prescribed pays a visit to a home, he is presumed to have sexual designs on the women of that household. One evening three young men planned to play poker at my home. I drove with them to the house of another acquaintance to ask him to join the game. Because the parking spaces in front of Filiberto's home were occupied, I parked down the street to permit Mingo to walk to the house and ask Filiberto if he wished to join us. Mingo stepped from the car, walked several paces toward the house, and then returned and re-entered the automobile. "Just drive up in front of the house and double park there," he said. "We'll do it chicano style." When we arrived in front of Filiberto's, Mingo peered out, but he saw only Filiberto's wife and another woman on the porch, no sign of the husband. Mingo then directed me to drive on, indicating that it would appear suspicious if he, a friend of both Filiberto and his wife, was seen approaching their home without an explicit invitation from the husband.

Many times the observer hears women express this value-laden sentiment, "I don't like to visit with my neighbors; if we have something to discuss, it is better done in the yard." In fact, during two years, only two cases were discovered in which a woman regularly visited the home of another to whom she was not related. In both instances the visiting pattern was asymmetric, that is, only one of the pair was the visitor, the other was always the visited. Neither of the visiting women had kin in town except those related through their husbands; one of the visitors had long since been deserted by her husband. Each of the visitors conceived of herself as a social isolate, for whom life was meaningless, hopeless, and without order. In fact, one of the women was contemplating suicide at the time of our acquaintance. In each of these two instances of irregular visiting, the husband of the visited woman peremptorily forbade his wife to admit the visitor any more. His action was a direct consequence of the gossip which arose from the unusual pattern. One of the women discontinued visiting her friend, but the other continued, and it is this case to which the next passages apply.

Mrs. Reyna, the visitor, was thoroughly upset by the order which curtailed her visits with her neighbor, Mrs. Salinas. Perhaps she was so much more upset than the other visitor because only a week before she had quarreled with a neighbor whose home bordered the other side of the Reyna house, a quarrel which had closed that friendship to her. This second prohibition from visiting added impetus to Mrs. Reyna's growing feeling that suicide would solve her problems. In spite of the order forbidding further visiting with the Salinas woman, Mrs. Reyna found excuses to go over to her home, although more surreptitiously than previously.

Mrs. Salinas had a sister-in-law, her brother's wife, who was also a close neighbor. The sister-in-law reported the continuation of the visiting, and once more Mrs. Salinas was warned by her husband not to admit the visitor. But so insistent were Mrs. Reyna's needs to visit with a friend, that Mrs. Salinas found herself unable to cope with the situation. The two women continued to chat and to confide in one another.

Mrs. Salinas' sister-in-law became increasingly incensed at the former's willful disobedience and, finally, waited one day at a window of her own home until Mrs. Reyna arrived next door. When Mrs. Reyna approached, the watching woman descended upon her. Amid shouts of "trespasser, trespasser!" Mrs. Reyna was pushed and slapped. Then a formal complaint was filed against the visitor; the charge: trespassing. When the case was heard in Commissioner's Court, the court found in favor of the complainant and fined the defendant, Mrs. Reyna, the nominal sum of five dollars. Both the women were advised by the judge not to continue the hostilities, and were warned that similar difficulties would result in a heavier fine imposed on each of them.

Of the people of Mexiquito it may be said that apprehension and anxiety increase as the distance between neighbors decreases. The closer the sites of two homes the less the degree of esteem between the residents. Relationships between immediate neighbors in Mexiquito tend to be unusually unpleasant.

Almost as soon as Telésforo had moved his small family into his newly bought house, he began to suspect his closest neighbor, an elderly woman, of hostility motivated by invidiousness. He noted that when he left the house in the morning to go to work the neighbor was sitting on her step watching him leave, but that she did not greet him. He presumed that her "hostility" was provoked by knowledge that Telésforo had purchased a bed, a television set, and a cedar chest to furnish his new home—furniture for which he paid installments of one dollar per week.

I am acquainted with one family in which two cases of mental illness have occurred in the recent past. Another member of the family is deeply concerned about the causation of such illness for, she advises, it is often said that mental illness is a consequence of a neighbor's invidiousness, and that sickness produced by malevolent intentions decimates an entire family. In this family's case the illnesses were attributed to the mother's financial success, which she achieved in several real-estate deals. As a consequence of those successes the family has become socially mobile and now lives on the south—Anglo—side of the tracks. According to the concerned informant:

> People don't want anyone to improve themselves. The trouble with the Mexican people is that they cut each other's throats. Nobody wants anyone else to improve, or to build a better home for themselves and their kids. You know, sometimes I don't blame the Americans for discriminating against the Mexicans. (We don't even help each other out, why should they treat us any better?)

Once during my stay in Mexiquito, Telésforo and his wife bickered, then came to blows. The wife suspected philandering on the part of her husband. When he came home late that evening, she met him and accused him of seeing another woman. According to the suspect, his wife shouted at him as he entered their home, "I will kill you, I will kill you." Thereupon she threw some crockery at him. He, in turn, reached into his pocket and withdrew a knife, which he opened. He grasped the handle and pretended to take several swipes at his wife with the weapon. Because the blade was bared and still in his hand, the movement of the weapon back and forth opened several wounds in Telésforo's palm.

Both individuals were very upset by the incident, which had serious economic implications in that the wounds prevented Telésforo from working for several days. The stitches which were required were costly, and the couple could ill afford either this expense or any loss of income. At approximately the same time they had quarreled, Telésforo's wife's hand broke out in large sores, which had to be lanced by a physician. Then several painful growths developed on Telésforo's skull, and those, too, required medical attention. All these medical bills diminished still further an already inadequate income.

The entire chain of events proved so upsetting that Telésforo's wife sought a fortuneteller. She wanted to find out "what was wrong with us," and the fortuneteller explained, "Someone was doing this to us, but she couldn't tell us at the time who it was. In a little while we will find out who is doing it to us and why they are doing it." The fortuneteller then told her to await a "big surprise," refusing to elucidate.

Not surprisingly, Telésforo and his wife were disturbed by the prognostication. He was fearful that some harm would befall their little daughter, for he felt that things of "this nature" come in threes, and so far his daughter had been the only member of the family unaffected. His wife's reaction to the ominous warning was to make plans to go to a store in a neighboring city to purchase the child a talisman. Meanwhile Telésforo planned to put his faith in God, "who has helped us along the way." Telésforo says that sometimes he prays so fervently in moments of crisis that he cries "just like a little baby."

Telésforo confided that *he* knew who was doing this to them, but for fear of hurting an innocent person he did not wish to make an accusation. Nevertheless, it required little effort to pry from him the identity of the suspected parties. There were two. The most likely source of malevolence, according to Telésforo, was the family of his wife.

Nos tienen mucha envidia. [They are very envious of us.] They can see all of the things that I have been able to buy for my wife and child. We're in our new home, and we have the refrigerator and the stove, and the TV set, and the furniture. And we have some money left over each

month. They are jealous of what we have, and of the fact that I am so
good to my wife.

Telésforo has sought to "improve" the diet of his wife's family—
in particular, her elderly parents—and so has brought them leftovers of meals from his own home. When he heard that his wife's
family was accusing him of poisoning the leftovers, Telésforo de-
sisted from such largesse.

According to Telésforo, the second possible source of the malicious
chain of misfortunes was the family of Abrám, Telésforo's oldest
and best friend. Although Telésforo excluded Abrám from the suspects, he attributed malevolent intent to that family because he was
sure that they were envious of his worldly goods.

Another young man's story illustrates the dissonance between aspirations to improve one's style of life and a fear of the invidious
sanctions such ambitiousness provokes. One of Mexiquito's small
businessmen, Prudencio, is recognized as one of the most ambitious,
aspiring, and conscientious merchants on the north side of the tracks.
Prudencio's zeal was recognized and encouraged by the award of a
plaque from the local Council of the League of United Latin American Citizens.

Prudencio was born and raised in Mexiquito. He followed his
older brother to Houston, where both worked in produce markets in
that urban center. Later he returned to Mexiquito, where he was
employed in a local produce shed, a job which provided most of his
livelihood. However, he also worked as a clerk in a retail store north
of the tracks. The owner of this store was an Anglo, who took an interest in Prudencio and encouraged him to help himself. When the
owner moved to another section of the country he offered to sell the
store and its stock to Prudencio, urging the latter to buy the enterprise. Prudencio remembers that his hesitancy was such that he rejected the plan, but the Anglo continued his encouragement. Finally,
the owner of the store offered the business to Prudencio at a very
low sum, to be paid in very reasonable monthly payments; he went
so far as to act as Prudencio's cosigner when he borrowed the money
from the bank. (Throughout his recollections of the business deal
Prudencio attributed to himself a passive role, and to his Anglo patron the active role.)

Several years later Prudencio accepted an additional position with
another Anglo as a driver and delivery man on an ice route, de-

pending on his wife to manage their store. Sometime later the Anglo owner made plans to move elsewhere and offered the small business to Prudencio. Once again, Prudencio refused to expand his commercial interests. The Anglo, however, insisted that if he left the business to anyone, it would be Prudencio. He offered the delivery truck to Prudencio on the following terms: if the purchaser could not pay for the vehicle during the first six months, the Anglo would present it to him as a gift. Prudencio agreed to the deal and says proudly that he paid for the delivery truck in the first five months.

Prudencio attributed his timidity and passivity in those business negotiations to knowledge that "your own race doesn't like to see you get ahead." He says that there is much invidiousness in Mexiquito, and people have come up to him on the street to tell him that his businesses would be failures within three months. Furthermore, he recalls that before he became an independent businessman, he was on very good terms with the other workers at the produce shed. When he took over the store and, later, the ice delivery route, the men acted as if they didn't know him. The unfriendly state of affairs continued for several years until a crew of laborers was transferred to Mexiquito from another branch of the same company. He claims now to associate most frequently and closely with the men who had been transferred from elsewhere.

The theme which depicts self-improvement by individualistic achievement as antithetic to the "wishes" or "expectations" of other Mexican-Americans is incessantly exemplified in Mexiquito. David, for example, is a young chicano whose hard work has led to professional and material success. Although David's progress to professional status is lauded by Anglo-American and Mexican-American alike, the latter group's laudatory comments are said to be veined with invidiousness. One of David's acquaintances, Tomás, comments that David was criticized when he built his new home "on the other side." Chicanos, according to Tomás, said that David was very anti-Mexican (*muy antimexicano*).

But, if he had decided to build it on the Mexican side, people, the very same people, would have said that he was a fool for building a $30,000 home in an area surrounded by shacks and dirt streets. But *what* can you do? If you do one thing they attack you, and if you do the other they attack you!"

Pertinent to the ambivalence associated with attitudes about David's success are two other stories about him, which were circulating during the period of the study in Mexiquito. People were recounting the discovery of nefarious activities in the cemetery. For several nights the suspicions of the caretaker were aroused by strange sounds emanating from the Mexican-American sector of the burial grounds. Afraid to investigate by himself, the caretaker prevailed on the Anglo manager to accompany him. At four in the morning (according to the story) the two sleuths entered the area and heard sounds of digging. They circled the stones until they came upon a bundled-up figure busily digging the earth away from a grave. Although both investigators were quite frightened, the caretaker found the strength to shout out: "Are you from this world or the other?" The figure turned out to be that of a young woman servant in David's household. The implication in context was apparent: David's success was to be attributed to the skulduggery on which he sent his servants, rather than to hard work and the acquisition of professional training.

The second story has to do with a remark supposedly made by David who, in his professional capacity as a physician, was attending a woman in labor. When the woman cried out in pain David was supposed to have told her "It didn't hurt when he put it in." David *might* have made such a remark; on the other hand my contact with David suggests that it is improbable. True or false, circulation of these stories deter Mexican-Americans from patronizing the successful David.

Crispín, another of Mexiquito's successful young men, recalled that during his days in high school he felt himself cast out by his Spanish-speaking acquaintances. He recalled that when he became active in high-school organizations and went around with Anglo friends he was "cast out by my own people. They all called me a traitor and all kinds of other things. It was really tough to have your own people turn against you."

Esteban, also a young chicano, expressed mystification that Anglos seem to help one another, whereas just the opposite seems to be true of the Mexican-Americans. He related that the other night he was driving home from work when he was stopped by a deputy constable.

The deputy constable—Ríos—came up to me with his little badge and gun on, but he wasn't dressed in any kind of uniform. I didn't even know who or what he was. [This last remark is patently untrue because Esteban speaks of the officer by name.] That guy came up to me and said: "Porqué pasaste allá?" I told him I had stopped and looked to see if anyone was ahead of me, and then he said to me: "Allí es un full stop!" That poor s.o.b. can't even speak one language or the other. *Un full stop*, what the hell! He makes himself out to be a big shot with his badge and his gun on in the Mexican town, but he would never do so on the American side. If guys like that could earn $5,000 or $6,000 a year they would right away build a house on the American side. That's the Mexicans for you, they'll cut your throat if you give them a chance.

Mingo, a young man of Mexiquito, remarked that he had been sent through elementary and high school with the assistance offered by an Anglo family and that he had attended college with the assistance of another Anglo. When he had won his college degree he sought employment and was recommended for a well-paying job by still another Anglo. But the personnel manager of the firm to which he was recommended was a chicano, like himself, and Mingo was turned down for the position. "That's the way Mexicans are."

Mingo and his family had lived for three years in a home owned by an Anglo landlord until one day the landlord asked them to move. Because the relationship between his family and the landlord had always been a very friendly one, Mingo suspected that they were asked to move because "a Mexican wanted the place for himself." That is, another Mexican-American had employed devious means to influence the Anglo landlord to oust Mingo and his family from the house.

Another of Mexiquito's residents commented bitterly that his neighbors and acquaintances were envious of his material success.

I work hard for the things I own. I didn't get anything for nothing! If people see me in a taxi every once in a while it's because I am tired after a long day of work. Sometimes my wife and I go downtown to shop and get a taxi back home. Sometimes when I have things to do downtown after work I eat a hamburger in a restaurant, like the other night. I just got off work and my wife wasn't feeling right and she couldn't cook. I had to have something to eat, I just got out of work. I was hungry.

By such comments Telésforo was voicing his anxiety that people who saw him in a restaurant concluded that he had aspirations of grandeur, a surmise from which invidious sanction might conceivably arise and afflict him or another member of his family.

The tales of invidiousness and bickering are countless, particularly those which occur between neighbors. The following example describes a series of arguments between two neighbors which culminates in the death of a member of one of the families, presumably a victim of witchcraft. Old Pedro's home and the house of a woman share the same lot. The two neighbors, who have had long arguments about their respective rights to the property, finally took the issue to court. The justice divided the property evenly between the two litigants. According to Pedro, the woman is now wont to dump her garbage on his side of the line, or else she spits on his property, or sometimes she mutters dirty words, which she directs at his home.

Pedro claims that once, as he passed his neighbor on the sidewalk, she hit him in the genitals. He was unable to move after the blow but, notwithstanding his condition, she and her son pounced on him and began to pummel him about the face and body. Pedro's two sons happened by at the time and saw what was taking place. They chased the other young man and beat him up; meanwhile Pedro rallied enough strength to give the woman a terrible punch on her jaw. She ran inside to telephone the police. When the officers of the law arrived, they took Pedro to jail, where he remained incarcerated for several days.

On his emergence from confinement Pedro erected a high fence between the two houses (the fence still stands and is approximately seven feet in height, and composed of strong planks). Then one day when Pedro was at work a big rock sailed over the fence and through his window. His wife permitted the missile to lie where it had fallen amid the shattered window glass, while she went to call her husband from his employment. When Pedro came home and saw the rock surrounded by fragments of his window, he took up the rock and, after carefully estimating the position and height of his neighbor's window, let fly. The rock, according to all reports, shattered her window.

Once again the neighbor called upon the police for assistance. The officers took Pedro to court, but the justice allowed him to leave on his seasonal migrations to work in northern crops, hoping that by the time Pedro returned to Mexiquito the affair would have lost its heat.

The first crop in which Pedro and his family worked that summer was Arkansas cotton. One evening, as they were resting after a long day's picking, Pedro's wife suddenly sickened. He was alone with her in their room on the night that she died. He was sitting by her bedside when all of a sudden he heard three knocks on the door and three blows on the floor as if someone was stamping. At that moment his wife "just shivered and closed her eyes and died right there." The door opened and shut again and then there were three blows on the porch outside the house. Pedro rose and rushed to the door, which he threw wide open. He ran outside shouting: "Who is it? Who is it? What do you want here?" He looked all over for the person but could not find anyone. Old Pedro is now certain that his wife's death was caused by his neighbor, but he has been unable to produce any evidence he considers admissible in a court of law.

Another interesting episode which sheds light on the relations between members of a household and the world outside is presented below. One key informant related that he and his wife brought to a physician's office their nephew's wife, who had already begun labor. The young woman immediately entered an inside room while her relatives remained in the waiting room.

During his wait the informant found himself in the company of, among others, a young woman of about seventeen years, who appeared to be verging on death. "They had asked the Father to come to confess her," said the informant, to give some indication of the gravity of her condition. The girl was moaning and writhing and appeared to be in terrible agony. She did not seem to respond to the ministrations of the physician.

The girl's mother began to discuss the problem with those who were with her in the waiting room. The mother was quite distraught and, according to the informant, she reiterated the following refrains:

She's a good girl. We have never done anything to harm anyone and she never has either. She has always been a good helper in the house, and never has meant harm to anyone. But there are always some rotters [cabrones] around who want to cause trouble just when someone is at peace with the world; when things are going well someone will always try to bewitch [poner mal] you.

Another of Mexiquito's people who contributed to this investigation related that her own mother had suffered bewitchment caused by neighbors. The mother was ill for seven long years, an illness which no one could diagnose or cure. Her symptoms were a swelling around the abdominal region. The patient's husband took her everywhere for curing—to cities and towns, to doctors, curers, and witch-es—but all to no avail.

The sufferer and her husband then sat down together to attempt a reconstruction of any incident in the past which might have pro-voked a neighbor to cause such a catastrophic illness. After some pondering, the wife recalled that once when her husband was away on a week's journey and had left her with just enough corn for the week, two old neighbor women came to the house to ask for some ground corn. She had to refuse them, because she had only enough for herself and her children. It was just after that incident that her stomach began to bloat out of all proportion to the rest of her body.

After reconstruction of that event, the couple agreed that the next step was to locate the two neighbors as quickly as possible. The hus-band set out immediately and found the two women herding their cows near-by. He warned them that they should cure his wife or he would see to it that they received their just deserts.

After several days he realized that his warning had gone unheed-ed; his wife remained seriously ill. He returned to the accused women, but this time accompanied by his wife's brother. The two men lassoed one of the women, and then the other. The trussed-up women were then tied by their hands and feet between two trees. They were advised that if they did not effect a cure of the patient they would be killed. Nonetheless, the neighbors swore that they had nothing to do with the illness. Several days later the husband of the patient again returned to the neighbors' home and began to shoot at the house, frightening the two residents, who entreated him to show mercy, but still swore their innocence.

By then the sick woman and her husband realized that there was nothing more that they could do to force the suspects to cure her. He took a straight pin and punctured the abdomen at the place of the swelling. From the puncture a trickle of yellowish liquid left the body; it was exactly the color of corn. The couple concluded that, without a shadow of a doubt, the guilty parties were, indeed, the two accused neighbors. After her "operation" the patient was as healthy as ever before.

More recently, a neighbor of Mrs. Kino became infatuated with the latter's daughter, but the girl did not respond. Soon the girl be-gan acting strangely. Her parents took her from doctor to doctor, but all that the medical men would advise was that she was suffering from a small hemorrhage in the head, about which they could do nothing. The young woman, it is said, was pronounced incurable by the physicians. As the girl's condition worsened, her parents took the advice of a friend and visited the home of one of the more prominent curers in this region.

At the time of their consultation with the *curandero*, the family explained to him their problem. He, however, was already well versed in the details of the girl's illness. He had known that they were coming to him for consultation; in fact, he had known it before they, themselves, had considered it. The *curandero* advised the parents to visit the cemetery located in the city of Thompkinsville at midnight that same night. They were to proceed to the fifth row of stones and to begin digging at a spot which he indicated for them on a sketch map. Digging was to commence at the stroke of midnight. At a depth of two feet they would find a tin can, in which would be two dolls, one with a rubber band around its head. They were told to remove the dolls from the can, take the rubber band from the head of the one, and put salt on the head of the other.

The parents of the girl wasted no time. They arrived at the cemetery that same night. As directed, they commenced digging at the fifth headstone. There they encountered the can with its two dolls. The rubber band that they found on the head of one of the dolls was removed, and salt was put on the head of the other. They quickly reburied the dolls and rushed to their home in Mexiquito. Early the following morning they visited the hospital in which their daughter was confined and inquired about her condition. They were advised that the girl had improved noticeably, beginning at midnight. Since that night the girl has not been ill.

Raúl, a young man of Mexiquito, reports that he was once requested by a woman to take her to a curer because she was having trouble with a neighbor. The neighbor was a bad sort, the woman told Raúl, and was "doing something to her." The *curandero* she consulted advised her to go out of her house at midnight, when she was to stand between the two houses and recite a number of prayers, including several "Our Fathers." Then she was advised to take two seeds given her by the curer and to place one of them at each corner of her home on the side which fronted on the house of the suspected neighbor. According to Raúl, the woman did this and now she is no longer troubled by her neighbor.

Another story which describes the view that residents of Mexiquito tend to hold of their neighbors is recounted by Orlando:

Some years ago my brother eloped with a seventeen-year-old girl, a very beautiful young woman. The girl's aunt did not like my brother because she wanted her niece to marry another.

Almost as soon as the couple were married, they began to get very sick. For a very long time they had an unhappy marriage. One of them was always sick and they didn't have any children, even though both of them wanted children. In those first years they couldn't get along with one another at all, and they kept arguing and fighting all of the time. They were married in 1933 and didn't have their first child until 1936.

Finally, they went to visit a curer for some advice and she told them that somebody had it in for them and they would have to try very hard to get along to overcome the malice that the other person had in his heart for their marriage.

They tried harder to get along and the marriage was more successful. Then, one afternoon, when my brother's wife was cleaning up the yard she spied an old doll, and discovered that it was full of needles. She put the doll on the fire and destroyed it, and they were able to have children and they got along better together. That doll was put under the house either by the girl's aunt or else by her former boy-friend.

The qualities believed by the chicanos of Mexiquito to inhere in relationships between an individual and the society outside of the nuclear family are clearly portrayed in the following account given by an old woman of the death of her favorite daughter. According to the elderly woman:

She was well educated, and we even sent her to business school where she learned to keep books and to notarize documents. She did very well at those things but she didn't last long after that. Perhaps in three years she lost her appetite, she didn't eat anything. She was only twenty-three when she died. The doctors never could find out what was wrong with her. We took her everywhere! We spent a great amount of money trying to find a cure for her. We tried everyone! We brought her to Monterrey, Victoria, Saltillo, Linares, San Antonio, Corpus Christi, everywhere!

She wouldn't eat, she would only drink water. After about a year and three months of this, she died, and the doctors never found out what had been wrong with her. I don't believe in such things, but the people here were talking and whispering that it was witchcraft [*mal puesto*] which caused her condition; perhaps so.

At the funeral parlor they performed an autopsy and, afterwards, they called in my oldest son and my older daughter to whom they showed the intestines. They were all sticking together, dried-up and dried-out, the way it happens when you don't eat anything. Perhaps it was witchcraft; she had had a lot of schooling and a good job. Perhaps it *was* invidiousness which caused it. I don't believe in causing harm to one's fellows. If someone doesn't say hello to me on the street—well— so he doesn't greet me. I don't think that things like that are cause enough to harm someone.

The stereotyped perception of neighbors in Mexiquito is perhaps exemplified in the following story, which describes the esoteric art of "witch fishing." Reina, a young woman, was describing the activities of those who know how to fish for witches (*Pescar brujos*). Such a person is acquainted with several prayers, which he uses in his fishing; each time that he recites one, he must tie a knot in a handkerchief (*paño*).

Once, when Reina's father and a friend were walking along a deserted road at night, they heard a whistling sound (*chiflando*) overhead. Her father's companion had the ability to fish for witches and so he recognized the whistling sound as that which is made by a witch when it flies about. The friend began praying and each time he recited a prayer he tied a knot in his handkerchief. Soon a huge, very ugly turkey fell to the ground near them. They grabbed the bird and secured it. Then they began to beat it and to cudgel it, for they knew that only by doing so would it be transformed into a person (*gente*). When it did change into a person, it turned out to be a woman neighbor whom they both knew.

The neighbor begged the men to permit her to leave because if her husband should wake and find that she was not in bed with him he would beat her severely. (At this point in her story Reina reflected: "Isn't it funny that he slept in the same bed with her and didn't know that she had left, but with this kind of person you just don't know those things about them.") The two captors were not anxious to release her because it isn't often that a person catches one of those people who are always doing bad things to others. But then their captive promised to give them as much money as they wanted if they would free her. She pointed to a pile of silver dollars near-by and was released by her captors. As soon as the men released her and she was on her way, the men turned to the pile of money and started running their hands through it. When they touched the silver it turned to clay.

There are also means other than witchcraft by which individuals are thought to be projecting their malice against neighbors in Mexi-

quito. During a ten-day period in 1958 a number of households received telephone calls of a calumnious nature from anonymous persons. The language of the callers was so vile and the insinuations so
dastardly that those who answered the telephone were left shaken
and ill. After receiving such calls several families petitioned a
change of telephone numbers from the company. After inquiries revealed the reasons for the petitions, the company notified the police.
Because none of the families would sign a formal complaint the police could not inaugurate an investigation. Although the persons
called, quite reasonably, were reluctant to divulge that they were
the targets of such vilification, some of the circumstances associated
with the calls were put together as described below. The nature of
the matter indicates something of the quality of interpersonal relations in Mexiquito.

Approximately six or seven Mexican-American families received
the defamatory telephone calls. Those families represented some of
the most successful of the socially mobile chicanos; in fact, all but
one of the families had moved from Mexiquito to the other side of
the tracks. Those who received the calls claimed that the information revealed by the caller about their personal lives was such that
only an individual who was a most intimate friend would have had
access to such details. One woman, who was placed under a physician's care as a consequence of such a call, believed that because
some of the insinuations made were about bastardy, fornication,
and such, the caller must once have been a very good and close
friend, because she certainly would not have revealed such information to another.

The mother of one of my friends in Mexiquito was a recipient of
one of those vilifying telephone calls. Her son related the story as
follows. "I had heard of those telephone calls before, but they had
never touched me so closely. The caller used language that even a
man shouldn't use." Immediately after his mother received the call
she telephoned him at home and told him to "come over right now
and pick me up."

When I got there she was all shaken up and could hardly speak to
me. A couple of days after my mother received that call, Junipero came
over to the house asking me for advice. His mother had received a call,
too. The language and the accusations against her were so bad that
she just burst out crying. Now, says Junipero, she won't even answer
the 'phone anymore; she just lets it ring.

Those members of the maligned families with whom I talked attribute the telephone calls to invidious motivations of a family whose social mobility has not kept pace with that of those whom they telephoned.

But insulting telephone calls and witchcraft do not exhaust the techniques which Mexiquito residents assume are used by their acquaintances to project hostilities. It is a common belief in the neighborhood that arresting officers of the United States Border Patrol often act with such prescience about the illegal presence of one's friends and relatives that the agents must have been tipped off by neighbors. Salazar, an older man in the neighborhood, is convinced that the Border Patrol was tipped off by his neighbor, Luis, when they came to arrest Salazar's common-law wife from Mexico. In another, similar case, a young woman who was picked up, charged, and deported, all within the space of two hours, was convinced that the agents acted with such celerity in her own case that someone must have informed them of her exact whereabouts. She accuses a woman whose own deportation was assumed to have made her invidious of the more fortunate informant's longer illegal stay in this country. There are many such accusations of willful malice lodged by residents of Mexiquito against others of the neighborhood.

The people of Mexiquito peer out from the security of their homes at a society which they view with distrust, suspicion, and apprehension. The fears of invidious sanction, witchcraft, tips to the Border Patrol, and calumnious telephone conversations all attest to the anxiety and apprehensiveness with which social relations in Mexiquito are viewed. In actual fact there are bases in reality for such anxieties and apprehensions; a sudden illness or a spate of bad luck demand explanation. The Border Patrol's visitations and consequent deportations of relatives and friends are not to be wished away, and there is no doubt about the reality of the terrifying telephone calls. Only within his or her own home is the Mexican-American in an environment in which he or she trustingly participates with others.

Summary

In Mexiquito the most important social units are the nuclear families, which consist of parents and their children. Ideally, each nuclear family resides in a separate household, although sometimes a widowed parent of one of the spouses lives with them. Visiting between households is discouraged, except by members of the close family or ritual kinsmen.

Within the household, interaction between family members is guided by well-marked channels of respect and deference. Status and role behavior are clearly marked for each member of the nuclear family, and the individuals interact with assurance, if not with ease. The older order the younger, and the men the women. Those values which order the conduct of the residents enjoin exhibition of levity or frivolity. The home is a place for serious demeanor, it provides an appropriate environment for one's wife and daughters.

The confinement of females within the home gives rise to a closely knit group of a mother and her daughters, a relationship which perdures throughout the lifetime of the individuals. The imminence of a daughter's marriage appears to provoke stressful consequences in the life of the domestic group. It is hypothesized that a daughter's impending marriage is stressful because it threatens to rupture the microcosmic group of interdependent women who reside together.

The individual households stand isolated from each other, socially if not spatially. Families perceive members of Mexiquito society other than close relatives as dangerous and antagonistic. Improvement in the well-being of an individual or his family is accomplished in the face of opposition from others of the society. The themes of invidious sanction and malevolent intent are incessant in Mexiquito, and the means by which such hostile intentions are believed to be projected are manifold.

4. THE PALOMILLA

U nlike their womenfolk, male chicanos are expected to engage in social activities beyond the confines of the household. The most important of the institutional settings, other than the family, in which young males engage is the *palomilla*.[1] The palomilla is a network of informal dyadic relations between age-mates. This chapter focuses on a consideration of the role played by the palomilla in the life of the individual, and its relation to the total social system.

The passage of a son from boyhood to adulthood and marriage is quite unlike the road his sister must travel. At an early age the boy begins to initiate contacts with the young males of the neighborhood in informal aggregations, which are quite fluid. Although some of the aggregations do bestow names on themselves, others do not. Neither is the proprietorship of a territory important as a general feature of the assemblages of men; for some it is present, for others it is not. The aggregations to which males, youths and adults, adhere are not based on social class, although there is some tendency for individuals of similar occupation, education, and income to interact with each other more frequently than they do with others with whom they do not share such characteristics. But social class exerts no more influence upon the formation of aggregates of boys or young men than does residential propinquity, attendance at the

[1] An earlier discussion of the palomilla appeared in the symposium The Presentation of Self in Hispanic Society. See Arthur Rubel, "The Mexican-American Palomilla," *Anthropological Linguistics*, 7, No. 4 (April, 1965), 92–97.

same school, or other factors. Finally, the institution of leadership is absent from these assemblages of males. It is precisely because of the absence of characteristics of corporateness that these aggregations are so difficult to define.

I shall follow local usage and call this type of aggregation a palomilla. The word itself is derived from *paloma* (dove), so that literally a palomilla is a covey of doves, but the word is used to indicate an association of boys or young men. The phraseology and the persons to whom the term is applied are recorded here as they are utilized by the chicanos of New Lots. "Palomilla," "the palomilla," "my palomilla," and *"el mero palomilla"* are terms used every day by the chicanos.

In New Lots the term "palomilla" refers to those males with whom any individual frequently associates in social activities. It is never used to refer to work groups, nor does it appear to include those rare Anglos who sometimes associate with the chicanos. The bounds of any one palomilla depend upon the individual elected as the fixed point of reference within a network of informal relationships.

One may, and people do, subsume under the rubric palomilla the assemblage of one or two close friends who are inseparable from one's self. Mingo and Peña comprised such a tiny palomilla. Neither ever seemed to be without the other, and they were very seldom seen in the company of others. On most nights Mingo and Peña were found on the corner outside Jesusito's clothing store, a corner of the street that was also frequented by another, larger palomilla. During the course of the evening when one of the palomillas moved elsewhere, Mingo and Peña either stayed on the corner or else moved off by themselves to another locality. The two palomillas happened to frequent the same locale, but each acted discretely.

The individual who speaks of his palomilla as containing himself and several others also speaks of "the palomilla" when he refers to those individuals who regularly frequent the same *cantina* with him. Furthermore, the same speaker applies the term palomilla to the aggregation of individuals who tend to be invited to the same barbecues and public dances which he attends. The last usage subsumes a number of smaller, otherwise discrete, palomillas. The characteristic absence of structure of the palomilla should not be taken to mean that any individual may at will interact with a palomilla. He cannot. The chicanos of Mexiquito recognize full well those eligible to interact with a particular aggregation. Others would be presuming.

Pains have been taken to utilize English descriptives such as "assemblage" and "aggregation" because such terminology betokens the noncorporate nature of the palomilla. The palomillas of Mexiquito are formed on the basis of the mutual likes and dislikes of the individual participants. There is no set of rules by which one requests membership, nor is one invited to join a palomilla. An individual who wishes to separate himself from his regular *palomilla* may do so at will, since there is no tangible bond between himself and the others of that assemblage.

Perhaps the quantity of aggregates to which the rubric "palomilla" is applied by an individual appears to diminish its discriminatory value. I, for one, believe that to be the case. One is justified in asking: What range of relationships does the descriptive term "palomilla" discriminate from other ranges of relationship? The difficulty is similar to that with which the English-speaking person is, confronted by such terms as "community" and "society." All three terms are susceptible to more precise understanding if one is acquainted with the characteristic interaction rates between the persons involved. Thus a palomilla may be defined as that aggregation of males with whom a chicano interacts with some frequency. The fixed point of reference for the definition of the bounds of any palomilla is any one individual.

If one were to question an acquaintance in Mexiquito as to who else had been at the bar he had just quit, the answer would likely be "Palomilla." The response would leave no doubt that the others in the bar were acquaintances of the respondent. But the answer would by no means imply that those others were more than acquaintances. However, one would receive the same reply, "Palomilla," if he were to ask the same individual: "With whom were you drinking?" He might also receive the responses "The Palomilla," or *"Puro palomilla."* The inquirer would then know that the other had been passing the time with persons with whom he most often interacted. In this way the range of possible companions is markedly restricted.

The following passages describe some of the activities engaged in by palomillas of Mexiquito. Telésforo, for example, remembered that as a youth he used to "hang around" with a palomilla comprised of some of those neighbors who were his same age. In Telésforo's neighborhood:

. . . we had almost all of our friends. When we were kids we used to fly kites, play baseball, and some of the guys from other *barrios* used to come to play with us. We used to play with nigger-shooters [sling shots]. We used to have fights with nigger-shooters against the fellows we called *Los Molineros*. The *molino* [public corn mill] was right next to Calderón's store, and one reason why we called them *Los Molineros* was because all of their names began with *M*. I remember that their names were Mário, Miguel, Monte, Morado, Mugro, Marín. They really knew how to make nigger-shooters and were crack shots around there. Aside from *Los Molineros* there were some friends of ours who lived in the little rooms behind the Calderón store and also behind the *molino*.

Telésforo's house was:

. . . the main house, the headquarters, I guess you would call it. The kids used to always hang around our place because my mother wasn't there—she got married again—and my big brother was a storyteller. We always used to sit listening to him. The guys would sleep at our place, too, and whenever a woman couldn't find her kid in the morning, she would just come over to our place.

Telésforo said that much of the time of his palomilla was spent in the construction of sling-shots, and much of the remainder was utilized to plan strategy against the Molineros.

When one of us would go through their territory, they used to gather like an army. Boy, we used to have the fights. One time we scared them so badly that they never went through our territory again. When they wanted to go downtown after that, they had to go out of their way and go around where we lived; and when they wanted to go to school, they had to go around by Calle Libertad or some other way, but they couldn't get to school by the most direct street; they had to go out of their way.

Later Telésforo's mother and stepfather moved to Puebla Street. Telésforo thought of the boys in his new neighborhood as "nice." "They never fought. They always went swimming and rode bicycles. They never got close to us."

Telésforo volunteered that when he lived in the home of his sister and brother-in-law, their neighbors were nicknamed *los rancheros*. The term *ranchero* means to Telésforo a person who is shy and withdrawn. In Mexiquito, persons whom Telésforo and others called *rancheros* tended to be agricultural wage laborers possessing little competence in English-language skills. Diffidence was another quality attributed to a person called *ranchero*.

The ranchero neighborhood in which Telésforo, the boy, found himself had residents who were:

... kind of like *pachucos*, kind of like sports. They try to be different from the boys downtown [*el centro*]. They try to have something different on their cars, different from downtown. Those boys don't go downtown like the others. They gather in Segovia's store and tell stories about what happened to them. They're like out in the country. The mailman doesn't deliver mail to the houses out there because they are not on a route. He leaves the mail in Segovia's store.

Joaquín volunteered that when he grew up, his palomilla was known as the Catholic School Boys. "We hung around together a lot more than with other fellows. There were some fellows who would come in and out, but they weren't really a part of the palomilla." Joaquín recalled that another palomilla consisted of other students who also attended the parochial school. That palomilla was associated in his mind with such escapades as playing hookey from school, turning outhouses upside down, and other acts, which earned it a deserved notoriety. The boys of the palomilla tended to oppose the policies of the school and the police; they all dropped out of school early in life, though *not* for financial reasons. Their reputation contrasted sharply with that earned by Joaquín's palomilla.

Other data support the contention that although delinquent conduct *may* be a feature of some palomillas of Mexiquito, delinquency is not a generic characteristic of palomillas.

In spite of the fact that the rubric "palomilla" does not delineate groups of persons as neatly as one might wish, the chicanos do use it to advantage when they seek to mark the people with whom they interact as differentiated from those with whom they act in distant fashion. One evening when Telésforo and I were walking about the streets of Mexiquito, we encountered Hómero, a friend of mine, who was one of the individuals in the palomilla with which I was commonly associated. Hómero was introduced to Telésforo, and when Telésforo and I parted from him Telésforo pondered:

I was always in-between. We were poor, but we weren't very, very poor. I didn't want to fight, and get into trouble the way the other boys around us were always doing; and I didn't have the money to dress real well and to have a beer whenever I wanted one [in contrast with Hómero and his palomilla]. I've probably seen him hundreds of times.

In such a manner did Telésforo let it be known that *he* took account of the activities of Hómero and his palomilla, but that the latter took no note of Telésforo. Other data, some of which are presented in the following pages, indicate that Telésforo realized that he could not interact at will with Hómero's palomilla.

On another occasion a public barbecue was arranged for Caldo. It was sponsored by Caldo's palomilla in celebration of his approaching wedding, and each member contributing money for the purchase of food and beer was entitled to invite one friend. I invited Telésforo, but he confessed that he would feel *muy feo* (very uncomfortable) in such a gathering. "I know most of them, but they don't know me. I wouldn't have anyone to talk to."

Coeval with Joaquín's palomilla at the Catholic school was another comprised of students of Joaquín's age who attended public school. Although the public-school palomilla was composed of the more "sports-minded" of his age group, one of the boys who formed the nucleus of approximately six lads was not very athletic. Therefore he was "only in and out of the palomilla."

To the same extent that the female of a household is expected to confine her activities to a small circle of relatives, young males are thrust outside that enclosure. It is in the world outside of the household that the young male seeks his comfort and enjoyment, yet his allegiance and responsibilities remain fixed to the household social unit. It is *only* on the members of this household that the man can surely depend in time of need. The institutions of the family and the palomilla, therefore, do not conflict with one another.

In the Mexican-American society of Mexiquito a male is expected to pursue the pleasures of the flesh as soon as he is able, and for as long as he has the strength. At each and every opportunity he is expected to assert and to certify his manhood. It is considered most desirable that a man function in as untrammeled a fashion as possible—*a cada cabeza un mundo*, they say (Each head is a world unto itself).

The pursuit of some masculine goals is antipodal to the concept of the household as a venerable institution, in which live those persons with whom a young man must interact most decorously. Although a young man owes allegiance and responsible behavior only to those of his household, he pursues his social activities away from that particular locus. It is with his palomilla that the young man may "display the full social personality of an adult male," to make use of Pitt-Rivers' felicitous phrase.[2]

The palomilla is considered to be the normal social grouping for the young Mexican-American male of Mexiquito. Even after marriage the palomilla, not the new household, is properly the focus of his activities. A young man whose attachment to his household interferes with the more manly activities with his palomilla causes serious concern to his family and to the others of his palomilla. When such a situation is feared to exist, members of the society exert pressures to pry the man from his home to the more appropriate palomilla.

In one instance a young man of about thirty-two years was believed to be too closely attached to his wife and children. His mother complained, accusing his wife (her daughter-in-law) of refusing him permission to leave the house during the night. However, in this case, the young man resented the allegation. He said, "I like to stay at home nights. I work hard all day and enjoy watching TV at home."

At a later date persons with whom that young man regularly associated in palomilla activities advised me that the young stay-at-home had begun to complain one night while drinking with his friends. On that night he took grudging note that his two married brothers were quite successful philanderers, and he claimed that he envied them their pleasures and freedom. At a still later date the field notes record that the palomilla viewed with approbation its observation that Ramiro had begun to do well himself: by now his philandering was rated as even more successful than his brothers'!

In another instance, Tony, a recently married man, was the cause of much denigrating conversation among his former palomilla, who complained that since his marriage he didn't leave the house at night, and that he was allowing himself to be dominated by the wishes of his bride. Often the conversation of Tony's palomilla turned to the discovery of means by which they could release Tony from the household.

In another case, a newly wed couple established their own home immediately after the wedding. The husband, previously notable for his successes with women, now took every opportunity to publicize piously his changed behavior. *He* was not going to "run

[2] Julian Pitt-Rivers, *The People of the Sierra*, p. 90.

around" any longer! Furthermore, he reproached the behavior of several others of the palomilla.

On the approach of the first Christmas after their marriage, his pregnant wife was insatiably anxious to visit with her mother, who lived in Houston. Since the young husband was unable to leave his work during the holiday period, he unwillingly permitted his bride to spend a week with her mother in Houston. Throughout that lonely period he was despondent, and the palomilla commiserated and lent moral support. They found the bride blameworthy, claiming that she should have stayed with her husband during the holiday period. It was during this lonesome, depressed period that young Jaime's palomilla discovered that he was unacquainted with Mabel.

The Mabel Caper

Mabel is a fictitious, young Anglo woman who is said to live in an isolated farmhouse. She is reputed to be married to an Anglo older than herself, and, furthermore, Mabel's husband is said to work on the night shift; he leaves his wife home alone every night of the week. If one adds these details of Mabel's personal life to the general assumption held by Mexican-Americans that Anglo men are notoriously insufficient bed partners, Mabel becomes a siren, indeed. Jaime had not yet been made aware of the fictitious Mabel, although his palomilla had introduced others of Mexiquito to that alluring creature. Jaime therefore became a target for the waggishness of his palomilla.

As is true in every other case in which an individual is brought to meet the apocryphal Mabel, various members of the palomilla accept discrete responsibilities. The occasion on which Jaime participated began when he was approached by Hómero, one of his good friends.. Hómero let slip to Jaime the facts about Mabel's youth, her beauty, her unrequited desires, and her isolated abode. Jaime was not slow to respond, and Hómero confided that he felt sure a tryst could be arranged for the very next night. He would keep Jaime informed.

After they separated, Hómero alerted the others of the palomilla —all except Jaime's *amigo de confianza*. Cars went out along the roads near Mexiquito in search of an unoccupied farmhouse and, finally, one was discovered. Hómero then informed Jaime that

Mabel was more than agreeable to the proposed meeting. However, Mabel had set one condition: Jaime must bring with him one full case of cold beer. Jaime accepted the condition, and the stage was set. While Jaime looked forward to the next night, the palomilla rejoiced.

In midafternoon Jaime was seen in the barber's chair. He asked for a haircut. He also solicited a shave, an unheard-of luxury. When Jaime confided to the barber that he had "something hot lined up for tonight," the barber shared his enthusiasm, for he was one of the men assigned to precede Jaime to the deserted farmhouse.

That night on the trip to the farmhouse Jaime asked innumerable questions of his friend and guide, Hómero, who answered as best he could. When they arrived at the farmhouse Jaime picked up the heavy case of beer, and with his two guides trudged up the pathway. Jaime was cautioned about the need for silence; the trio could hear only their own low whisperings.

Hómero tapped lightly on the door with his fingers. There was no answer, and Jaime looked nervously at his guides. Both were perfectly solemn. Hómero again tapped lightly, calling softly, "Mabel? Mabel? It's me."

Then a powerful beam from a six-cell flashlight shone full into Jaime's blinded eyes as a voice barked angrily, "There you are! You Mexican s.o.b.! Now I have you, you Mexican bastard! I'll teach you to fool with *my* wife!" The thunder of a .45 contributed to the unexpected din. As the third shot rent the air above, Hómero lay on the ground, apparently in agony. He cried out to Jaime for help, but Jaime was no longer present.

It was several hours before one of the searching parties could locate Jaime. Scratched, weary, fearful, and soaking wet (he had attempted to hide in a deep irrigation ditch), Jaime refused to believe that he was the victim of a caper. He blamed himself fully for his good friend Hómero's perhaps mortal injury; he inquired whether the police were yet aware that he was the guilty party. Only with the greatest reluctance did Jaime enter the car of the search party. Later, when he encountered Hómero gleefully relating the prank to other patrons of the Rio Bar and Grill, it appeared that Jaime's anger knew no bounds.

According to all reports of similar visits to the fictitious Mabel, the preparations made by the palomilla for Jaime's visit with that siren were no different from those undertaken on other occasions, nor was Jaime's reaction singular. The palomilla recalled a number of instances in which the target had responded in a manner even more inglorious than Jaime's.

The narration of Jaime's visit with Mabel still evokes laughter, and to participate in such a hazing is unforgettable. The moral which the palomilla draws from such a prank is most illuminating. The participants moralize that in spite of the most pious assertions to the contrary, it is in the very nature of the Mexican-American male to transgress the marital bond. Each time that a married man embarks on the adventure the thesis is validated, and one of the major charters of the institution of the palomilla is buttressed. When field work in Mexiquito neared termination the palomilla was making serious efforts to introduce Tony, the wife-dominated husband mentioned previously, to Mabel.

Marriage and the Palomilla

Although the institution of the palomilla competes with the institution of the household, the two are not in conflict. Furthermore, although marriage is important to the individual, it does not affect his status within the palomilla one iota. Indeed, marriage is a rite of passage for the individual, a rite marked by his palomilla, but unlike that of a young woman at marriage, the palomilla marks not the passage of an individual from one institutional status to another. There is none to mark.

At the time of a young man's wedding, his palomilla initiates a barbecue and beer-bust. Often those of the palomilla closest to the fiancé will actively participate in his wedding, as well.

When Jaime announced his wedding plans, for example, three of his palomilla organized a barbecue. Only one of the three was a particularly close friend of Jaime, that is, a person in whom Jaime would confide his intimate life. The three organizers made plans to meet together, and at the organizational meeting the names of twenty men were selected as those closest to Jaime. It was stipulated that each person who was invited would be taxed five dollars, and that the money would be used to buy food and drink. Meat and beer were subsequently purchased; each item was solicited from a businessman-relative of one or the other of the organizers. Another member of the palomilla who was noted for his skills at barbecuing was requested to act as the cook.

On the afternoon of the party the meat was barbecued at the home of Jaime's *amigo de confianza*. Beer supplied by the host was consumed by those preparing the food, and when the meat was ready the cooks left for the site of the celebration, which was held on the lot where Jaime's home was being constructed.

After consumption of a goodly amount of beer, the food was served, and when the men had finished eating they broke into small groups to discuss topics of common interest. That is, until Hómero began to tell jokes, attracting all of the men to where he was standing. Many of the jokes referred to marital affairs, especially the nuptial night.

The author attended other barbecues meant to serve the same function: celebration by a palomilla of an imminent change in personal status of one of its participants. All had the same pattern of organization and attendance, although some were more luxurious than others; occasionally a trio of musicians entertained the crowd. The following passages illustrate the great importance members of a young man's palomilla may have for his wedding.

Lorenzo was soon to be married. He had two very close friends, Júlio and Raúl. Previously, the three youths had taken an oath "to become compadres when we got married." Although all three were very close friends, Júlio considered Lorenzo his *mero amigo de confianza* (true or outstanding best friend). "When I have something on my chest, I go to tell Lorenzo about it, and the same for him when he's got some trouble."

When Lorenzo was in the process of making arrangements for his wedding, he asked Júlio to act as sponsor of the ceremony. If Júlio had accepted that office, it would have made of him and Lorenzo *compadres de casamiento*.

Júlio outlined the reasoning underlying his refusal of his best friend's offer. If he had agreed to sponsor his best friend's wedding, he explained, he would thereby become a *compadre de casamiento*. Júlio felt that the relationship would somehow lessen the probability that he would be the baptismal godfather of his best friend's first-born child. The latter sponsorship would enlace Júlio and Lorenzo as *compadres de pila*, by far the most important fictive kin relationship which the chicanos of Mexiquito recognize. Júlio calculated that he would prefer to forego the immediate prize of the lesser relationship, and wait one year for the baptism of the first child so that he could enter into particularly close *compadrazgo* bond with his very best friend. Interestingly enough, Júlio was somewhat offended because Raúl *had* accepted the lesser responsibility and the inferior relationship. Júlio said that he had "told off" Raúl for accepting the role of sponsor of Lorenzo's wedding.

Approximately two weeks after Júlio had elucidated his reasons for having refused Lorenzo's proposal, the latter was honored at a barbecue and beer-bust sponsored by his palomilla. The affair was splendiferous and lasted well into the morning hours. Then two weeks after the barbecue and beer-bust, a dance was held to honor Lorenzo. The dance was sponsored by Júlio and Raúl, Lorenzo's two best friends, each of whom had contributed forty-five dollars in order to rent Veterans' Hall, the largest public hall in the city. An orchestra from northern Mexico was hired to play for the celebration. No special invitations were issued to the dance, but each man in attendance was expected to bring his own liquor. The public nature of the dance in honor of Lorenzo was in contrast with the exclusiveness of the barbecue.

In another illuminating exchange on the subject of the role of the palomilla in a man's wedding, Manuel, a participant in quite a different palomilla from Lorenzo's, was asked to be best man at the wedding of his *amigo de confianza*. Manuel, a bachelor, remarked to others, "He wanted me to be best man, so I said OK. I said, 'I'll give you away, and I'll take you back, but I won't follow you [into matrimony]'."

A better understanding of the meaning that the *amigo de confianza* relationship holds for the chicanos may be garnered from the following discussion that I had with a young resident of Mexiquito. I asked Báldemar whether he had ever heard of an *amigo de confianza*.

Oh, yes. I used to have two of them. He's someone you always go around with, a person you tell everything to. You talk everything over with him. He's a special friend. With the palomilla, well, they're your friends and you go around drinking beer with them, but this is a special friend. He's sort of your best friend.

"Is the *amigo de confianza* more important than a compadre?"

Well—with a compadre, it's kind of like that. People think that you choose a compadre just to have someone to drink beer with. But that's not the way it is; at least that's not the way I feel about it. With a *padrino*, he should be there to guide your kid. Sometimes when the kid won't listen to the father, the *padrino* should be there and slap the kid on the back and say to him, "I hear that you haven't been such a good boy lately. What's up?" Then he'll talk to the kid, and the kid will talk to him. All my compadres are like that. They're people I feel I can depend upon in case something happens to me, so that they will watch over my kids.

Marriage in the culture of the Mexican-Americans of Mexiquito is an important rite of passage for the individuals involved. As such it is celebrated by ceremonies appropriately public. In the case of the bride, the rites celebrate both individual and institutional changes, whereas the rites for the boy are restricted to the changes in his individual life cycle. Those most affected by the change in the status of the girl—her own parents—announce publicly the institutional change which her marriage portends, but the family of the groom participates little, if at all, in the celebration of his marriage.

The rites celebrated for a bride recognize symbolically that she is about to pass from one social unit to another, from her family of socialization to her family of procreation. (In the words of one oldster "She becomes just another sack of wheat." However, even in the family of *that* wit, his married daughters preserved a very close bond with their mother, his wife.) The passage of the bride from the family of her parents to that of her own household is enclosed within ritualized procedures; the *portadores*, the *diario*, and the euphemistic waiting periods are all tokens of the delicacy of the transition of the bride from one series of allegiances to another. They are also recognition that a new household in which she will be wife and mother is imminent. These rites are cultural mechanisms which cushion the separation of a female member from the domestic group with as little trauma as possible. That such mechanisms are inadequate has previously been demonstrated.

Such problems of courtship and marriage do not exist for the groom, who has passed gradually out of his parents' household. Within his palomilla the youth reached manhood and learned to express himself as a male. Since marriage does not curtail the palomilla activities of the husband, he continues as before. By means of one or several celebrations, the young man's approaching marriage is duly noted by his palomilla, for it helps him to celebrate any important change in his personal life cycle. However, palomilla celebrations make no note of an institutional change, or of any innovation in the rate with which the subject interacts with the membership of different institutions. Such an institutional innovation is absent. The society recognizes the palomilla, an aggregation of age-mates, as the appropriate group for the more social activities of the young men, whether or not they are married. An unduly warm relationship between a young man and his wife and children is frowned upon. Gossip, the Mabel caper, and more direct reprimand function as adequate sanctions to prevent such an attachment. The institution of the palomilla competes with the institution of the family only for the time and affection of a youth, but these two institutions are complementary. They are not at cross-purposes.

Bereavement and the Palomilla

The palomilla is of crucial importance to an individual young man during several of his life crises. In this section will be described the important role played by palomillas during the bereavement of a member. The descriptions are all based on participant observations.

Milo's paternal grandmother passed away. During the young man's childhood Milo and his mother had been deserted by his father, and they both went to live with the deserter's mother. During the years a very affectionate relationship developed between Milo and the old woman. Milo spoke of his paternal grandmother as *abuelita,* and addressed her in that manner, instead of by the more formal term often reserved for paternal grandmothers— *mamá grande.*

On the evening of his grandmother's death, a *velório* was held at one of the funeral parlors and was attended by a large number of persons. Milo and the other men remained outside the building, where chairs and benches had been placed on the lawn and walks of the grounds. Against the building sat a group of older men, the paternal uncles of Milo, while younger men either sat or stood separated from their elders. During most of the evening the bereaved Milo stood on the main walk leading from the street to the funeral parlor, but he never stood alone. Around him stood the young men with whom he most frequently interacted. Although Milo was silent, they smoked and chatted, yet never left his side. Only twice was Milo observed to leave the palomilla: the first time in order to sit down on a chair next to mine to introduce his father to me (the father had returned for the funeral); the second time to attend the more formal rites of the *velório* inside the chapel.

The people who came to the funeral parlor that first night parked their cars and trucks on the street, then walked up the pathways to the parlor. The men approached Milo and shook his hand. Often, they patted him on the back, meanwhile murmuring their sympathy. The women, too, approached Milo and expressed their sympathy for him in murmured phrases.

After greeting Milo the men found themselves places in the assemblage outside the funeral parlor. His male relatives joined his paternal uncles or began to chat with his father. Milo's palomilla, on the other hand, joined the cluster which surrounded the young mourner, and chatted with each other. Without exception the women passed immediately to the inside of the parlor, where they knelt or sat to pray for the soul of the deceased. The women remained inside until they departed for home.

During another service for the dead the following observations were made. In this case the deceased was the father of Ramiro, with whom I had interacted in the same palomilla. We two were also members of the League of United Latin American Citizens (LULAC). On the afternoon following the loss of his father an automobile containing Ramiro and others of the palomilla passed me on the street. Their countenances were grim as Ramiro asked me my destination. When I answered that I was then on my way to my own car and thence to the funeral chapel, Ramiro peremptorily told me to enter their car, saying that they would take me to the mortuary. I received the impression that Ramiro thought me lax; as a member of the palomilla I belonged at his side, with the bereaved. Nevertheless, after assuring him that the chapel was my destination, we parted company.

At the funeral parlor was almost the entire palomilla, those men with whom Ramiro interacted with the greatest frequency. Ramiro was standing between two members of his palomilla, part of an open circle of six young men, all of whom were seen regularly with Ramiro in social activities. A short distance away stood a small group of four other members of Ramiro's palomilla. On chairs located at the entrance of the parlor sat another group of three or four other young men, some of whom were members of LULAC, but others who were not. On the basis of the previously observed rate with which the last mentioned four young men interacted with

Ramiro, they could not be considered a part of his intimate palomilla. Within the funeral parlor sat some older men who occupied the left-hand side of the room and chatted with one another in quiet voices, while the women sat on the right-hand side of the chamber. The women prayed, but did not engage one another in conversation.

People began arriving in increasing numbers. Each man stopped to shake hands warmly with Ramiro, and usually squeezed him about the shoulders. None of the women stopped to say or do anything to Ramiro, however; they passed directly into the building.

After each man had stopped for a brief moment to greet Ramiro, he quickly joined one of two clusters of males. Later, three clusters could be distinguished, one of which surrounded Ramiro. In this aggregation I knew every individual, for as both Ramiro and I belonged to the same intimate palomilla, we had interacted with far greater frequency with the individuals in this cluster than with any other person present at the service. The men now around him were those with whom Ramiro chatted at the bar after the weekly LULAC meeting. When he had a barbecue at his home, these were the individuals he consistently invited, and at public barbecues and dances Ramiro spent most of his time with this small group. During his bereavement, then, these men stood close to Ramiro.

A second discrete cluster of young men stood apart from Ramiro, gathering around Nacho, Ramiro's older brother. I was unacquainted with any of those standing around Nacho, and even though all were residents of Mexiquito, I recognized few even by sight.

Later in the evening a group of six or seven younger men arrived at the funeral home; all were complete strangers to me and to the others of Ramiro's palomilla. (This conclusion was based on the observation that their entrance caused some of those of Ramiro's palomilla to stand on tiptoe and to question one another in an attempt to ascertain the identity of the newcomers.) The younger men went directly to the funeral parlor from their automobile. They did not stop en route to shake hands with either of the chief mourners, Ramiro or Nacho, but when the youths departed they approached the palomilla ranged around Ramiro, and then each of the young men murmured his sympathies to Ramiro. Although they stood with our palomilla for approximately ten minutes, they said nothing to anyone except the bereaved Ramiro. From their conversation we learned that they were the palomilla of Serafino, Ramiro's younger brother, who had not yet arrived from Cleveland.

Later in the evening the women in the funeral parlor began to rise and walk to their automobiles, and the young men of the various palomillas moved off the walks in order to clear a way for them. None of the women stopped to say anything to the bereaved brothers. Then the older men also left the building, but not before each one approached Ramiro and Nacho to shake hands again and to express condolences once more.

Throughout the evening Ramiro was surrounded by his palomilla. Several times he wept unashamedly, and occasionally he, or another of the palomilla, remarked that so heavy a loss is made more bearable when one is backed (*respaldado*) by friends. Not once during the watch over the bier did the relatives of the two brothers stand near them (the brothers' wives were inside with the other women), nor did the brothers stand together to comfort one another. Each stood apart with his palomilla.

Several things had to be arranged for the funeral, and some of these Ramiro entrusted to members of his palomilla. For example, several of the wives had to bring the distraught widow from her home to the *velorio*, and Ramiro delegated to two of his palomilla the task of driving the automobile for the women. Another of his palomilla was asked to drive to the airport in Randolph to meet Serafino when he arrived from Cleveland.

On the second evening following the death, the body was brought home from the funeral parlor. At 10:30 that night I arrived at the house and found a small crowd of men standing outside on the sidewalk, while the womenfolk, relatives of the widow plus some of the wives of the palomilla, remained inside. At approximately eleven that night, Ramiro and his palomilla went to a restaurant for sandwiches and coffee.

On the following day the funeral took place. At the appointed hour the sidewalks in front of the Methodist church were crowded with men. Inside, the church was crowded by the relatives of the deceased and by members of the congregation. Outside, two groups of men could be distinguished by their relative ages. Alongside the Methodist church were the younger men, many of whom consistently interacted with Ramiro. Across the street were older men, dressed uniformly in black suits and white shirts. They were said to be friends of the deceased.

When the casket was brought from the church it was placed in a hearse; then the widow and the three sons of the deceased followed. Together they trailed the body to the cemetery in their automobile, followed by the automobiles of relatives and, finally, by those of the palomillas of the three sons.

Summary

The aggregation of persons in Mexiquito with whom an individual male interacts with some frequency is known as a palomilla, a network of informal relationships between younger men. The fixed point of reference in any palomilla is an individual, and no two individuals will participate in exactly the same palomilla. Within the palomilla is found a close, but not necessarily enduring, relationship between two individuals; they are *amigos de confianza*.

Furthermore, the palomilla of Mexiquito is characterized by the absence of corporate features. A young man owes no obligations to his palomilla, nor is he responsible for any of the acts of another member of his palomilla. He can, and sometimes does, move freely in and out of a palomilla. The palomillas of Mexiquito display none of the attributes of hierarchized status, of leadership and followership, or of other characteristics of corporate unity, which seem so much a part of the youth gangs which often find their way into the daily press. Such features are alien to the palomilla, but they are definite attributes of the domestic group to which the young man belongs as son, husband, and father.

The importance of palomillas as a major organizing feature of Mexiquito social life contributes to the atomism of the social system because these aggregations organize a minimum number of individuals into ongoing, loose relationships. An absence of a sense of obligation between associates and an inability of participants to exercise leadership over one another hinder the coherence of more effective and durable social units other than the small family.

5. POLITICAL BEHAVIOR

The chicanos of Mexiquito sometimes attempt to cope with felt needs by acting in concert. The previous chapter described how two, perhaps three, participants in a palomilla act in concert to arrange such affairs as dances, barbecues, and the Mabel caper. This chapter describes attempts to activate the Mexiquito electorate during three campaigns.

This discussion is based on observations of chicanos' efforts to mobilize the voting strength of Mexiquito during two municipal elections and during a campaign for a seat in the state Senate. Because it is so often true that an understanding of leadership is of primary importance in any study of local political behavior, inquiries were made about leadership and leaders in Mexiquito. Joaquín, a particularly perceptive observer of his own society, was asked about the importance of the roles played by Martín and David in Mexiquito. Martín and David are considered by Anglo-Americans to be outstanding leaders across the tracks in Mexiquito. I asked Joaquín: "You know, I have the feeling that Martín and David may be the leaders for *some* things over here, but they're really not as important as the Anglos would want you to think, are they?"

No, I don't think they're very important at all as leaders. Of course, they're successful men, and they're important for the Latin to be able to point to and say "This is what we can do, too." But I don't think people pay too much attention to what they have to say. You know there's a lot of resentment about them because they built their homes on the Anglo side of the tracks. People say they are very Anglicized. I was real surprised the other night to hear somebody frankly state this. But Roberto was telling me. He was saying that David got all his money on our side and yet he lives with the Anglos.

You know, it's hard to put your finger on a leader over here; there's no really good way. I've been thinking about that before and I don't know how you could figure that out.

Joaquín was then asked about Abel's status as a leader. Abel, who is very much a part of the local political scene, publishes a four-page mimeographed broadside. The sheet is entitled *La Garrapata* (The Tick). He is thinking of changing the title to *¡Epa!* (Ouch!), reflective of its often stinging commentaries on Anglo-chicano relations. *La Garrapata* has as its publicized purposes the providing of a local news medium for Mexiquito, and the public shaming of those chicanos thought to be too closely associated or identified with the Anglo way of life. *La Garrapata* functions latently to quicken the sense of in-group identity of the chicanos by constantly opposing the ways of this group with those of the other, the Anglos.

To return to the status of Abel as a leader in Mexiquito, the following conversation with Joaquín was recorded.

Well, I guess you could call him a leader, but a lot of people, me included, don't pay much attention to him. He's a kind of troublemaker, a rabble-rouser. But you take Eloy now, people watch what *he* does, and he never raises any noise about what he's doing. It's funny too. You'd think that nobody would be interested [influenced] by what he thinks, living where he does. [Eloy lives in a large home on the Anglo side of the town.] I think he's a leader here, but I don't see how he manages it because you never hear from him.

Then you take Esteban. He's probably the most important person in town as a leader, but you never hear him say anything openly. He runs a Mexican-type store.[1]

Esteban speaks real good English and so does his wife, but they haven't changed much. They're not trying to get up there with the Anglos, to become Anglicized. I don't know how he does it, but he's real important in that neighborhood, much more important than Abel.

---

[1] It is appropriate to mention that several other chicanos commented that Esteban was a very influential person north of the tracks. Their indication of his importance was usually in association with description of his store as a "Mexican-type store," in other words, one which appears like stores in Mexican towns and cities.

Then you take Teodora. She's right up there. She's real class here in town. She's just a little old lady, who walks around town with a shawl over her head, and speaks Spanish all the time, and talks loud, and laughs a lot. Real Mexican, just like Esteban. But she's real powerful here on the Mexican side of town.

During elections she'll come out for a representative or a governor, but the rest of the time she doesn't say much, publicly. When Shivers and Price Daniels were running for [gubernatorial] office, there were people down here from Austin who went to talk with her.

Then Joaquín was asked: "Does Teodora belong to any clubs or political parties? How does she keep her political position?" He answered: "I don't know how, but I know that she doesn't belong to any of the civic groups or political clubs."

The quotations above indicate that the organization and leadership of politics are informal, not formal. The data which follow support a preliminary conclusion that the chicanos of Mexiquito display little aptitude for the formal organization of political behavior.

In the first of the observed electoral campaigns there were two vacancies on the City Commission. Héctor and Martín were the chicano contestants. Héctor's opponent was an Anglo, but Martín was running unopposed. The passages which follow are from the field notes.

The rally in support of the chicano candidates was to take place at Sunrise Hill, a county park. Martín and I made plans to attend the rally, which was scheduled to begin around one in the afternoon.

Martín called for me at one o'clock, but inasmuch as I was not yet ready, he left, saying he would return. By half-past two Martín had not yet returned. When he did come he told me that he had found Benjamín with several others of the palomilla and he had been unable to tear himself away from them. Our friends were awaiting word that the rally and barbecue had started. Finally, Martín and I left my home and went once again to call for Benjamín. Another young man, whom I knew only by sight came along with us. On the way out to Sunrise Hill we each bought a can of beer at the grocery store and then continued on our way, until Benjamín and his companion told us that the location of the rally had been moved from the park to Gregorio's house. We changed direction and went to Gregorio's.

When we arrived, there were approximately thirty automobiles parked in front of Gregorio's. The men were standing around in the yard, chatting and drinking beer. There were no women to be seen. Martín and I went over to the improvised bar, where Chico handed each of us a can of beer. There were still no women to be seen. Martín and I were informed that the tripe was cooking, but that it would need to be cooked for several more hours.

I was acquainted with the great majority of those present, among whom I discerned at least three palomillas. There was the palomilla of Chico, Abel, and Larry. There was another of Lázaro and Martín. Then, there was my intimate palomilla; those present were Roberto, Baldemar, Héctor, Hómero, Jaime, Prudencio, Mireles, Miguel, Idelfonso and Ramiro.

I went over to chat with the bartender, Chico. He thrust into my hands *two* cans of beer; it was a gesture of friendship. I noted that those at the rally were talking about politics *among* other things.

Idelfonso called me to his side and introduced me to two young men with whom I was not familiar. Each of them spoke faultless English. They were well dressed. Apparently, both youths had been drinking for some time. One, who tended to sway when we talked, was a student at a local college. Because Idelfonso had introduced me as an anthropologist from The University of Texas the student showed himself anxious to discourse on such academic subjects as anthropology, sociology, and history. The collegian began to complain about discrimination in the Valley. He equated discrimination against the chicano with the same behavior against Southern Negros. He then asserted that the only reason he came back to the Valley to live was that his parents and family lived there.

The student then commenced to denigrate the political rally.

This is no way to hold a rally! Nobody is saying anything! Nobody is telling them the problems we face! Nobody is offering a platform with which we can solve our problems! Anglos wouldn't hold this kind of a political rally!

Later in the afternoon the two young men approached me again. They asked whether I attributed to inherent biological differences the fact that "the Anglos are always ahead of us." I asked them whether *they* thought that to be the reason. They did not. Then both of the youths began to shake their heads from side to side. They continued to shake their heads negatively as if silently asking: What is it that we do wrong all the time?

Still later in the afternoon I was approached again by the collegian. He asked:

What do you think will improve us? What do you think will make us better [vis-à-vis the Anglos]? Don't you think that it has to come from within, from a part of the group? Don't you think that's where your leader has to be from?

Fifteen minutes later I was approached by the same youth. He said:

You should run for City Commissioner; we need someone to guide us. We don't have leaders. We need someone who knows his way around! Well, whatever we may not have, at least we're always happy.

A local band began to entertain the crowd. The band— La Música Incógnita—played traditional ranchero tunes. When the music terminated, entertainment was provided by an impromptu group consisting of a guitar, a bass, and a violin. *Gritos* (jubilant cheers) signified that this music was well enjoyed. The beer and conversation flowed more freely. The atmosphere was becoming more charged with excitement.

I noted that some of those present were walking several hundred feet to a large chicken house, and I surmised the trip was to relieve themselves; others performed that function behind the parked autos. I wandered over to the chicken house; why should anyone walk to the chicken house when the automobiles were closer? Within the house no fowls were in evidence, nor was there any indication that there had been any there in the recent past. The building was very clean, with sheets of corrugated paper spread over the clean cement floor. In one corner sat the players in a costly crap game; in another corner were seated the poker players.

From outside rang the announcement that the food was ready (lunch was late—the cooks had been drinking). At that, the games broke up and the players dispersed. Everyone went to the barbecue pit to be served lunch. When all had finished eating the barbecued tripe, the tortillas, and the beans, a master of ceremonies mounted a table. He announced that Héctor, sponsor of the barbecue and candidate for the City Commission, was going to make an address. The announcer's voice was charged with emotion. In his introduction he informed us that Héctor's opponent was a *bolillo*, an Anglo. We were told that if we did not vote Héctor into office we could not expect to improve the condition of the chicanos with respect to the Anglos. His tirade was a call to support Héctor, the man whose food and beer we had just enjoyed. A vote for Héctor, our friend, was a vote for a chicano; a vote for Héctor was a vote against the Anglos.

Héctor then mounted the table. He commenced with the assertion that he was acquainted with most of those present. He knew their problems well and he wanted to help them with their problems. Héctor promised that if he was elected he would always act in such a way that his friends would benefit.

Héctor then spoke at some length portraying his rise to a present position of responsibility as a purchaser of crops of vegetables from farmers. He ascribed that mobility to two causes: his own earnest efforts to improve his condition, and the help he had received from Anglos sympathetic to his social aspirations. Héctor stressed his relationship with Anglos influential in the region. He made much of the fact that his position as agent was so trusted that his employers awarded him a power of attorney. Héctor used his position of trust with Anglos as a certification of his worthiness for public office. He identified himself, a poor working man, with the members of his present audience. Several times during his sentimental speech members of the audience sought to generate enthusiasm by shouting the campaign slogan: "All the way with Héctor!" When Héctor terminated his speech the *grito*, that virile huzza resounded. Most of those in the audience appeared to be unmoved by the effort.

Several times during Héctor's speech persons were seen to shake their heads ruefully when he made use of such rubrics as *bolillo* and *gavacho*, apparently because of my presence. After the speech Rolando captured the attention of the crowd by stating in a loud voice that he had "kept an eye on Arturo [author] and seen his back rise at mention of those derogatory terms." No one responded to Rolando's gibe (*mosca*).

Once again the master of ceremonies climbed onto the improvised platform. He introduced Martín, who was running unopposed for the City Commission.

Martín's address was quite unlike Héctor's. He made no mention of the rift between the two sociocultural groups, Anglo-American and Mexican-American. He stressed the fact that he and Héctor were not candidates for the *same* office. A vote for Martín was *not* a vote against Héctor, and vice versa. Martín reiterated that point. His plea for votes was a request for support from his friends. He did not present issues as a basis for choosing a candidate any more than did his two predecessors. The rally dispersed when Martín had finished.

Another rally took place several days later. This one, also, was in support of Héctor's candidacy. The locale was a barrackslike hall, which usually was utilized for public dances during the harvest season. Approximately fifty men comprised the audience. Again, no women were present. With the exception of myself and two others, all of those present were chicanos. The other two Anglos were Abe Cohen, owner of a small clothing store in Mexiquito, and a Mr. Gruel, who was the manager of the bus depot. It was strange to see Gruel here. An irascible man, he changed from employ to employ during my residence in New Lots. Gruel did not seem to participate in the social life of either side of the tracks. He did not seem to have the respect of either of the groups which comprised the population of the city.

The meeting was called to order. Unexpectedly, the master of ceremonies introduced as a speaker the aforementioned Gruel. From the kind of introduction given him it was evident why he had been asked to speak in favor of Héctor's candidacy. He had been invited *because* he was an Anglo. (Probably Gruel was the only Anglo willing to publicly support Héctor's candidacy.) In his turn, it became apparent why Gruel had accepted the invitation.

Gruel's address made only passing reference to Héctor's candidacy. He began to read lengthy passages from several newspapers. The gist of the readings was that Chief Justice Warren of the Supreme Court represented a clear and present danger to the nation. Gruel concluded that portion of his presentation with: "If he isn't a Communist, he thinks like one!" Gruel then spoke at length of a presumed Jewish-Communist conspiracy, which held this nation and the "free world" in a deathlike grip. His other readings were of similar ilk.

Several members of the audience became restless. There was a good deal of yawning and moving about on the benches. Renaldo left his bench to sit next to me in the rear of the hall. He whispered: "Tell me, Art, does this guy make sense to you?" Renaldo then volunteered that he did not consider Héctor a worthy candidate for the City Commission. *He* was not going to vote for Héctor. Renaldo and several others left the hall before termination of the rally.

At the conclusion of Gruel's address, Héctor was introduced. Once more he identified himself with the other young chicanos. He stressed the fact that, although he had been born in Mexico, he was proud to be an American citizen. Héctor emphasized the trusted relationship he had always held with Anglo employers. He then loosed blasts at several influential chicanos who had not lent their support to his candidacy. He descried as "millionaires" those persons who had permitted money to go to their heads and who had built their homes on the other side of the tracks. In other words, those people who had not supported him were also traitors to Mexiquito. (By implication, Héctor contrasted himself with the "traitors" because he had built his home in Mexiquito, although it was a well-known fact that he *could* have built south of the tracks.)

On the day after the rally I visited Héctor's campaign headquarters located in Justino's home. On my arrival four men were present, all members of Héctor's palomilla. They were the young men one commonly saw in association with Héctor on social occasions. The campaign "workers" were not working; they were conversing. They were engaged in a discussion of the importance of electing Héctor to the City Commission. (Martín was running for re-election.)

Sometimes the conversation of the campaigners focused on strategy. At such times there was much talk of *hacienda movida, hay mucha movida,* and "moving the people." Such phrases implied that the Mexican-American electorate—the *chicanazgo*—was a dormant mass, which had to be stirred into activity. As a matter of fact, one of the young men compared the chicano electorate to "an ant hill," which had to be stirred up. Each of those present sought to generate the enthusiasm of the others. Each urged his companions to insure that every voter in his family was guaranteed transportation to the polling station. Each worker told the others in no uncertain terms that they were responsible for every person in their families casting his or her vote. That was their real responsibility! Also, those who worked in industrial plants with other chicanos were asked to bring those voters to the polls. No great pressure or sense of personal obligation was associated with the last admonition.

Héctor was defeated by a large margin. After the election Abel confided that he had visited the polling station during the balloting. He had noted the mayor, the city manager, and one of the city commissioners standing together. They seemed nervous to Abel.

Nicéforo, also, had spent time in the polling station on election day. He was a self-appointed poll watcher in order to "prevent" chicanery by the Anglo electorate. Nicéforo said that he had noted a certain "nervousness" on the part of the Anglo municipal officials as they observed the voting.

Nicéforo complained that Héctor had lost the election because the Anglo city officials had "called out the vote." He explained: During the afternoon of the election, while Nicéforo was acting in his self-appointed role of poll watcher, he saw the three city officials hurriedly confer with the election judge, another Anglo. Nicéforo believed that they were apprehensive because of the light voting. In an election characterized by little interest and consequently little balloting, there is a chance for the chicanos to win simply by casting more votes than the Anglos, if each group votes as a block. Table 5 depicts the number of poll taxes purchased in New Lots by year and by ethnic group.

Table 5

OWNERSHIP OF POLL TAXES BASED ON SURNAMES

	1956	1957	1958
Anglo-Americans	1400	1433	1470
Mexican-Americans	1100	1125	1144

After the conference the city manager left the scene. Within an hour, according to Nicéforo's calculations, "The line began to form." Nicéforo surmised that the city manager had telephoned a number of Anglos in order to communicate to them his fears. They had responded by casting their ballots.

Later on in the week in which the conversation with Nicéforo was held I visited with the city manager. As we discussed the recent election, the official volunteered the information that in pre-election conversations that he had held with some chicanos, they had expressed doubts about the worthiness of Héctor for city office. The city manager confided that the people of New Lots have little interest in the elections, a disinterest which he considered unhealthy for the city. The manager then volunteered that his concern over the election had been so profound that he had taken the initiative and made a number of telephone calls to officers of the more active social and fraternal groups on the Anglo side of the tracks to induce the citizenry to cast their ballots. Nicéforo's surmise was confirmed. During that election 700 Anglos voted and 326 Mexican-Americans

balloted. When Abel was asked about his analysis of the dispropor-
tion he answered: "A lot of chicanos don't want to vote for someone
because then someone will get hurt. These people don't want to
cause trouble by voting." In other words, in elections in which personal esteem overrides impersonal issues (as in Mexiquito) a vote
for someone is a ballot against another.

More acculturated chicanos are well aware of the potential
strength of the Mexiquito electorate. At a meeting of the League of
United Latin American Citizens (LULAC) held during the campaign, several members urged the local council to support a drive
to induce the chicano voters to purchase poll taxes in the following
year. The move was voted down on the strength of Ray's argument
that such a drive would be construed by Anglos as having political
overtones. The LULAC council, he argued, would no longer be accorded the esteem of Anglos who conceived of the group as an educational and citizenship-oriented organization. Ray announced that he
was for the members acting as individuals and getting their friends
to buy poll taxes, but that he was not in favor of the Council having
circulars printed which would urge the purchase of poll taxes. Ray's
argument carried the day.

The description which follows is the result of observations of the
campaign of Henry B. González for a vacancy in the state Senate.
At the time of the race González was a state representative from
Bexar County. (Bexar County, which is approximately three hundred miles north of Mexiquito, is comprised almost entirely of urban
San Antonio.) González was running for office against an Anglo
incumbent. González' public pronouncements took little note of the
rift between chicanos and Anglos in the state. Although the candidate attempted to appeal to all sectors of the electorate—chicanos
and Anglos alike—his attractiveness to Mexiquito rested squarely
on the fact that he, like them, was a chicano.

Early in the González campaign for the Texas Senate I was
speaking with Hómero, a Mexiquito voter. My companion became
incensed when the conversation touched on the election. He contended hotly that the *chicanazgo* would not cast a bloc vote for González, even though it was in their best interest to do so. Bitterly,
Hómero offered the following explanation why the *chicanazgo*
would not vote in the manner he thought best. Many chicanos, said
Hómero, suckle (*mamar*) the politically powerful, and such chi-

canos cannot afford to vote for González even if they wished to. They cannot take a chance. Hómero added: "Mexicans never do anything together, because they are too self-centered and rancorous (*egoísta y rencorista*)." Then he lamented the presumed inability of chicanos to discuss matters of importance with one another. "When two chicanos begin to discuss something, it isn't two minutes before one pulls a knife on the other." Hómero claimed to have witnessed the following incident (it was probably an aprocryphal story):

Two close friends, they were either *primos* or *cuñados*, sat down together to have a beer. In no time at all one had thrown a beer bottle at the other, breaking open his head. The police arrived immediately and took down their names, one, two, three. Then the two were carted off to jail.

From that story, Hómero drew the moral that the chicanos owe their subordination by Anglos to their own inability to cooperate in common cause. "Even though we're improving, they have their foot on our necks."

An organizational rally to inaugurate the local González campaign was held in Edinburg, the county seat of Hidalgo. Narciso attended the rally. When describing his experience there to the palomilla, Narciso said that he felt "like a damn fool, to hear those chicanos talking about this and that; about 'I'll be on this committee and that committee'." Narciso spoke of the Anglos laughing up their sleeves at the "big talk" of the chicanos: "You have to be somebody, you can't just be a worker or a clerk and say 'I'll serve on this committee with so-and-so,' as if those big-shot Anglos would serve on such a committee with you."

Narciso then derided the melodrama of several of the influential chicano speakers at the rally. He recounted one such address, as follows:

We are mexicanos! We have our roots here! This is our land! This is where we have always been! We can't allow strangers to come and take it away from us! Any man here who doesn't vote for the chicano I will personally slap across the face!

According to Narciso's account, another influential announced: "Any chicano who does not vote for Henry B. González, I will brutally kick in the gonads." Narciso told how the audience responded to those sallies with *"Que vivas!"* for González and his erstwhile supporters.

Later in the campaign a political rally was held in McClune, the largest city in the county. This rally was attended by several hundred chicanos. Among those present were eighteen men from Mexiquito who, with one exception, ranged between twenty and forty years of age. Every one of those present from Mexiquito was bilingual. None of them were engaged in agricultural field labor. The only Anglos present, besides myself, were candidates for county offices, who addressed the rally in support of their own candidacies.

When González arrived at the rally in the late afternoon he was greeted by a sustained ovation. Speaking in faultless English, the candidate devoted his speech to his proposed program of legislative reform. He spoke to the point. When he had finished he was saluted by another ovation. González then left the platform, but was prevailed upon to repeat his speech—in Spanish. Apparently, the audience was far less interested in *what* he had to say than in the way that he said it. On our way home to Mexiquito one of the palomilla remarked: "See, Art, not all Mexicans are dumbbells."

Once during the González campaign, Abel looked out the window of his store and spied a chicano lawyer, a visitor from another town. Abel decided then and there that he would call a rally for that very evening, to be held in the plaza. The lawyer would be the principal speaker. Abel dashed across the street to welcome the lawyer, and described his plans to the visitor. The lawyer agreed to speak in support of the González candidacy. Abel then sent word around Mexiquito that a rally would be held in the plaza that very evening. It was held but very few attended. Renaldo, the only person in Mexiquito to have committed his time to González' support, did not attend the spontaneously organized rally because, he explained, "I had a date."

The second municipal election which I observed took some unexpected turns. Two vacancies were to be filled, of which one was for the office of mayor and the other was for a post on the City Commission. Both incumbents were Anglos who were running for reelection. The mayor was running unopposed. Then, two weeks prior to the balloting a young Anglo businessman entered the mayoralty race.

The latter was almost unknown to the voters of Mexiquito because he was a new resident of the city. He was a member of a number of civic clubs, but only one of these contained chicanos with whom he interacted.

Ten days before the mayoralty election several young chicano men initiated a candidates' night at the El Casino bar. Invitations were issued to all candidates. The purpose of the meeting was to introduce the various candidates to the Mexiquito electorate, and to permit them to present their programs to the chicano voters. Only two of the campaigning candidates accepted the invitation. One of these was the young newcomer; the other, an Anglo who was a long-time resident and was running for the City Commission. Both men were fledglings in politics.

On the night of the function at the El Casino the atmosphere inside was informal. Beers were enjoyed and conversation waxed. Some members of the audience bought the candidates beer and they reciprocated. After several hours of conversation the two Anglo candidates were transported around Mexiquito and introduced to several of the more influential chicanos. On the next day the palomilla was enthusiastic about these two candidates; the others were disparaged.

One week before the election one of the candidates appeared at a LULAC meeting and expressed a desire to address the Council. To accommodate the campaigner's request, the meeting was adjourned. (The adjournment was in keeping with the constitution, which prescribed political nonpartisanship for the local Councils.) In effect, the speaker addressed an aggregate of voters, not a corporate entity.

This speech was in English. He stressed that he was "for an open town." By that he meant that he favored a proposal to facilitate credit for new residents who wished to build homes valued at more than twelve thousand dollars. (Only one member of the Council owned a home whose value even approached such a sum.) Although the candidate was obviously enthusiastic about his program for liberalizing credit facilities, no one else seemed particularly interested. When he had terminated his speech, the floor was opened for questions and discussion.

Several members of the audience castigated the present administration of the city. Their attacks were based on the common grievance, so much a part of Mexiquito's ethos, that the residents of the north side of the tracks were not being treated fairly by the present city administration. Specifically, the complaints took note of the absence of paving on many of the streets north of the tracks, a paucity of sidewalks, and the lack of service from the municipal sewage system. The candidate, Miller, promised to "find out about" the problems; he did not otherwise commit himself.

When the questions were exhausted, everyone turned to less serious pursuits. Some men began to play poker, others clustered around the bar to talk. One of the clusters around the bar was composed of the more angry critics of the administration. The candidate listened to their grievances without comment other than: "It is good to hear representations from your side of the tracks." When the office seeker had departed it was apparent that his socializing with the Council had left a very good impression.

The next regular meeting of the Council coincided with election day. In the middle of the meeting Mr. Miller, the candidate who had addressed the group, appeared. He jubilantly announced his victory by a margin of thirty votes. Commissioner-elect Miller thanked the members for their support. He also announced that the dark-horse aspirant to the mayoralty had been elected. The victor and the members of the Council were mutually cordial.

That very night several supporters of the mayor-elect celebrated his victory in La Frontera Bar. One youth was designated to telephone the victor, congratuate him, and invite him for a drink. The invitation was cordially accepted. The mayor-elect even set up a few beers himself. The next day those who had celebrated the victory at La Frontera waxed enthusiastic over the cordial relations they held with the mayor-elect. One of the palomilla commented: "There's one thing about our people. They'll vote against anyone they feel doesn't like them. They don't care who they vote for, but if they feel that a man doesn't like *la raza* they'll turn against him."

Another young chicano, an active supporter of the mayor-elect, narrated the following pre-election incident. The Sunday before election day he and four others were sitting in Veterans' Hall. They were passing the time of day, chatting and drinking beer. Late that afternoon the incumbent mayor strode into the hall. He marched directly to the bar.

He walked right past our table without as much as saying "How're you boys doing?" or "What are you drinking? Here, have a beer!" He must have felt pretty sure of himself, . . . ! There's something I'll tell you about our people; if they feel that a man doesn't like them they'll do him in!

Soon after the election Abrám, a young clerk and former collegian, was discussing the outcome with another salesclerk. The latter claimed to have overheard the Commissioner-elect tell the Anglo manager of the store: "Today is my day to be friendly with the Mexicans." Abrám commented stiffly: "If I had known that, I wouldn't have voted for him."

Those in the city who follow politics consider Tomás to be that city's most sagacious observer of chicano political affairs. He is consulted by aspirants for municipal, county, and state offices, Anglos and chicanos alike. When the recent election was discussed with Tomás he expressed anger with Abel's tactics. He was disgruntled because Abel had not agreed to throw his support to the candidacy of the Commissioner-elect. Instead, Abel had supported an Anglo by the name of Simpson. Tomás surmised that Abel was forming a political faction of his own. Then Tomás remarked that as much as he "respected" Abel, the latter was obstinate and not very intelligent.

Abel is a hardheaded fool. I don't believe he knows Simpson at all and probably wouldn't recognize him if he saw him. Simpson refused the invitation to come to the El Casino on Candidates' Night, so Abel has probably never shaken his hand and that's important amongst our people.

Tomás continued his diatribe. In spite of the fact that Abel is a compadre of David, the former had rejected a request from David to back an Anglo candidate supported by David. Instead, Abel had supported another Anglo:

. . . and as a matter of fact Abel is a compadre of mine too. Even then he wouldn't go along with David! You know a compadre is a pretty important thing. You're supposed to respect a compadre. I don't know what you think about it, some people don't care for it. But it's supposed to be pretty important and I go for it. I think you should support a compadre whenever the time comes for it.

Analysis of Political Behavior

The data concerning Mexican-Americans' political behavior and attitudes which have been presented are a product of participant observations and informal interviewing conducted during the course of three electoral campaigns. Two of those campaigns were for municipal offices, and the third for a vacancy in the state Senate. The subjects of these observations were chicanos actively engaged in

Mexiquito politics during the campaigns. It is possible that other members of the north side of the tracks were equally active, perhaps even more so, but it is improbable, as I undoubtedly would have been aware of such activities.

It is a reasonable assumption that the attitudes which were overtly expressed by Mexican-American citizens during the election campaigns are reliable indications of the manner in which they voted. Moreover, if such attitudes are indeed reliable, it follows that chicanos vote for the man, but not for the issues he represents. Recall that all overtly expressed political attitudes were *personalistic* in nature. For instance, Abrám would not have voted for one aspirant if he had "known" the candidate's "real" attitude with respect to chicanos. Also, the palomilla voted for the mayor-elect because he interacted with them in a personal manner. Conversely, they voted against the deposed mayor because he saw fit not to socialize with them in Veteran's Hall. On still another occasion, an appeal by two chicano candidates at a barbecue-rally was directed to the recognition by the chicano electorate that they were all friends, the electors and the candidates. The appeal for support was directed to those with whom the office seekers had just shared food and drink. Moreover even though Representative (later Congressman) González advanced his candidacy in terms of an impersonal program for legislative reforms, and carefully refrained from appeals to ethnic loyalties, his legislative program provoked no discussion or comment on the part of the palomilla attending the rally from New Lots. What did impress his audience, however, was the manner in which González delivered his speech. In fact, so impressed was the audience, that the speaker was prevailed upon to display his virtuosity by repeating the same presentation—in Spanish. In this, as in all instances observed during the three campaigns, impersonal issues were subordinated to the personal qualities of the candidate. The concept of personalism helps to answer a puzzle posed by one prominent Anglo: "There isn't one leader among the Latins who can pull a large group of people along with him. There isn't one! Why is that?" That puzzled concern finds its echo on the north side of the tracks, as well. Witness the matter-of-fact observation by a prominent chicano merchant: "The trouble with this town [Mexiquito] is that whenever we have an election we split a thousand ways; nobody likes anyone else after it."

Besides personalism, other salient regularities are observed in chicano political behavior. One of the most striking is that their grievances are consistently expressed as complaints, not demands! In spite of the tiresomely often repeated grievance that municipal services in Mexiquito are either inadequate or in disrepair, I do not recall anyone discussing the possibility that the complaints might be transformed into demands. Nor does anyone suggest that municipal services might be obtained or improved by the application of political leverage, or by influencing the election of officials by means of strategic voting behavior. The concept of forming and utilizing pressure groups for purposes of bargaining for improved service appears to be absent in Mexiquito. Contrarywise, that concept is fundamental to the political thinking of Anglos who live across the tracks.

Another finding of interest is the absence of instrumental groups in political activities. Honigmann defines instrumental groups as people organized together for "the achievement of some relatively specific goal . . ."[2] During the observed election campaigns individuals were discovered to adhere to the personality of an individual candidate and, also, to the symbol of *la raza*, but not to organized instrumental groups in support of either a campaigner or his platform. Moreover, Honigmann comments that some societies display a certain "flair" for organizing and proliferating instrumental groups.[3] Clearly, the chicanos do not.

However, one would not be justified in concluding that because chicanos do not organize themselves into instrumental groups, they are not concerned with social issues, or do not mobilize their forces to cope with felt needs. During the elections each chicano activist was observed to rally to his side those persons whom he could influence in his behalf. He rallied them by means of the only instrumental technique in his repertoire: personal appeals to acquaintances or kinsmen. Chicanos concert their efforts to achieve goals, but they fail to organize one another for purposes of such achievements. Organization of groups for the attainment of goals, whether diffuse or particular, is not one of the instrumental techniques made available to them by their culture.

In Mexiquito, individuals concert their efforts in interaction with others; their ties to those others are of a personal nature. But, given the importance of the personal aspect of those ties, unless persons are linked by bonds of real or fictive kinship, the strength and relia-

---

[2] John J. Honigmann, *The World of Man*, p. 422.
[3] *Ibid.*, p. 423.

bility of the bond varies as the appreciation one person has of another varies. Personalism in Mexiquito contributes to unstable, shifting alliances which, at a glance, appear to be motivated by whimsy. By extension, the personal quality of the relationship between elector and candidate does, in fact, seem almost whimsical; personal aspects seem to subordinate impersonal issues in elective campaigns. However, an explanation that chicanos' voting behavior is based *simply* on the call of friendship or obligations to kin, that is, *A* votes for *B* because they are friends or kinsmen, lacks cogency because it appears to be an oversimplification of a complex matter.

It is more compelling to argue that the characteristic personalism of Mexiquito political behavior (and, by extension, that found in other Latin American areas) is a dynamic and instrumental kind of behavior which is oriented toward the attainment of some more or less specific goals.[4] But in this case goals are not sought by means of organized groups, a technique so much a part of Anglo society on the south side of the tracks.

In sum, the importance of a personal quality to elective and other kinds of instrumental behavior in this type of society is an obverse of the absence of organized special-interest groups. Where personalism displaces other instrumental tools, as in Mexiquito, what is done as a favor is not to be demanded, nor is the favor to be retained by force.

Thus far it has been argued that temporary adherence of individuals in Mexiquito to a strong or otherwise engaging personality is the major means whereby social forces are mobilized. That way of coping has been traditional in the lower Rio Grande Valley for many years among the Spanish-speaking population; however, the region is now bicultural and the traditional personalistic coping techniques have been rendered relatively ineffective by the events of the 1930's, during which Anglo political groups, for example, the Good Government League, assumed mastery of local politics. As is true of all types of social behavior, personalistic coping techniques are optimally effective when all parties are agreed on the premises

[4] Compare with relevant comments in John Gillin, "Ethos Components in Modern Latin American Culture," *American Anthropologist*, LVII (June, 1955), 488–500; René Williamson, *Culture and Policy;* George I. Blanksten. "Political Groups in Latin America," *American Political Science Review*, LIII (March, 1959), 106–128.

and then act in a manner which is logically predictable. Chicanos in Mexiquito continue to cope personalistically with political problems, despite the fact that their understanding of appropriate behavior is in radical opposition to that of the superordinate Anglo group.[5]

Other Views of Chicano Politics

Traditional chicano voting behavior has not always been as ineffective as it is now in South Texas. Such a conclusion receives firm support from several articles by Professor O. Douglas Weeks.[6] Professor Weeks' firsthand acquaintanceship with local political history in the *chicanazgo*, and his insightful understanding of it, are enviable, indeed. More than a quarter of a century ago Weeks expressed his optimism that in the course of acculturation of South Texas chicanos to the superordinate Anglo society, the former would learn to adapt their political behavior to accord with that of the Anglos. Much more recently, another student of chicano political behavior found reason for concern because of the slowness with which the Texas chicanos were developing "effective" political behavior.[7] But the latter author, Donald S. Strong, also found room for optimism as did Weeks before him. According to Strong:

> The majority of this Spanish-speaking group both in San Antonio and in south Texas simply do not "get the score" politically; they are herded to the polls and "voted." They have to date developed practically no group-conscious political leadership. While the group is entirely capable of producing effective leaders and will surely do so in future years, at present the Negro is much more politically advanced than the Mexican-Americans.[8]

It seems that what these political scientists anticipate is not more effective behavior, but different behavior. That personalistic ties to

[5] For a definition and discussion of the concept of radical opposition, Godfrey and Monica Wilson *The Analysis of Social Change*.

[6] O. Douglas Weeks, "The League of United Latin-American Citizens; A Texas-Mexican Civic Organization," *The Southwestern Political and Social Science Quarterly*, X (December, 1929), 257–279; "The Texas-Mexican and the Politics of South Texas," *The American Political Science Review*, XXIV, No. 3 (August, 1930), 606–627.

[7] Donald S. Strong, "The Rise of Negro Voting in Texas," *The American Political Science Review*, XLII, No. 3 (June, 1948), 510–522.

[8] *Ibid.*

candidates and party "bosses" can be effective behavior, indeed, is supported by the previously cited material gathered by Weeks, and by other documentary material.[9] However, personalism in Mexiquito continues as a major kind of political instrumental behavior, in spite of the protracted, bitter, and successful campaigns by Anglo settlers to destroy the traditional political organization which characterized the lower Rio Grande Valley previous to 1940 (and which can still be found in such South Texas locales as Rio Grande City, Laredo, and Duval County).

The description presented of contemporary chicano political behavior in Mexiquito accords well with those provided in other locales and in different eras by Weeks and Strong. We do not disagree on description but on interpretation. Our differences in interpretation of the same or similar data are a function of differences in the way the materials are handled. This sort of problem is by no means restricted to the analysis of data from South Texas. In fact, a similar difference of interpretation prompted William F. Whyte to pen a stirring "challenge," in which he called attention to the value gained by interpreting political behavior in the context of more general social-structural principles derived from on-the-scene observations of politics.[10] Both Whyte and I analyze political behavior of our respective populations (Italian-American and Mexican-American) in a holistic framework, taking account of the social-cultural context of interpersonal relations. Thus, political behavior is not viewed isolated, as it were, from other aspects of social behavior, but rather as intimately linked to those other behaviors and as derived from the same sources. On the other hand, it would appear that political scientists comprehend political activities by lifting them from sociocultural context, then comparing those from one society with those obtained from another; for example, comparing Mexican-American political behavior with that of Anglo-Americans or Negro-Americans. These are different procedures and they give different results. The disparity between the present interpretation of chicano politics in Mexiquito and the evaluations of Professors Weeks and Strong is therefore understandable and to be expected.

---

[9] Weeks, "The Texas-Mexican." See also, *Glasscock* vs. *Parr*, Supplement to Texas Senate Journal, 36th Session (1919), pp. 846–851.

[10] William Foote Whyte, "A Challenge to Political Scientists," *The American Political Science Review*, XXXVII (August, 1943), 697.

Summary

In observations made during three election campaigns it was noted that the personal esteem in which a voter views a candidate overrides campaign issues. Personal esteem is conceived of as a mechanism whereby the behavior of others is subject to influence. However, inasmuch as the esteem in which individuals hold other individuals is volatile, voting behavior is equivalently labile. Given the personal nature of social relations in Mexiquito, chicanos vote for the candidate who appears to them to be the individual most likely to respond favorably to instrumental activities characterized by personalism. The importance of personalism in elections is a converse of the absence of special-interest groups organized to bargain and exert pressure for group advantage. In Mexiquito politics what is done as a favor is not to be demanded, nor is the favor to be retained by compulsion.

Such an understanding of the manner in which chicanos organize themselves to cope with political matters differs from a view advanced by political scientists. The latter stress that Mexican-Americans in South Texas represent a disorganized sector of the electorate but that, in time, they will become more organized. My own understanding is that chicanos respond to situations of a political nature in the very same manner as they do to other kinds of demands: by attempting to exert influence on those to whom they are related by kinship (real or fictive), or by acting in concert with friends and acquaintances. Furthermore, unlike Anglo-Americans, chicanos vote for persons with whom they feel they can establish relationships amenable to personalistic instrumental activities. Finally, chicanos seem no less interested in political issues than do Anglos. They simply organize their activities in a different fashion.

6. FORMAL ORGANIZATIONS

Mexican-Americans in Mexiquito, and elsewhere, tend not to organize corporate instrumental groups, although a few are found scattered in the history of the neighborhood. Moreover, when chicanos *do* join such voluntary associations their participation is short-lived and discomforting. Unlike their Anglo-American counterparts, chicanos participate in secondary associations as if they were of a primary nature.[1]

Two Mutual-Aid Societies

The earliest corporate groups in Mexiquito's history were two mutual-aid societies: the Sociedad de Beneficéncia General Ignácio Zaragoza, and the Sociedad Mutualista Amigos del Pueblo. The two organizations had much in common, but each was short-lived and, according to all reports, meetings were scenes of bitter, rancorous argument. In fact, when inquiry is made, former members tend to

---

[1] Compare Paul Lin's material from Kansas City and Professor June Macklin's discussion of chicano participation in formal associations in Toledo, Ohio. In Kansas City "These voluntary associations were characterized by ephemerality . . . 'They come and go' " ("Voluntary Kinship and Voluntary Association in a Mexican-American Community," p. 92). And, in Toledo, even when chicanos ". . . appear to have formed relationships, e.g., in voluntary associations, which are . . . [in structure] secondary groups, I have found these to be functioning as primary groups; *i.e.*, one votes with brothers and compadres, not according to issues" (June Macklin, "The Curandera and Structural Stability in Mexican-American Culture: A Case Study").

recall the dissolution of those societies and the bitterness of their associations far more quickly than they recall the reasons why the societies were formed in the first place.

In the year 1925 the first mutual society was organized and named Sociedad de Beneficéncia General Ignácio Zaragoza. Its hall now stands empty and desolate, the windows boarded and doors locked. According to its bylaws, the Zaragoza was founded as a mutual society which was open to persons of Mexican descent between eighteen and fifty years of age. Associates contributed small sums of money each month to a treasury, which, in turn, provided funds to be dispensed to ill or destitute members, or to the families of deceased members. In order to manage the fiscal affairs, a treasurer and a financial committee were elected each year. Some other committees of importance were the Health Commission and a Commission of Public Instruction.

The Sociedad Zaragoza had two major purposes, the first of which was to help protect the Mexican immigrants in the new society. It was stipulated that members of the society were to give preference in employment and commerce to other members. In case of a member's illness he was to receive from the treasury a sum of one dollar daily for the first ten days, and then fifty cents daily for the subsequent ten days. If a person remained ill beyond that length of time a collection was solicited from the others in behalf of the patient. In case of a member's death each of the deceased's associates was asked to give one dollar. Those former members with whom I spoke complained bitterly about individuals who solicited aid for legitimate needs but did not receive it, and suggested that the undeserving had no trouble in securing funds.

As an example of the above, old Pedro, a former member of the Zaragoza, believed that the Society was dissolved because the treasurer was suspected by the membership of purchasing land which cost beyond his income. Pedro, who quit the Society before suspicion fell on the treasurer, gave two reasons for his own dissatisfaction with the mutual society; the first was ostensibly because of a rejection of a widow's petition for assistance. Her request was denied "because she had a business," said old Pedro. He was in agreement that she did, indeed, have a business, and he realized that the bylaws stipulated that the Society was organized for members of the working class (*clase obrero*) and not for the merchants. On the other hand, the income she earned from her peddling was inadequate to support herself and her children. Pedro recalled with vividness how disgruntled he felt about the rejection of his friend's solicitation.

The other reason given by Pedro for his leaving the Sociedad Zaragoza was an action taken against another of his friends. The friend "was a very intelligent young man who owned books and read a lot." According to Pedro the younger man demonstrated a capacity to interest the membership in various programs he initiated. The young friend also spoke publicly in such a manner as to exhibit a great amount of common sense. In the short time of his membership the young man performed many tasks beneficial to the Society. In spite of his services, the older members of the group banned him from the meetings. Pedro surmised that that action was taken because his friend "outtalked" the older members and because the younger presumed to offer his elders counsel. Old Pedro said that his young friend's ouster from the Sociedad Zaragoza was a consequence of the *envidia* felt by his elders. When the young man's membership was curtailed, Pedro and eight others severed their own membership in the mutual-aid society.

Aside from the protective functions for which the Society was organized it was also intended to sustain the interest and allegiance of the immigrants to the motherland: Mexico. It was considered that Mexico, its culture, and its political constitution provided the ideal foundations for a better world, and members of the Zaragoza were admonished to maintain a truly Mexican-style home, a respectable household, as their contribution toward assurance of a better world. ("Esta sociedad, como todas las de seta [sic] indole, procurará tener un mundo mejor para vivir, es decir un hogar respetado.") Note that the range of social responsibility stipulated did not extend beyond the range of the home, a narrowly circumscribed area, indeed!

Within the framework of the Sociedad Zaragoza, its Commission of Public Instruction had as its primary duties hiring instructors to teach members' children the Spanish language and the history of Mexico. In order to carry out its functions the Commission solicited books from the Secretary of Education in Mexico City. The Sociedad was quite active in promoting cultural affairs, such as the Mexican Independence Day celebration and other events with patriotic motifs. Furthermore, every member was required to learn the Mexican national anthem, and to instruct his children in Mexican traditions and history. Each meeting of the Society was opened by a rendition of the Mexican hymn which was followed, "out of courtesy," by singing "The Star-Spangled Banner."

Less is known about the other, smaller, Sociedad Mutualista, the Amigos del Pueblo. Its members wore pins emblazoned with the Mexican national colors of red, white, and green. Its membership, unlike that of the Zaragoza, was not restricted to laborers, but included a few vendors and petty merchants from Mexiquito. The former president of the Amigos del Pueblo organization remembers that some members used to dominate the discussions because they found it easier to express themselves and that others were taking money out of the treasury as fast as it was being put in, but he remembers little else about his association with the Amigos del Pueblo. The small mutual-aid society has long been defunct, and today no one even remembers where meetings were once held.

Unquestionably, the most important function of both of the mutual societies during the early days of Mexiquito was the provision of funeral and sick benefits. Each member paid a stipulated amount into the coffers of the Society, an amount which was used to defray the costs of a funeral of any one of the members. At the time of a member's decease all the others were expected to accompany the body to its grave. Each of the mutual societies, furthermore, had a special funeral oration read at graveside. The oration read over a deceased associate of the Sociedad de Benificéncia Zaragoza, for example, extolled the closeness of the tie between a member and his Society and between the latter and the motherland—Mexico. Furthermore, the oration pointed up the altruism of membership in such a society of "working-class" men. In sum, members were exhorted to depend on their links with their Mexican heritage and with their fellows in the working class.

At the present time another civic-minded group holds meetings at irregular intervals in Mexiquito. Nine public-spirited citizens hold meetings in the basement of a small kiosk located in the middle of Mexiquito's plaza. This is the Comité Pro-Plaza, which, as its name suggests, is charged with the responsibility of maintaining the lawns, trees, and bandstand in the plaza. Originally, the Comité was founded by immigrants interested in the creation and presentation of a plaza in which Mexican national holidays and public dances might be celebrated.

Today, the Comité comprises nine men, four of whom are past middle age and are immigrants from Mexico; the remainder are young American citizens. To the older men the plaza is a place of some pride and they perceive it as a link between Mexiquito and old Mexico. The younger men feel no such pride, nor do they deign to attend the plaza dances, which they feel are for the benefit only of field laborers and their families, especially those recently immigrated residents of Mexiquito.

At one meeting of the Comité Pro-Plaza a recently deposed treasurer of the group was accused of misappropriation of funds. The Comité's only source of income is taxes levied on those who participate in the weekly dances. Outdoor dances in the plaza can be sponsored only in the spring and summer because of inclement weather so that the Comité's only income is limited to one-half of the year. Furthermore, on some weekends during spring and summer a dance is sponsored by groups other than the Comité; for example, on one occasion the LULAC was a sponsor. In such cases proceeds from a dance are shared equally between the sponsor and the Comité Pro-Plaza.

At a dance each vendor of ices or soda pop is taxed ten cents, but the number of vendors observed at any single dance in the plaza never exceeded five. The second source of income is provided by dancing couples; every male dancer (with the exception of young children) is charged twenty-five cents for the evening. Although the weekend dances attract several hundred spectators, the number of dancers never exceeds forty, most of whom are untaxed children. It may readily be noted that those sources available provide slender income to the coffers of the Comité Pro-Plaza.

Moreover no dance is free of its costs. For instance, at each dance, music is provided by a band of between three and five musicians. Each musician is paid for his services, an entire band receiving ten dollars or thereabouts for its night's entertainment. Furthermore, the electricity used to illuminate the brightly lit plaza is charged to the Comité Pro-Plaza. When one accounts for the costs and the gross profits from the dances it seems a wonder that any surplus ever does accrue in the treasury.

Let me now return to observations of the meeting at which accusations were leveled against the former treasurer of the Comité Pro-Plaza. During that meeting the former treasurer was openly accused of fraud, and elections were held for a new treasurer and other officers. Apparently the elections were called as a consequence of antagonism and outspoken suspicion by some of the membership against the now deposed treasurer; he was accused of peculation. During that meeting most of the accusations were expressed euphemistically, but others were not. For example, one newly elected officer expressed his concern that "there were no funds in the bank account," another said that the treasury had "somehow evaporated," and "the funds have been used in some unrecorded manner." Only one of those present suggested the possibility that an alternative explanation for the shortage of funds might provide the answer. The newly elected treasurer voiced the cautionary opinion that "It is true that during his administration we painted the inside of the bandstand." The new officer's tone clearly implied that even such an expenditure was not great enough to account for the depletion of the treasury.

After an airing of the accusations the treasurer-elect was instructed to visit his predecessor and to request from him the books and records of his office. Another member suggested that the former treasurer should be ordered to deliver the books and records to the Comité as a body. Others advanced the suggestion that the most appropriate procedure would be to have the deposed officer deliver the books and records to his successor and, later, to appear before the Comité, which was to sit in extraordinary session. Finally it was resolved that the suspected officer be instructed to deliver the books and records of his office to his successor, and to appear before the entire committee on the following Thursday night. Needless to say, the deposed treasurer did not appear before his committee nor has he delivered the books and records to his successor.

At the same meeting of the Comité Pro-Plaza described above, the following incident took place. An elderly member confided that he was a former president of the organization. He advised that during *his* tenure of office the Plaza was improved in such a manner that it was a beautiful sight to see. Now that he was no longer president, however, the present officials were not devoted to the maintenance of the park, but were interested only in the exploitation of the plaza for their own personal gain: "They charge the people for the privilege of dancing and then divide the proceeds amongst themselves." The old man said further that it was "wrong" for those officers to reap a profit from the proceeds, and he claimed to be so outraged that he seriously contemplated initiation of a petition to be signed by twenty-five or more *chicanos* for the recall of the officers, despite the fact that they had just been elected to office. He planned to present the proposed petition to the city manager across the tracks, in the hope that the latter Anglo would remove the present slate of officers and place the speaker in charge once again.

Of course, it is possible that the deposed treasurer of the Comité Pro-Plaza had indeed misappropriated funds from the treasury. On the other hand, an independent calculation of the proportion of costs to gross profits demonstrated the unlikelihood that such funds ever existed. It was also a possibility that present officers of the Comité did, indeed, plan to exploit the plaza for their own advantage. Such accusations, however, that some members of a formally structured organization benefit themselves at the expense of the others recurred so often that I infer it to be a patterned device whereby individuals expressed the point of view that membership in a corporate group was detrimental to the individual. Chicanos *do not*, in fact, sever their associations with instrumental corporate groups because of actual peculations; rather the calumnious accusations serve the purpose of validating their desire to quit the organization.

The largest, most active organization in Mexiquito with an entirely chicano membership is the League of United Latin-American Citizens. To Mexican-Americans of the neighborhood, "It is a miracle" that the local council of LULAC has remained viable for as much as two years.

LULAC in Mexiquito is a corporate group, which developed from a palomilla. In 1946 many of Mexiquito's veterans of the Second World War returned from military service; they resumed interactions in palomillas. One evening several members of one of the palomillas were drinking at Rusty's, a bar outside the city limits. As so often happens in gatherings of palomillas, the conversation turned to the relationship between Mexican-Americans and Anglo-Americans. This particular palomilla consisted of young bilinguals, all of whom were American citizens and overseas veterans, none were agricultural wage laborers. All of those present were disgruntled to discover that intergroup relations in Mexiquito were exactly the way that they had been when the men had left to enter the various military services.

That night at Rusty's one of the young veterans deplored to his companions the fact that the chicanos tended to berate the Anglos because they did not help the chicanos, but the chicanos themselves did not help the members of *la raza*. At that point in the conversation, Niño, one of the palomilla, advocated the formation of a club for benevolent purposes complete with officers, a constitution, and dues. Niño said that for some time he had wished to participate as a member of a benevolent society, but that the only one in town was "run" by older men, "And they won't listen to a younger guy!" When the others present agreed with Niño that beginning a club was a good idea, arrangements were made to hold an organizational meeting.

The following week at the organizational meeting the group adopted "The Volunteers" as its formal title; officers were elected, and a bank account was opened. The Volunteers viewed themselves as a group of enlightened leaders of *la raza*. During the next year the club held raffles and barbecues to raise money, some of which was spent to assist the indigent of Mexiquito.

Approximately one year after the founding of The Volunteers as a formal institution, the Unified School District's Board made arrangements to resolve one of its most pressing problems. More school rooms were urgently required to meet the demands of the expanding Mexiquito population. But the Board preferred not to raise and spend the large amount that a new school building would cost; instead they searched for alternatives. The School Board discovered several abandoned barracks that had been built for the United States Air Force during the recently terminated hostilities. Following the end of the war the barracks had been turned over to the Health Department which utilized the buildings as an isolation center for tuberculars. Several years passed before a permanent isolation center was constructed, and then the barracks were placed on sale.

Without fanfare the School Board purchased the barracks, and it was not until the contract was signed that word of the purchase leaked to Mexiquito. The consequences were profound and immediate; not since the lynching of Villareal many years before had Mexiquito been so united in sentiment.

The chicanos of Mexiquito interpreted the School Board's action as a deliberate slight to the north side of the tracks. Purchase of the obsolete buildings seemed an indication that the Board did not believe that chicano children deserved first-class educational services. Furthermore, knowledge that the barracks had formerly housed victims of the dreaded tuberculosis, or *tis*, exacerbated an already open wound. The great mass of the population of Mexiquito gathered on the plaza to hear inflammatory speeches inveighing against the School Board in particular and Anglos in general.

Individually and collectively the members of The Volunteers felt strongly about the School Board action. To The Volunteers the purchase of such obsolete and assumedly infected buildings epitomized the disdainful manner in which the Anglos treated the chicanos of the city. It was unfortunate that the self-appointed leaders of New Lots' north-side neighborhood were put to the test almost as soon as they assumed the mantle of leadership; they had not as yet learned how to cope with that first challenge to their leadership competencies. They had, however, learned about the League of United American Citizens, a national organization.

The inexperienced young veterans requested advice, sending details of the problem to LULAC, whose lawyers investigated and found that the purchase contract had already been signed. Since the purchase was legal, LULAC advised The Volunteers not to pursue the matter; there was nothing to be accomplished. Made aware of their incompetence to deal with a matter so complex as the purchase of the obsolete barracks, The Volunteers voted to become a local council of the national LULAC organization. Several Volunteers, including some who had been most active in the protest against the School Board's action, quit the organization rather than affiliate with the LULAC. Those dissidents joined forces with a more radical group of Spanish-speaking Americans, the "G.I. Forum," which met in a near-by town. To this day the dissidents seldom associate with their former palomilla comrades.

The Volunteers, now the LULAC Council, continues to be beset by problems. One day a special meeting of the officers was called. Two members had been delinquent in their dues for six months and, despite repeated requests that they rectify the matter, had steadfastly and publicly refused to comply. Their refusal, however, was not the underlying cause of the crisis. Six or seven other more reliable members had seized on the refusal of a few to pay dues as a reason to withdraw their own memberships from LULAC; the latter complained that the delinquents were receiving special consideration.

One of the complainants, Mireles, a founder of The Volunteers and charter member of LULAC in Mexiquito, was reputedly quite discontented with the organization. He said that recently he had been approached by a friend, a non-LULAC chicano, who asked him about the progress the organization was making toward the first of its sponsored civic-improvement projects. Money for the project had already been raised at several large barbecues rendered by LULAC, and the funds turned over to a city commission for purchase and installation of needed materials. Mireles answered his friend that the matter was now "out of LULAC's hands" and the other answered that he ". . . knew all along that LULAC was just a bunch of wet-dogs." The sally struck a responsive chord in Mireles and he began then to voice his own suspicions that the money had never been turned over to the city commission but, instead, had been pocketed by those LULAC members in charge of the project.

Mireles expressed his discontent with the LULAC Council in other ways. He complained that someone was stealing earnings made by the Council's bar-and-refreshment stand. He reasoned as follows. Each month one or two members of the organization were delegated to attend the bar. It was the bartender's obligation to purchase bottled beer and ice at wholesale prices, then on meeting nights to sell the beer at retail prices, a quarter for a bottle of beer. Profits from the bar were destined for the Council treasury. Mireles claimed that his suspicions of pilferage were aroused because during the month in which *he* had served as bartender the weekly gross receipts amounted to between twenty-five and thirty dollars. Since termination of his tenure gross receipts amounted to much less. He concluded that the bartender was pocketing some of the receipts. (On the other hand it was my observation that receipts had been lower because bartenders since Mireles were not nearly as aggressive salesmen as he.)

Whichever is the better explanation of the lower receipts, Mireles diminished the frequency with which he interacted with the Council. When questioned, he muttered darkly about pilferages and he also complained that some members of the Council who were more fluent in English dominated the meetings.

Another reportedly disgruntled member was Abelardo. His disaffection with the LULAC Council led him to volunteer the following attitudes about chicano society in general. His remarks refer to his impressions of states in which he once worked.

Up there [Illinois] it's different. If a guy wants to work, they don't ask questions, a guy has a chance to live a decent life, to live like a decent person. With a job he can get himself a nice home, send the kids to school, live nice . . .

Those poor people up there [speaking about the farmers he had seen in Arkansas], they don't have any money. They keep buying at the store, and then when the crop is in they owe more than they can pay. They don't know how to read, or how to write, nothing! But they come down here, and they get a chance. They can be something down here. It's not like a Latin. You can do all of those things down here, and work, and save, and everything, but you don't get a chance. Of course, some of the guys are doing all right, but they don't help the others. On this side of the tracks if a guy sets up a dry goods store he only stocks cheap merchandise. Why? Because a Latin will go to the other side of the tracks to buy his good clothes, he won't help out over here. You can't make any money, a decent living, over here.

Francisco, another member of LULAC, was incessant in his complaints that the president at that time was pocketing receipts from dues collected. He accused previous officers of having done the same. Renaldo, another young member, contended that money provided by the Council as a scholarship to a deserving young man was given to the cousin of the treasurer *because* he was a relative. The rancor and accusations, which appear to be important aspects of group memberships, seem to be a product of the failure of individuals to adjust their requirements to those of others: chicanos in Mexiquito have learned to join groups but they have not as yet internalized the necessity to accommodate individual differences and the acceptance of majority rule.

One meeting night, LULAC's membership decided to hold a barbecue in order to raise money for the Council. Raymundo and Ubaldo were appointed cochairmen of the Arrangements Committee. At a subsequent meeting the Committee cochairmen reported their plans, proposing a date for the event. Réal then sought permission to speak. He reminded the membership that persons of Junipero's palomilla had already scheduled a barbecue on that very same date and, because many members of the Council interacted with sponsors of the other barbecue, the events would conflict. Réal proposed an alternate day for the LULAC affair. A vote decided in favor of the alternate date. Two members voted in the minority: the cochairmen of the Arrangements Committee. After the vote was tallied, one cochairman leaned across to the other and whispered loudly, "Let's not do a thing to help them! They voted against us the whole way!" The other nodded his head in a fierce affirmative.

On the day of the barbecue I was called for by Raymundo. He drove his automobile *away* from the proposed site of the barbecue and announced that he was taking me to a bar and that *we* would not appear at the barbecue! He then stopped at the home of another LULAC member, a friend of his, urging the newcomer to join us and to abdicate his plans to attend the Council barbecue. Finally, Raymundo was persuaded to attend along with the others of the Council.

On an entirely different occasion, the LULAC Council nominated Guillermo to head a committee to plan another barbecue. At a later meeting Guillermo reported his plans, one of which was to serve beef as the main course; however, some members expressed a preference for chicken. When the issue was put to a vote by the president a majority voted for chicken as main course at the barbecue. Guillermo was plainly discomposed by the vote. For the remainder of that meeting and during the one which followed, he acted obstreperously. Each time that a suggestion was proposed by one of the officers, Guillermo bickered. On some matters so unequivocally in the interest of the Council that a vote was perceived a mere formality, Guillermo voted consistently as a minority of one. Finally, he became so patently out of order that the solemn Calvo, a member never before known to speak in public, asked for the floor. Calvo sardonically asked the presiding officer why he did not offer his chair to Guillermo inasmuch as the latter was running the meeting. On termination of that meeting several members came over to the author to say, "We don't know these things, but we're trying to learn." And Hómero said;

You know, people talk about discrimination this, the damned [*fregados*] Anglos that, discrimination here, and discrimination there. But, our worst problem is among ourselves! Why is that? I don't know. But before we talk about solving the problem of discrimination by the Anglos, we have to start right here among ourselves, there's where the first problem is!

An athletic-minded palomilla in Mexiquito once formed a club which they called the Stardust Club. Its membership was composed solely of Mexican-American boys and girls. It elected a slate of officers, and held regular meetings in rooms provided by the Catholic school. "They were the nicer palomilla. Some had to work, but they were all going to school, and they were planning to stay in school. Some of them were thinking of going on to college."

After a short while one of the founders of the Stardust Club dropped his membership and was thereupon ostracized by the others. Then *envidia* (envidious sanction) developed against the president of the Stardust Club, and eventually the club split up. The youth who had been subjected to ostracism then formed another club called the C. and R. Club (Culture and Recreation), whose membership was provided by the very same crew that founded the Stardust Club. "*That* didn't last long."

Abrám was asked, "There are not a lot of clubs on this side of the tracks, are there?" He answered, "No. Not much more than the Catholic War Veterans, the Knights of Columbus, and LULAC." I then asked Abrám, "How about the Roundtable? I hear that that was a pretty good club."

Yeh. I used to belong to that one. The trouble with that club was that the big shots in it, the guys who were big shots in town, would slap you on the back, and talk real friendly with you while you were together, but as soon as your back was turned, they would talk about you.

Another informant who discussed the Roundtable volunteered the information that the members of the Roundtable Club invited a young chicano to join *because* he was a college student. That action was taken to lend prestige to the Roundtable Club. The young man was requested to draw up a code of behavior for the membership. "You know, Art, college and all that!"

Originators of the Roundtable Club were a palomilla of three. Because they were originally so small an assemblage, they decided to invite several extraspecial friends of each of the founders. When Joaquín introduced to the Roundtable Club one of his own buddies, Abrám, he sensed some disapproval on the part of the others because Abrám's pigmentation was darker than any of the three founders. But because Abrám was such an especially close friend of Joaquín, he was accepted. Others who were later introduced and accepted as members of the Roundtable Club were also darker than any of the three initiators of the organization.

Now, to more of Abrám's recollections about the Roundtable Club:

We [the Roundtable Club] had a lot of money; it was a hundred and fifty dollars. That's not much, I suppose, but we weren't together too long, either. We did some nice things with it; once we went to Mexico on the Club's money. But then after a while we didn't meet, and that hundred and fifty dollars stayed in the bank.

Well, a couple of years ago I was running the Boys' Club at the church, and we needed money. I thought I would ask the club for some money to help it. They were mostly—no, they were all—Catholics. I went to ask about the money and found out we didn't have any at all in the bank. I guess the president got it; Cruz must have gotten it.

There are several other groups in which some chicanos of Mexiquito are members. A Veterans of Foreign Wars post claims ninety members but I have never observed more than eight at any one meeting. A very few chicanos, perhaps three, may be considered actively engaged in the American Legion post, whereas the remainder of the membership is composed of Anglo veterans of the world wars. Anglo and chicano veterans concur that several years ago the Veterans of Foreign Wars, composed of representatives of both ethnic groups, played a prominent role in civic affairs. According to those views, however, chicano veterans began to predominate in the Veterans of Foreign Wars in New Lots and the Anglos withdrew to revitalize the dormant American Legion post. Whatever the truth of that analysis, today people in the city consider the Veterans of Foreign Wars post as representative of chicano veterans, and the American Legion as an Anglo organization in which are to be found several chicanos.

Only one instrumental group of women attracts the attention in Mexiquito. The Lucky 13 Club is composed of thirteen young women, whose activities entail card parties and several dances during a calendar year. Organized instrumental groups are even less significant among Mexican-American women than among their menfolk.

Summary

The personalistic approach to social relations is reflected in the small number of formally organized instrumental groups which have sporadically appeared in the history of this neighborhood. Today there are approximately fifty chicanos who participate actively in corporate organizations.

Members of contemporary instrumental groups express anxiety that elected officers dominate discussions, and accuse the latter of misappropriating funds from the treasuries. It is suggested here that such accusations are more likely reflections of the anxiety felt by members who perceive their autonomy threatened, than a reflection of reality. In spite of the foregoing, an increasing number of chicanos are learning to join formal secondary groups, although they have not as yet internalized the procedures whereby each member modifies his desire for autonomy and so adjusts to group procedures.

Failing to internalize such requisites for group participation, some members continue to feel anxious about their presumed exploitation by those in positions of elected leadership, while others are so discomforted that they sever their association. In whichever manner the individual adjusts to the circumstances of formal group procedures the qualities of anxiety and disaffection associated with social behavior are nurtured.

Anglo society across the tracks from Mexiquito, to which upwardly mobile chicanos aspire, organizes its social life in terms of an individual's multiple membership in secondary associations of a formal character. Until chicanos learn to organize their social behavior in this way, also, they cannot expect to participate in the segment which effectively controls the social, economic, and political system of the total society, in which Mexiquito is enmeshed. So long as chicanos continue to act as if the larger society was organized on the basis of small family units and as if Anglos engaged one another in personal dyadic relations, they will continue to be frustrated in their attempts to secure some modicum of predictable control over the social environment beyond the bounds of their family.

7. ILLNESS BEHAVIOR AND ATTITUDES

Preceding chapters have discussed aspects of social life in Mexiquito; illness and health may also be understood as integral parts of social life. In Mexiquito, sickness is not isolated as a unique type of phenomenon. Instead, to these chicanos, illness is only one kind of misfortune which, along with other kinds, threatens the well-being of an individual and the tranquility of his nuclear family. Consequently, illness, barrenness, automobile accidents, continuous bickering between husband and wife, and loss of a breadwinner's job are all members of a class of events which, to chicanos, may be a product of natural causes but, on the other hand, may be caused by another chicano. Thus, illness, the kind of misfortune on which this chapter concentrates, is perceived as a product of the undue influence one individual exercises over another, just as well as it is thought to be a consequence of the improper functioning of one's body, or of those unseen forces to which a physician refers as germs. Furthermore, an illness may also be interpreted as a consequence of the hostility which obtains between two chicano individuals, or between their nuclear families. The empirical data indicate that when one focusses attention on topics of illness and health he discovers a new and intriguing vantage point from which to view the social system and the emotional qualities found within it.

Every specific pathogenic condition is associated with a cluster of symptoms, but no single symptom (with the probable exception of dramatic mania) is the exclusive property of any one illness. Because of overlapping symptoms chicanos have difficulty in arriving at definitive diagnoses and precipitating causes for any one condition. Consequently, as in more orthodox nosological systems, a diagnosis is, in the final analysis, validated by the favorable response a patient makes to the regimen of healing that the diagnosis demands. On the following pages informants describe the procedures whereby one diagnosis after another is arrived at for a given set of symptoms until that condition responds satisfactorily to healing techniques. In Mexiquito, as elsewhere, the proof of a diagnosis is in the healing.

Telésforo, a young man, was asked to describe how his mother knew that any of the children were ill. He replied, as follows:

> You would have a pain in your head and would touch your hand to your head and say "Mamá, Mamá," and maybe you would cry a little. Then mother would get some aspirins and she would put you in bed to keep you warm and comfortable. If you didn't hurt anywhere in your body then there was nothing the matter with you. Then during the middle of the night mother would get up and go over to the bed and see how you were doing. In the morning if you didn't get out of bed she would give you more aspirins, and if you were still sick, she would start on the herbs. She would go through all the teas that she knew, and then she would ask the neighbors. If none of these things worked, and you had tried all the teas and medicines that people knew of, then they figured that you suffered from *ojo*. *Ojo*, also, is very dangerous. The people would start praying for you, and they would start rubbing your body and making a big cross on your chest with an egg. After that you might be swept with branches of a *pirul* tree. Then if this didn't help the sickness, and if you're not dead yet, they would turn you over and start curing you for *empacho*. All this time you were kept in bed. This is because you were to be warm and kept comfortable. You couldn't walk around because you would have your little strength drained out of you. After all this treatment and after you were well again mother would give us a purge to clear the stomach of all the herbs; this was to allow the stomach to start new again.

On the following pages are described concepts of illness which reflect social behavior and its qualities, and, also, the nature of the social ties which exist between chicanos and those who provide them preventive health and medical-care programs. In Mexiquito, illnesses are clearly divided into two categories, natural and unnatural (*mal natural* and *mal artificial* or *mal puesto*).[1] Those which fall

---

[1] Arthur J. Rubel, "Concepts of Disease in Mexican-American Culture," *American Anthropologist*, 62, No. 5 (October, 1960), 795–814.

into the first category are considered to be within the realm of God, whereas the latter, witchcraft, is considered "one of the others," the realm of the devil.

Mal Natural

Mal de Ojo

In Mexiquito, certain persons are thought to possess "strong" power over "weaker" individuals.[2] Strong glances, covetousness, or excessive attention paid by one such person to another exposes the actors to the hazards of an unnatural bond. This bond causes the stronger to unwittingly drain the weaker of his will to act, and, consequently, the latter comes under the power of the former.

Although all chicanos are looked upon as susceptible to the virulence of evil eye (*mal de ojo*), the weaker nature of women and children subjects them to greater danger than mature males.[3]

As we sat discussing *mal de ojo*, old José explained:

Once I went hunting for rabbits with my compadre. It was he that wanted to hunt, although the area was swarming with rattlers. Anyway, we arrived at the grounds where he had planned to shoot and soon saw a rabbit running across our path, first in one direction, and then in another. I pointed out the running animal to my compadre and told him to shoot it. He fired once and then a second time, but each time the bullets skittered harmlessly by. I told my compadre: "Don't shoot again! There must be a snake nearby that has the rabbit in his charm [*liga*]." Sure enough! In a moment we saw a tremendously long rattler coiled by a rock, with its jaws wide open. That snake had the rabbit in his charm and was bringing it closer until finally it could devour the creature. That's what *mal ojo* is like!

Old José also recalled another incident in which *mal de ojo* was a factor. Once as his wife's uncle was walking about the ranch he happened on the sheeppen just as his little nephew rose from the ground covered with manure. The uncle took one long disapproving

---

[2] People in this part of the world, unlike those in other culture areas, do not consider *mal de ojo* to be a power used deliberately by persons of evil intent, nor do they confuse it with a pathogenic disorder of the eye, possibly conjunctivitis, in which liquid is exuded. Both are referred to as *mal de ojo*, but the former and not the latter is always caused by another person; consequently, when referring to someone presumed to have caused a *mal de ojo* condition, one says "*Me hizo ojo.*"

[3] Cf., Florence Johnson Scott, "Customs and Superstitions among Texas Mexicans," *Publications of the Texas Folk-Lore Society*, II (1923), 75–85.

look at the filthy child and returned to the house where he informed
the child's mother of what he had seen. He then returned to his own
house located near-by. Shortly afterward, the child's mother came
dashing to his residence urgently requesting him to come to the
child, for she was about to lose him. The boy was suffering from a
very high fever and diarrhea. The uncle dashed to the child's side
and immediately commenced to touch him about the temples and
to make the sign of the cross. The patient recovered almost immediately.

At the conclusion of his narration, José and his wife joined in a
deeply felt admonition that *mal de ojo* is mortally dangerous. However, they were careful to specify that the condition itself is not what
precipitates death, rather the problem lies in whether one attends
it with speed. Hesitancy to cure the patient of *mal de ojo* or—equally
dangerous—an improper diagnosis, such as a physician might make,
permit development of the terminal stage of this illness. The last,
mortal stage of *mal de ojo* is a coughing fit so violent that the patient
coughs up green bile (*hiel*), for which there is no known cure.

A young father of Mexiquito told how he took his entire family
to the Mexican town of Rio Bravo, just south of the border, for a visit
to his wife's parents. All went well until they arrived back home in
Mexiquito, when they discovered that their infant daughter was
suffering from a high temperature. At this point in his narrative the
young man stated firmly that he did not believe in *mal de ojo*, but
"that is what was the cause of Olga's sickness." Olga's parents
thought back to their visit and decided that their daughter's condition had been precipitated by her having been looked at endearingly
by a woman in Rio Bravo, a woman who had reached out for the
child but had not succeeded in touching her, much less caressing
her. Inasmuch as Olga's fever remained high, her parents returned
to Rio Bravo in order to have Olga touched and caressed by the presumed agent. After this had been accomplished, the difficulty ended.

Telésforo, a young man who has appeared previously in these
pages, has begun to doubt the realities of such things as *mal de ojo*.
Nevertheless, he relates an incident which could have convinced
anyone.

You know, the other day before I came to work I shaved, took my
whiskers and all off. When I was outside I met a woman who looked
at me and said, "You just shaved, didn't you? Took your whiskers off?"
Well, I went on to work, and pretty soon I was feeling sick, and then I

felt real hot. Well, I went up to Mrs. Brown, my boss, and said, "You know, I don't think I'm going to make it today!" So she put her hand up to my head and said, "Wow!" Boy, my head was really burning! I went on home and got into bed and around nine my brother came home and said, "Come on, let's go see the doc." So I went to see the doc and he gave me a shot, and gave me some pills and I went on back to bed. I wasn't feeling any better, so I told my wife to go on over to that woman's house and bring her over here. She came over with my wife, and she ran her hands over my face and said, "Well, you looked so young and cute that I guess that's why I noticed you." Well, she went away then, and pretty soon I began to feel better. I went back to work the next day and Mrs. Brown said, "Well, you sure were sick yesterday!"

Another young man, one of Telésforo's palomilla, described the latest instance of *mal de ojo* in his own family.

Last week my cousin's cute little baby had *ojo*. In the hours of the late afternoon my cousin was holding her child out in their front yard. One of the neighborhood men returning from work stopped to talk with the couple, remarking on the child's cuteness. Then he went on his way. That night when they put the child to bed, it began to cry and remained inconsolable through most of the night. Even though I slept in the other part of the house I could hear them moving about with the child. Very early the next morning I could hear my cousin leave the house as she went next door to speak to our neighbor who is a relative of the man with whom they had chatted the evening before. She asked the neighbor to do her the favor of requesting the man to stop at our house on his way to work. The neighbor went and roused the man with strong eyes. On his way to work that man stopped at our place and went into the other room where he ran a hand over the child's face and forehead, cooing to her and talking to her. He didn't remain any longer than about five minutes. When he left the baby had stopped crying.

In another case, a young matron provided an account of an occasion on which her child contracted *ojo*.

One morning my son—the middle one—awoke with a cold and fever. I had to go downtown to run an errand and left the child with his father. My husband took some cardboard from the house and spread it out on the ground for the child. The child was cutely dressed in checked shirt and shorts, I remember, and looked very handsome. My husband went across the street to chat with one of our neighbors and the little boy followed his father. When the boy and his father returned to our house the child began to tremble and had convulsions. My husband recalled that during his conversations with the neighbor, the latter had commented favorably on my boy's appearance. With this in mind, my husband returned to the other house and asked our neighbor to accompany him to the child. Our neighbor agreed to come, saying, "I guess I can *really* cause *ojo!*" My neighbor took the boy in his arms and fondled him, touching him upon the forehead.

Old, weatherbeaten Marcos said:

You never see *ojo* work on an adult, but then—one time I was working on the loading platform of the Green Garden shed. I was sitting there with Mr. Ronald and another, equally bald. The other workers were laughing at the picture presented by the three *pelóns* (bald ones) sitting together. One of the onlookers approached me and suggested that I have the others touch me about the head to protect me from *mal ojo;* but I told him that something like that wouldn't affect me, for I was an adult and too strong for *ojo*. But when I got home that night and started to go to sleep I had a terrible ache in the head. Someone from the house went right out and called one of those fellows who had been staring and laughing at me over at the shed and brought him over to the house. He rubbed his hands all over my forehead, and above the eyes, and within five minutes I was no longer bothered by the pain.

It would be incorrect to assume that a person with "strong" power must look a "weaker" individual in the eyes in order to establish an unnatural bond between them. The eyes of the former are simply instruments of unfulfilled covetousness; they need not meet the glance of the victim. Moreover, although a relationship which contains elements of covetousness is the classic cause of *mal de ojo* in Mexiquito, this is generalized to include any kind of special attention paid one individual by another—El ojo es de bello y de feo (Evil eye affects the beautiful and the ugly in equal measure).

Cures for *ojo* flow logically from a premise that this condition is a consequence of an unnatural bond established between a strong and a weak person. So strongly held is the premise, so often is it reinforced by the logic of events, that even those who doubt the validity of the premise cannot afford not to take its consequences into account.

When a person manifests sudden severe headaches, inconsolable weeping (in the case of children only), unusual fretfulness, and high temperatures, the family attempts, in anxious fashion, to retrace the patient's social activities of the previous few hours. If they are so fortunate as to recall a significantly affective relationship, the suspected agent is hurriedly brought to the patient to rupture the charm by which each is held to the other. At this, early, stage of the infirmity the linkage may be ruptured by the stronger simply passing a hand over the forehead of his or her victim, or by patting the latter about the temples. Ideally, no stigma attaches to an agent of *mal de ojo* unless he refuses the family's request to break the charm. On those many occasions in which the actual agent cannot be recalled to the patient's side, the tie is broken by means of sympathetic magic and religious prayers. Such is the case when the child has associated with a great number of strangers or has been seen by them during the course of a day's activities ("Every time my wife goes downtown to shop with the children, the littlest child suffers from *mal de ojo* when they get home"). What follow are examples of treatments actually undertaken in specific cases of *ojo*. Note that in each citation a major effort is devoted to rubbing the patient with hen's eggs, the purpose of which is to drain the power of the stronger agent from the body of his victim.

In the first case, as an example, a young mother said that she had "never wanted to believe in such things as *ojo* or *susto* because they are just superstitions." On the other hand, she recalls vividly a time when her child cried inconsolably and she had no idea what was troubling him. But when she began to diagnose and cure for *mal de ojo*, she met with quick success. In spite of the fact that before then she had never performed the requisite rites, she broke a hen's egg in a glassful of water. It looked to her as if it had been cooked in an "over" style, that is, well-fried with the yellow of the egg showing as if it was an "eye." The form assumed by the egg in the water accorded well with what she had been told by others was a diagnostic criterion for *ojo*. Satisfied with the diagnosis, she rubbed the patient with whole hen's eggs, made the sign of the cross, and recited the Credo three times. After these rites she threw away the egg-water mixture and from then on had no further trouble with her child's condition.

Susto

In Mexiquito an incident which has an unstabilizing effect on an individual often causes a part of the self, the *espíritu*, to leave the body.[4] The precipitating experience is portrayed as one in which the

---

[4] An earlier and more general discussion of soul loss appears in Arthur J. Rubel's "The Epidemiology of a Folk Illness: Susto in Hispanic America," *Ethnology*, III, 3 (July, 1964), 268–283.

victim proved unable to cope with circumstances despite strong motivation to do so. Oftentimes such situations are of a frightening nature. Although helplessness is a salient feature of all cases cited, it is significant that helplessness is perceived only in association with some kinds of problems, but not with others. That is, in no instance did I discover a victim who was helpless when presented alternate ways of coping with a problem that was a consequence of his or her cultural marginality. No doubt such a confrontation is stressful, but it does not manifest itself as soul loss. The problems which do seem to precipitate soul loss are those in which an individual is expected to perform adequately because he has been socialized to do so.

The first case of *susto* that we shall study involved a middle-aged man, a baker by profession. One day as he delivered his wares he fell into an open hole in full sight of a group of lunching workers. Their laughter made his ludicrous situation even more inglorious. After the gleeful onlookers had come to his assistance, he was taken to his mother's home. She commenced to rejoin his presumedly departed soul to the body, to massage his leg, and to administer a potion. Lest there be any question of the relative importance attributed the various facets of the disability, the narrator (sister of the victim) thought the laughter of the workers and the consequent mortification and helpless anger of the patient important enough to repeat three times during the course of her short story.

In another case, that of a little boy by name of Ricardo Montalvo, soul loss was assumed to have occurred as a consequence of a family Sunday outing at a local pond. Although the rest of the family played in and about the water, Ricardo demurred. Despite the coaxing and taunts of his family, in particular those of his older sister, Ricardo would have nothing to do with the water and returned to the automobile, where he fell asleep. He slept through the afternoon, not even waking when he was taken home after dark and put to bed. That night he slept fitfully and several times talked aloud in his sleep.

On the following morning the parents decided that Ricardo had suffered a soul loss, though not out of fear of the water. Rather, they reasoned, it was caused by the family's insistence that he enter the water, demands to which he was unable to accede, as the father later explained. On that day Ricardo was taken to a lay healer to be cured for soul loss.

In another case, a young agricultural wage laborer was stricken with an acute respiratory infection, which caused him to be admitted to a local hospital. One night while in the hospital Arturo awakened to discover a change in the appearance of his wardmate. Although the informant desperately attempted to attract the attention of the attendants he was unsuccessful. Later, when attendants did note the death of the other, they wheeled the corpse out of the room; not, however, before Arturo suffered a severe trauma from his association with the cadaver and his inability to do anything about it.

As soon as Arturo was discharged from the hospital he immediately went home and promptly requested the presence of his mother. He complained of listlessness and lack of appetite, his teeth chattered involuntarily, and his body shivered. Furthermore, he found himself jumping above his bed though still in a prone position. As soon as his mother arrived she diagnosed his condition as *susto*, precipitated by his inability to communicate the condition of his wardfellow and his continued association with the cadaver. She promptly initiated procedures designed to rejoin his soul with his body. After discussing that incident, Arturo reflected, as follows:

> When someone is in a hospital with an illness, it is easy for *susto* to occur. The doctors can cure you of the disease that brought you to the hospital, but you may come down with one that is more grave due to complications from *susto*. Doctors can't cure a person of *mollera*, or *empacho*, or *susto*, because they don't believe in them.

A woman, Mrs. Benítez, suffers from a long history of *susto*, a condition she, and others, attribute to the vexations (*mortificaciónes*) of everyday life. It is of interest here that the epileptoid seizures from which she suffers are perceived only as unusually extravagant displays of *susto*; but neither she nor her neighbors consider those acute episodes the most important symptoms of the illness. According to Mrs. Benítez' self-diagnosis, the seriousness of her condition—*susto pasado*—is a consequence of several *mortificaciónes* imposed one on another.

She places the blame for her *asustado* condition squarely on her husband. During the years in which she lived with him and bore his children, her husband beat her regularly until, at times, she was unable to raise her arms because of the pain and bruises. During those years, as she lived in mortal fear of him (*vivía asustada*), her first intimation of *susto* occurred. After a number of such years her husband left, never to return. She and her five daughters were left on their own, dependent on agricultural field work and Aid to Dependent Children assistance from the state of Texas.

In December of 1958 a welfare worker threatened to remove the four youngest daughters from their mother's care because of her inability to adequately provide for them. On the very night which preceded the particularly violent seizure which concerns us here, Mrs. Benítez' son-in-law visited her one-room apartment in a drunken condition. He had become involved in an argument with another in a neighborhood bar and came to his mother-in-law for the revolver he had left with her for safekeeping. Mrs. Benítez refused to give the weapon up, and the altercation became frenetic. The angry, but unsuccessful, young man left the apartment in a rage, but not before punching his wife.

On the following morning, before dawn, Mrs. Benítez suffered a severe headache presaging the seizure which followed. This spasmodic seizure exhausted her and left her with a desire to be completely isolated from others. The incident of the preceding evening had caused her a *susto nuevo*, which, combined with her older *susto*, created the very dangerous *susto complicado* or *susto pasado*.

During curing procedures a major effort is devoted to coaxing the soul of the patient back to his or her body. In Mrs. Benítez' case, the following procedures were observed. Mrs. Benítez went to the home of one of Mexiquito's lay curers, an elderly woman of some renown. After introductions were exchanged, the curer sat with her patient in a corner of her living room, away from those others of us who were present. There she asked her patient to describe her symptoms, and, as each symptom was provided, she nodded her head wisely. After the full set of symptoms had been presented, the patient was asked whether she had seen a Catholic priest to ask for an *ensalme*, or blessing for the sick. An answer in the negative prompted the healer to suggest that it would have been a good idea.

After the preliminary phases of diagnosis the healer began to elicit something of the patient's background and the nature of her vexatious life. Then the two passed into another room, from which the curer called out, requesting her daughter-in-law to bring a branch of the tree known as *palo blanco*, and a towel. Inside, the patient lay prone on the bed facing her attendant, who sat alongside speaking in a low tone of voice, both of them discussing the *mortificaciónes* of Mrs. Benítez' life. Then the practitioner stripped the leaves from the branch of *palo blanco* and, holding them just over Mrs. Benítez, began to make sweeping motions the length of her figure, from head to toe. While sweeping she prayed in a voice so low that the actual words were inaudible in the next room.

Following that, the practitioner took down from her shelf a bottle in which was a clear liquid that she sipped until her mouth was full. Then, suddenly, she spit the liquid over the upper part of the patient's torso and on her face, continuing to sweep and pray as she did so. Another swig of the liquid was also sputtered over the patient and then the low murmur of prayers died away. The curer commenced to talk again in an ordinary tone of voice, the patient adding her own voice. Then they emerged into the living room, the healer's face wreathed with smiles, and Mrs. Benítez looking very tired but elated. The healer's parting words to her patient were: "Above all, it is faith that counts, and if God is not willing, there is nothing that can be done." (Parenthetically, that credo of faith and others like it, for example: Santos no puede si Dios no quiere—[Even] saints can't heal if God proves unwilling—are commonplace in Mexiquito and stated by healers and patients with equal conviction. Nonetheless, as the Benítez case exemplifies, such *apparent* fatalism in no way impedes a flurry of activity as individuals pragmatically seek alleviation of their ills. In their search for healers and healing, the pragmatists of Mexiquito leave no stone unturned.)

In the case of Arturo, the young man who developed *susto* while in the hospital, his mother cured him as follows: First she lay him on the earthen floor of his shack, arms outstretched. Then she swept him from head to toe, using an ordinary household broom. After that she dug four holes (*pozos*) in the floor, one at each of the hands, one at the feet, and another at the head. These she filled with tap water and bade her son drink from each in turn. Finally, she began to pray for his soul to return to his body.[5] During these prayers each called out to the wandering soul: "¿Donde andas? ¿Donde andas? [Where are you? Where are you?]" until the patient felt that his soul had rejoined the body at which time he began to shout "Hay voy, hay voy [I'm coming, I'm coming!]"

Empacho

Empacho is an illness produced by a complex interaction between

[5] Cf., Scott, "Customs and Superstitions," for an earlier report on healing for *susto*, pp. 83–84; for additional data on *susto* in Mexiquito today, see Rubel, "Concepts of Disease," pp. 803–805.

social and physiological forces. Specifically, permitting another individual to override one's personal autonomy gives rise to a condition in which the digestive system fails to perform adequately, allowing a chunk of food to "stick to the passage" and block the normal digestive processes. In the chicanos' own words:

Empacho is caused by eating something that you don't really want, as if I went outside and called one of the children, and told him: "Come in and eat!" Well, if he didn't really want to, then empacho might result. Empacho is like having a ball form in the seat of your stomach; it burns like a fire [lumbre]. Empacho has to be taken care of as soon as possible for it is dangerous. After three months it is beyond cure, and one would die from it. If you allow too much time to pass, then you lose all the flesh, all of your weight, and you become thinner and thinner. Your body is drying out.

A young woman takes a view just as serious as the above:

Empacho occurs when you eat something that you do not want to, or don't like. For example, if you are visiting someone's house for dinner, and they serve something for which you have no desire, you will eat it rather than offend your host. You also will have empacho as a result!

Previous to diagnosis, a condition of empacho is often confused with other common indispositions, such as "gas on the stomach," or "indigestion." However, a clear-cut diagnostic procedure factors out empacho from other digestive difficulties. During the diagnosis a patient reclines facedown on a bed with his back bared. The diagnostician lifts a piece of skin in the rear waist region of the patient between two of her fingers. This skin is pinched between the two fingers as the practitioner listens attentively for a telltale snap or crack from the abdominal region; such a noise clearly identifies empacho as the cause of the discomfort.

Once the identity of the illness has been established, efforts commence to break up and disengage the offending piece of food from its clinging position. In the course of treatment the body is used as if it were a beaker as the curer attempts to redress the imbalance between opposing qualities of "hot" and "cold" within the organism.[6]

---

[6] For discussions of the concepts of "hot" and "cold" in Latin American cultures, George M. Foster, "Relationships between Spanish and Spanish-American Folk Medicine," *Journal of American Folklore*, 66 (1953), 201–247; William Madsen, "Hot and Cold in the Universe of San Francisco Tecospa, Valley of Mexico," *Journal of American Folklore*, 68 (April–June, 1955), 123–139.

The back is carefully pinched, stroked, and kneaded along the spinal column, as well as around the waist. The massage is interrupted only long enough to permit the attendant to administer an oral dosage of lead protoxite, which is sold in the pharmacy as *la greta*. This preparation is useful to penetrate the chunk of food, softening and crumbling it. Although valued for its penetrant abilities, *la greta* is disvalued for its recognized toxicity; furthermore, the "cold" quality assigned this medicinal in the local pharmacology disturbs the "hot-cold" balance of the organism. Because of its toxicity some, more timid, women prefer another penetrant, equally cold, but less dangerous—*azogue* (quicksilver). In many cases an additional purge in the form of castor oil, also attributed a "hot" quality, is taken by the patient. When castor oil is administered, "cool" fruit juices (citric) provide a counterbalance to the "hotness" of the castor oil. Meanwhile, the patient continues to be kneaded, pinched, and rubbed along the spinal column and around the waist. *Empacho*, though potentially fatal due to desiccation of the organism, is clearly enough understood and easily enough treated so that prayer is not mandatory. Still in all, it is by no means treated lightly even by those chicanos whose traditional views of health have changed so very much in the past few years.

There are many other natural illnesses of which chicanos are fully aware and about which they evidence real concern. For example, among others are measles (*sarampión*), pneumonia (*pulmonia*), high blood pressure (*presión*), heart disease (*ataque de corazón*), and malignant tumor (*tumor*). These conditions are considered here not so much as illnesses but, instead, because they help illuminate the closeness of the association which obtains between sickness and social life in Mexiquito.

Mal Puesto

At the beginning of this chapter it was stressed that examination of a great number of case histories, and viewpoints which informants express about those cases, leads to a conclusion that chicanos make a clear distinction between illness which is of natural cause and that which is artificially induced (*mal puesto*). However, it is equally clear that chicanos may and often do change their understanding of causation of an illness from one of natural origin to *mal puesto* during the course of the sickness. This seeming confusion is resolved when we introduce another variable: chronicity. In Mexiquito the longer the duration of any type illness the more probable that it will eventually be diagnosed as *mal puesto*.

Mal puesto is presumed to arise as a consequence of one of three kinds of social relationships: a spat between lovers, an unrequited affair, or as a reflection of invidiousness between individuals or nuclear families. In either of the first two instances the culprit is usually specified as an individual with whom such a relationship had, indeed, been maintained at some time in the past. On the other hand, illness believed to be a function of invidiousness is generally attributed to ill-defined others, usually "the neighbors" (*los vecinos*) or "the people" (*la gente*), or "someone" (*alquien*), and less often to a specific individual. In any case, a person who feels that he or his nuclear family has been victimized readily ascribes the reasons for such activity. In the case of one lover's leaving another, the former assumes that he or she has thereby incited the other to a hostile, covert action. An individual who feels disinclined to return the overtures of a suitor assumes that by such a rejection he or she incurs trouble in the form of *mal puesto*. The length of time which has elapsed between the occurrence of an illness and its presumed precipitating incident is of little importance when attempts are made to explain any given illness. In the case of an individual who assumes his misfortune to be a consequence of maleficence projected by "the neighbors" or "the people," there may or may not be a single precipitating event. For instance, an award won in school or at employment or, perhaps, a decision to move one's residence across the tracks are all specific occurrences which are likely to incite *envidia*; on the other hand, a family which has been enjoying a long period of good health assumes that a case of illness has been provoked by its state of wellbeing. "Things were going well for us," they reflect. Too well!

In Mexiquito, *mal puesto* assumes many different forms. The most clear-cut symptom is a presence of dramatic mania—the only symptom which is exclusively the property of *mal puesto* and, moreover, that symptom which is accompanied by the patient's understanding that he or she is controlled by another individual. Contrarywise, in those cases of *mal puesto* where dramatic mania is not present, the patient does not feel himself to be possessed by another individual. Besides dramatic mania and its concomitant, there is a wide gamut of symptoms which also may be interpreted as *mal puesto*. The problem which confronts chicanos and anthropologists alike is how to discriminate between *mal puesto* and natural illness when the symptoms of any given condition may lead to either interpretation.

The following account of a case of *mal puesto* associated with dramatic mania comes from a young man who prefaces it by the usual disclaimer: "I don't believe in *susto* or *brujería* or things like that."[7] The informant told how he set out to investigate a rumor that an attractive eighteen-year-old he sometimes escorted to dances was acting bizarrely, presumedly a victim of *mal puesto*. He, in company with several of his palomilla, went to her home, to which she had been confined by her parents. At the door of the house they were met by the girl's mother, who advised them that her daughter had been acting strangely and that it might be best if they did not visit with her. After conversing with the visitors, however, the mother relented: "Maybe it would do her some good if she were to see you."

After gaining entrance, the youths stood in the doorway of the bedroom and chatted with the patient, she clad only in a bra and a pair of pajama bottoms. Apparently the parents had removed the bedclothes and pajama tops in response to a suicidal attempt by the patient. The girl recognized her visitors readily enough, and greeted them: "Hello boys, how are you." Then she added: "He's got me and he won't let me go." "Who has you?" they asked. At that, she responded eerily by laughing and laughing in uproarious fashion and throwing herself onto the bed from time to time. During this violent period she would answer none of her visitors' questions, although she continued to recognize their identities. After ceasing her laughter, she resumed the conversation until once again lapsing into laughter.

Recollection of the above incident brought to the informant's mind another, during which he happened on a man who was standing in the business section of a near-by town and deliberately striking his head against the fender of an automobile. Covered by blood and grime, he continued to shout: "She's got me, this girl's got me and I can't get away." His bizarre activity continued until he was restrained and led away by the police.

A young woman describes a case in which the victim, who was one of her acquaintances, failed to return the affection of a suitor. He, aware of her lack of interest, offered her an orange soda. After drinking the soda she became demented (*se volvía loca*), surely he

---

[7] *Brujería* is an alternate term sometimes used for *mal puesto*.

had placed something in her soda (*echó algo*). Her face turned color, her eyebrows drew tightly together, and her eyes became huge; she was, in fact, a very ugly sight. She had appetite only for orange soda; all other food was rejected because of her suspicion that it contained hairs and insects (*cabellos* and *animalitos*). Her nights became sleepless nightmares because of the dogs and turkeys which she thought crawled upon, leaped, kicked, and bruised her body. Inasmuch as only she was aware of those creatures, her family proved powerless to protect her despite their concern. On the mornings following such attacks she arose covered by bruises and other marks of her anguished travails. She was taken from one healer to another; from *curandero* to physician, physician to *curandero*, without respite and to no avail.

It was previously noted that although dramatic mania is a symptom exclusively the property of *mal puesto*, there are other symptoms which that condition shares with natural sicknesses. For instance, a swollen abdomen, loss of weight accompanied by a rasping cough, painfulness in various parts of the body, and conversations with persons unseen by others—all were diagnosed as *mal puesto* during the course of field work. On the surface they appear to have nothing in common, yet in each case the condition was characterized, also, by its failure to respond satisfactorily to a series of treatments and by its chronicity. A syndrome which satisfactorily responds to a regimen of healing exercised or prescribed by a recognized healer removes it, *ipso facto*, from the realm of *mal puesto*. Because of the characteristics listed above, it is helpful to think of *mal puesto* as a residual diagnosis.

As quickly as an individual suffers chronic illness which fails to respond to treatments logically called for by diagnoses of natural illness, patient and family seriously begin an evaluation of the former's social relations with persons who are not members of his nuclear family. Attention centers on a jilted or unrequited admirer, or on an individual who may have reason to envy one's financial success, educational achievements, or general state of well-being. More often than not, some unspecified others—*los vecinos* or *la gente*—are the cause of this invidious sanction.[8]

In one case of *mal puesto*, which terminated in death, the victim was a man whose family and friends firmly believed him to be a

[8] Charles J. Erasmus discusses the concept of invidious sanction in his *Man Takes Control*.

victim of *mal puesto* following his failure to respond to surgery after a diagnosis of malignant abdominal tumor. In this case, the condition was attributed to a jilted girl-friend, who had blown a lethal powder his way.

In another case, an older man was said to have simply wasted away, despite intensive treatment by a series of physicians and lay healers. His condition was assumed to have been brought on by neighbors envious of his home.

In connection with this discussion of *mal puesto,* it must be remarked that the present study uncovered no evidence of specialists whose sole or even major responsibility was to cause or cure *mal puesto.* Material from this neighborhood indicates that fears of witchcraft and attribution of illness to that source are very common, but, in accord with evidence from other Spanish-speaking communities in the United States, witchcraft is far more often presumed than practiced.[9] Such a finding fits well with current anthropological theories of witchcraft and sorcery. In fact, those theories would lead us to expect a fear of witchcraft to be extremely pervasive in a society such as Mexiquito's, in which residents have no formalized techniques whereby to control the behavior of persons not members of their own small family units.[10] As has been noted in earlier chapters, the largest effective social unit in Mexiquito is the nuclear family household, the autonomy of which is jealously preserved by its members. *Mal puesto* functions as a social device by means of which members of one household perceive others outside it as attempting to influence and sanction their behavior.

The preceding discussion of health and illness demonstrates that those sectors of life in Mexiquito are intimately linked with social relationships, and are reflective of them. In light of this finding, it is of considerable interest to note that when a patient or his family consider an illness to have been precipitated by faulty interpersonal relations, the presumed agent of that condition is never portrayed as an Anglo. Furthermore, in spite of the saliency of intergroup antagonisms between chicanos and Anglos in New Lots, there is no evidence to indicate that such hostilities are symbolized by illness.

---

[9] Margaret Clark, *Health in the Mexican-American Culture,* 174–175; Sam Schulman, "Rural Health Ways in New Mexico," in *Culture, Society, and Health,* Vera Rubin (editor), Annals of the New York Academy of Sciences.

[10] Beatrice B. Whiting, "Paiute Sorcery," *Viking Fund Publications in Anthropology,* No. 15.

In Mexiquito, illness is appropriate to communicate intragroup, but not intergroup social stresses.

The following is an *ensalme* used today by the women of Mexiquito.

Ensalme

Criatura de Dios,
Yo te curo y te ensalmo,
En el nombre de Dios y El
Espíritu Santo.
Tres personas distinctas y un
solo Dios verdadero.
San Roque y San Sebastián
y once mil Vírgenes.
Por su glorísima pasión y
ausención [Ascensión] te vengo a
curar a tí afligida criatura
de ojo, calentura y espanto
y cual quierer otra corrucción . . .[11]
no refiriendo su sacreasanto
misterio.

Jesús Criatura de Dios
    acúerdate de Dios.
Jesús Criatura de Dios
    acúerdate de Dios.
Jesús Criatura de Dios
    acúerdate de Dios.
Con tu amante esté Jesús.
Con tu amante esté Jesús.
Con tu amante esté Jesús.

Criatura de Dios
Yo te curo y te ensalmo
En el nombre de Dios
    Y el Espíritu Santo
    Que Jesús sea tu Doctor,
Y María Santísima tu Doctora.
que esta enfermedad
    Sea curada y avententada [aventada] . . .[12]

[11] Final words of this line were not included because they were illegible in the original version.
[12] See Note 11.

Por el amor de Dios
Por el amor de Dios
Así Sea!
Amén.

Prayer for the Sick

Child of God,
I heal thee and I pray for thee,
In the name of God and the
Holy Spirit.
Three different persons
one true God.
San Roque and San Sebastián
and eleven thousand Virgins.
Through His most glorious passion and
ascension I come to
heal thee, suffering child,
of evil eye, fever, and soul loss
and of any other illness . . .
without alluding to His sacrosanct
mysteries.

Jesus, child of God
   remember God.
Jesus, child of God
   remember God.
Jesus, child of God
   remember God.

May Jesus be with this lover of God.
May Jesus be with this lover of God.
May Jesus be with this lover of God.

Child of God
I heal thee and I pray for thee
In the name of God
   And the Holy Spirit
   May Jesus be your Doctor,
And may Holy Mother Mary be your Doctor.
may this illness
   Be healed and expelled . . .
For the love of God
For the love of God
   May it be so!
   Amen.

The following prayer is used by numerous residents of Mexiquito to whom it has been distributed by a commercial processor of herbal remedies.

ORACIÓN AL TODOPODEROSO
y Evocacíon al Espíritu puro de
DON PEDRITO JARAMILLO

Oh! Dios de infinita bondad y misericordia. Yo os suplico la gracia de que, el espíritu purificado del que fue en el plano terrenal DON PEDRITO JARAMILLO, asistido por el Ángel de mi Guarda, venga en estos momentos angustiosos a prestarme el auxilio y consuelo que necesito; que él atienda a mi enfermedad, que me preste su consejo para curarme, como por Tu Bondad Infinita pudo hacerlo cuando se encontraba en el plano de la vida terrena. Oh, Espíritu purificado de DON PEDRITO JARAMILLO, si te lo permite el Altísimo como yo fervientemente lo suplico, acércate a mí y ayúdame a curar mis dolencias! (O por el enfermo por quien se la invoque.)

Yo rogaré por el mayor desenvolvimiento de tu espíritu para que cada vez te eleves a superiores planos de perfección. Alabado sea el Santísimo! AMÉN.

PRAYER TO THE ALL POWERFUL GOD
and Evocation addressed to the Pure Spirit of
DON PEDRITO JARAMILLO

Oh! Lord of infinite goodness and compassion. I pray that you lend me the aid of the unsullied spirit of he who was, while on earth, DON PEDRITO JARAMILLO, that he, with my Guardian Angel, may come to me at this grievous time to lend me the help and comfort which I require; that he attend my illness; that he lend his counsel to cure me, in the same way that You, in Your Infinite Goodness, were able to accomplish while here on earth. Oh, pure Spirit of DON PEDRITO JARAMILLO, if our Lord permits as I so fervently pray He will, come to me! Help me to heal my misery! (Or, lend your healing aid to the patient whom I represent.)

I will pray for the continued development of your spirit in order that you may reach ever higher levels of perfection. Glory be to God. AMEN.

Healers

We move now to a discussion of the healers available to the chicanos and of the manner in which these people discriminate between them.

Although chicanos do often contrast physicians with lay healers, the contrast is more philosophical than behavioral. Lay healers are an essential part of the traditional context with which one is familiar, whereas the behavior and expectations of physicians are alien to the traditional context of life. But, in actual fact, the nature of the individual who cures one is of far less moment to chicanos than whether the healing has been successful. From the chicanos' point of view, their wanderings among healers, some of whom hold premises about health and illness which are in startling contrast to those held by others, are not at all incongruous behavior. Treatment of a patient by his mother on one night, a physician on the next, and a spiritualistic *curandero* on the third seems to them not at all inconsistent. The cure is the thing; by what means or by whom is purely academic. Some examples of the various kinds of healers to whom a chicano has recourse for a single disease entity are presented below. If the accounts are unique in any way, it is because they are expressed in an unusually lucid fashion.

The first account is one rendered by an elderly man who is now nearly eighty. He has been working for many years in Mexiquito as a caretaker; as a young man he worked in the produce fields as a stoop laborer. This is how he views the variety of health resources available to chicanos like himself and his aged wife.

I don't have any faith in doctors. They're interested only in curing the pockets, and only afterwards are they interested in curing you. They ask you whether you have any money before they cure you, and they ask how much you have.

One time, long ago, when I was still working in the stoop labor I was very, very ill. It was while I was moving some crates of tomatoes around that I felt this excruciating pain in my left side. I ached very much for many days throughout my thighs and my abdominal region. I began to swell in the legs and arms, and my limbs began to turn yellow. I went to see a chiropractor two or three times, but he didn't do me much good.

Then I read about a doctor in Mexico who can cure you without seeing you. I don't believe in such things, I don't believe in them; but you know the saying, El perdido se va a todo [He who is lost tries anything]. I wrote to Mexico City, and he wrote back and said I was to send a dollar, so I did; and he sent back a prescription, and wrote that I was to send another two dollars, which I did. Another prescription followed, and a request for more money, so I didn't use him any more and he didn't do me any good with his prescriptions. I couldn't do anything for myself, and pretty soon my condition was so bad I couldn't even walk around.

Next I went to visit my brother and sister in Monterrey [Mexico], but I could hardly get out of bed once I was down there. Still, I had to visit a doctor, so my brother broke off a spade handle and tied it to my leg so that it was like a crutch. Then he and I went down the street together, where we passed an old man; a very old man with a long white beard and a very wide-brimmed hat made out of straw. As soon as we saw him, my brother and he exchanged greetings. Well, when the old man saw me all swollen-up, on my crutch, he inquired about my condition, and we told him about it. We told him, also, that we were on our way to visit a doctor. The old man, however, told me that my condition was not at all serious, and that all I had to do was to follow the prescription he would present to me.

Well, he started to recite the prescription to me, so my brother pulled out a pencil and piece of paper to note it down. It was a very simple prescription, and the whole lot of ingredients didn't cost me more than one dollar. The prescription was as follows: A little bit of gasoline, some alcohol, three cloves of garlic, three fingersfull of pepper, some camphor, and some *energine*. These all had to be mixed together, placed in some bottles, and left in the sun to dry. When they had remained in the sun all day I was to apply the potion to the swellings. Then, before going to bed I was to take an onion and place it in the hot ashes of the fire. The hot onion was to be laid against the sole of the foot throughout the night. After three such treatments in eight days, I was feeling quite strong and walked where I willed! I was thinner, but I was strong.

Well, after I had been cured by the remedies, not too long afterwards, I went to seek out the old man who had proved to be my benefactor, but I could not find him anywhere. I went to my brother to ask his assistance, but all my brother said was "What old man?" He remembered nothing about the incident which had brought us together with the old man. So then my brother and I went to my sister; we felt that she would remember, naturally, because she had purchased the ingredients for the remedy from the stores. But she couldn't remember anything at all about the incident! We decided that the old man must have been my guardian angel [*angel de guarda*]. Those remedies of the old folks, of our fathers, are the best. I don't trust doctors over here.

You know my wife feels the same way about them; she doesn't have any more faith in them than I do. When this town was first started we had two doctors here—*americanos*—and they were compadres, they were partners in the office. They were good; they cured me many times, and they cured my wife many times, of bad illness. They saved me from dying, although God was most important (¡*Primero Dios!*). Once, my lung was all swollen up and I was about to die, but that doctor saved me from dying!

You know my wife lost her sight completely and we despaired of her ever seeing again. But I read in a newspaper that there was a doctor in Monterrey [Mexico] who could restore eyesight by placing new eyes in the head for those which are no good. He had what they call an eye bank there. I wrote to my sister in Monterrey to ask her about that doctor and she found out that the doctor has to see the patient first, before he can do anything for them. My sister didn't even bother to write me after she had spoken to the doctor, she just came straight up here to take my wife back with her.

Well, the doctor examined her and told her that he wouldn't have to put a new eye in the one socket because it was obstructed by a cataract and he could cure that, but that the other eye didn't have a chance because it was dead, and the nerve was dried-up. He said that even if he did put a new eye from the bank into the other socket it wouldn't do any good because the connection was bad. He cut out the cataract and it was this big [approximately one-half an inch], and my wife keeps it at home in a glass bottle.

He also gave her glasses, which she was to wear for two years, and then she was to return for a new prescription. But she sees better than I do now and its been five years, so there is no sense in her going back there for new glasses.

The preceding account in which individuals are described as peripatetic shoppers among physicians, chiropractors, and lay curers is by no means unique. Rather it depicts the actualities of health-relevant behavior in Mexiquito. Amelioration of a condition is what counts for the chicanos, whereas, the type of specialist who actually performs the cure is of little moment.

Telésforo, who is almost six decades younger than the preceding informant describes a similar set of attitudes. In this case, however, the problem of raising funds for a physician's fee was a crucial factor in the decision as to the priority given the alternate healing resources. What follows is a description of the manner in which Telésforo and his family sought to resolve a health crisis.

When he was ten, Telésforo stepped on a sharp object, which penetrated the callous of his foot, but he paid the wound little heed. As time passed, however, the callous re-formed and he began to experience sharp pains. He now recalls a number of sleepless nights, during which he cried until morning.

Telésforo's married sister, with whom he was living, became more and more concerned over her younger brother's condition. She began to probe the foot with a needle and other sharp tools, but to no avail. The pain worsened, the foot swelled, and from time to time pus was extruded. The next step in the healing process found the sister soliciting advice from the neighbors. On their counsel she bought and applied to the injury a few cents worth of balsam but this, also, proved of little use. As time passed without relief, the swelling spread from the foot to the leg and soon the boy was unable to use his limb at all.

Next, Telésforo's stepfather, with whom the boy's mother was living, offered advice. He suggested that Telésforo collect his own urine in a tin can, and that this be applied to the wound in order to penetrate the calloused skin. Some neighbors then suggested that after the urine had penetrated the callous, chicken feces be applied directly to the wound. This last was intended to "draw" (*chupar*) the pus. These procedures were duly carried out under supervision of Telésforo's sister but, once again, without success.

As the family's concern worsened, Telésforo's eldest brother returned to Mexiquito and visited the boy. He discovered the youngster in tears and the remainder of the family terribly anxious about the condition. After one look at the swollen limb, he advised his sister to prepare Telésforo for a trip to the local hospital. In the meanwhile he would attempt to borrow money to pay for treatment. As soon as the estimated fee was borrowed, Telésforo was taken to the hospital, where the physician lanced the swelling and removed the pus. He took pains to advise the family that if they had waited longer he would have been forced to amputate.

Because other cases in Mexiquito that were characterized by extensive swelling and large amounts of pus have been attributed to witchcraft, Telésforo was queried as to whether *mal puesto* might not have been a factor in his own condition. He dismissed the suggestion out of hand.

Because *mal puesto* is only when you go to a doctor and he scratches his head and tells you that he would prefer you to go to someone else, that he can't tell what is wrong with you. When the thing is *mal puesto* you can go to all the doctors and all the nurses anywhere and they can't do anything for you. But *this* was different, we just didn't have the money to see a doctor. That's a different story. We knew that if I had gone to a doctor, he could have cured it. We knew that if we could find the money, the doctor could have cured it.

The above account is illuminating for several reasons. First, Telésforo implies that from the very beginning his family defined the situation in such a manner that it was clearly understood to fall within the province of a physician. Mitigating against such action was the lack of money estimated to be required by a physician's attention. The decision to take the boy to the doctor was founded on the judgment of Telésforo's oldest brother, head of this fatherless family. Another of the reasons the above account is instructive is that, as in a great number of similar situations, it is presumed that in the absence of adequate funds to pay a physician his fee, he will not attend one in time of emergency. Such a presumption has great currency in Mexiquito. (Yet, in two years of field work I never once heard of a physician refusing to treat an emergency case because of the patient's inability to pay the fee charged.)

Finally, another case is presented in which a chicano family struggled as best it could to cope with mortal illness. Like the others which preceded it, this example depicts the flexibility and pragmatism with which chicanos make use of available health resources.

In this account a very young boy was ill, and all efforts to improve his condition had met with failure.

Everybody was sitting around the house with tears in their eyes. They didn't have any money to go to the doctor, and they had tried a lot of different remedies, but the little boy was ready to die. He had terrible pains, and there was sweat on his face, and he just lay there and cried, even though they held him in their arms. They just didn't have any money for a doctor, and they were ready to see him die.

My sister went over to their house and asked them whether they had tried a suppository (*vela*). They didn't know what that was, so she came back to our house to get a suppository. Then she inserted the suppository into the child and told them to carry the boy outside to the commode, which they did. All of a sudden the boy defecated; everything came out (*hizo cuerpo*); it was terrible! That little boy just sat there and sighed.

He stopped crying and looked around, and then he laughed with the people. Then they gave him a bottle and he went right off to sleep. He was all right after that. Right then, they began calling my sister comadre. Later, she baptized that baby, but even before she baptized him, they called her comadre.

There are four categories of healing agents to whom chicanos of Mexiquito appeal for assistance. First on the list are housewives, whose ordinary family responsibilities include home cures for their own relatives. A second class is represented by other empirical healers, whose clientele consists of relatives as well as neighbors for the treatment of whom a gratuity is offered. This latter class includes seven older women, who also perform as midwives (*parteras*). A third kind of folk healer consists of those whose special qualities clearly distinguish them from all other classes. These are the *curanderos*, who differ from all other classes of healers in this region by virtue of the fact that they practice their art as a divine calling, received as a gift (*don*) from God.[13] Secondly, each curandero is closely identified with the spirit of a deceased healer and, thirdly, curanderos are characterized by personal qualities of a deviant nature. The fourth class of healer from whom chicanos seek assistance are physicians, individuals who are rigorously trained in concepts and techniques of modern Western medicine and who receive formal certification of their competence from supervisory agencies. Now, each of these respective categories of healing agents will be discussed in turn.

Folk Healers

The healer most often utilized by chicanos of Mexiquito is the ordinary housewife. In Mexiquito all housewives list among their primary responsibilities the curing of members of their own households: Parents expect a daughter to have mastered such procedures by the time that she is ready for marriage. As a matter of fact most, but not all, matrons of this side of the tracks do indeed understand the more fundamental techniques which enable them to serve as their family's first line of defense against sickness. Housewives in this society represent the first step in the lay referral system.[14] I will not dwell further on the role of housewives in medical care because of earlier lengthy references and discussions in this chapter.

The second class of folk healer to whom chicanos resort for health

13 Note that this usage of *curandero* refers to a class of healer different from those to whom Clark refers by that term in San José, on p. 163 of her book, *Health*. Clark's *curanderos* are equivalent to those herein referred to as neighborhood healers, whereas that class of healer in South Texas referred to as *curanderos* appears to be absent in California and elsewhere in the Southwest. However, the importance of spiritualistic curing in Mexico is clearly attested by Isabel Kelly (*Folk Practices in North Mexico*).

14 See the discussion of lay and professional referral systems in Eliot Freidson, *Patients' Views of Medical Practice*, pp. 132–151.

Photo courtesy of John Avant.

9. The shrine of Don Pedro Jaramillo in the Los Olmos cemetery.

10.   An humble dedication to Don Pedro.

11.   Portrait of Don Pedro in his shrine.

12. Inside Don Pedro's shrine.

13. A contemporary *curandero*.

14. Patients in the Hidalgo County Health Unit.

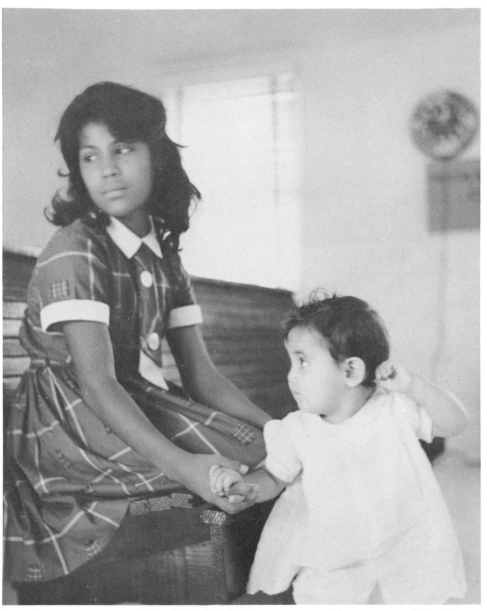

15. Two youngsters in the Well-Baby Clinic.

16. The Well-Baby Clinic.

aid are the neighborhood healers, who possess some repute and expect a gratuity in return for services. As is true in other similar Mexican-American neighborhoods, these empirical healers "are members of the community who are regarded as specialists because they have learned more of the popular medical lore of their culture" than have others.[15] The closeness with which these pragmatic healers are identified with others who are not healers may be calculated by the absence of special generic terms of reference or address by which to discriminate members of this class from nonhealers. The most usual way to refer to such a specialist is by the very ordinary terms of reference: *un señor* or *una señora, el señor* Garcia or *la señora* Robles. Sometimes when one makes reference to such a healer who is also a midwife, she is called by a more specific term, one which emphasizes the midwifery aspects of her duties: *partera.*

Neighborhood healers are resorted to after a housewife's curing efforts have proven ineffectual. Sometimes a healer is sought to read a patient's fortune, a skill not controlled by ordinary housewives. However, fortunetelling plays a minor role in those expectations which chicanos hold for their local healers. On the other hand, midwifery is very important to the people of Mexiquito and is a competence which they look for among their neighborhood female healers.

One gains some idea of the importance of midwifery skills when he understands that in 1955 more than twice as many Mexiquito infants were delivered by registered midwives than by physicians. The seven Mexiquito women recognized as practicing midwives by the Hidalgo County Health Unit are all past middle age, with pragmatic *partera* experience, which ranges between five and thirty-one years.[16]

The table which follows discloses some of the personal characteristics of these midwives.[17]

Although there are, of course, certain difficulties associated with relatively untrained and unsupervised midwives, the really important problems which the chicanos face are the diminishing services provided by aging midwives and the continuing demand for those

[15] Clark, *Health*, p. 207.

[16] Figures are from files of the Hidalgo County Health Unit, and from "A Study of the Midwife Problem in Cameron and Hidalgo Counties" by James D. Wheat.

[17] I am grateful to the Hidalgo County Health Unit for these data. Spaces in which question marks occur indicate that relevant data were unavailable.

Table 6

MEXIQUITO MIDWIVES

| Subject | Age | Years Experience | Literacy | | | |
| | | | Reads | | Writes | |
			English	Spanish	English	Spanish
1	54	15	Yes	Yes	Yes	Yes
2	58	27	No	No	No	No
3	58	5	?	?	?	?
4	67	?	No	Yes	No	Yes
5	68	?	No	Yes	No	Yes
6	73	30	No	Yes	No	Yes
7	78	31	No	Yes	No	Yes

services by women of childbearing age. Note that all seven midwives are past middle age, and that four out of the seven are past sixty. Furthermore, with one possible exception, not one young woman intends to take up practice as a midwife in Mexiquito. During the course of a series of open-ended, structured interviews administered to mothers in attendance at well-baby clinics, four reasons become salient why women prefer midwives to physicians.

The first and most often proffered reason is that the midwife is a woman and usually a mother. Consequently, it is reasoned, midwives understand the fears and pains which are associated with delivery better than can a male physician. (Chicanos lack acquaintance with female physicians.) Secondly, a strong element of embarrassment attends exposure of the female genitals to a male, even though the latter be a medical specialist. Thirdly, midwives are said to show more patience than physicians; midwives, unlike some doctors, permit a delivery to follow its natural course. Physicians on the other hand are perceived as harried by a busy schedule, and consequently they are accused of a readiness to hasten birth by utilization of the dread forceps (*los fierros*). Finally, midwives are relatively inexpensive birth attendants, whereas physicians remain more expensive, in spite of erstwhile efforts by a few to lower their fees on deliveries.

Although, as has been emphasized, a major role of the neighborhood healers is midwifery, by no means all such healers are midwives. Some of these curers have gained their repute in the healing of *mal de ojo, susto, caída de la mollera, mal puesto,* and other folk ills. It is worthwhile once again to draw attention to the fact that these neighborhood healers are but a little above the stature of housewives, who confine their assistance to members of their own families. The former simply understand more and are more experienced than the average housewife in the traditional curing techniques.

On the other hand, although housewives and neighborhood healers do share premises of health and illness with highly acclaimed curanderos, the latter possess quite distinctive characteristics which separate them from all others. The respect which curanderos today command among chicanos reminds one of the reverence accorded the charismatic Tatita a century ago.[18] Although today one never hears reference to the ephemeral Tatita, healing specialists similar to him are very much a part of contemporary life in Mexiquito and the remainder of the lower Rio Grande Valley.

The most important of the curanderos who play so strategic a part in the contemporary life of Mexiquito is, strangely enough, deceased. Years ago, the sage Don Pedro Jaramillo practiced his healing arts in an adobe hut ninety miles north of Mexiquito on the ranch known as Los Olmos. Near that site there now stands his shrine, which attracts pilgrims from many parts of the United States. Many are the stories which glorify his memory, two of which must suffice here because of shortage of space.[19] These two themes were chosen because they provide a social framework within which curing is currently carried on in the region.

The first of the two stories describes the occasion when three Anglo physicians, jealous of Don Pedro's reputation and large clientele, paid the curandero a visit. Their mission, although professedly friendly, was not only to divest the curandero of his distinction by proving him unworthy, but also to kill him.

After the physicians had been introduced, Don Pedro said to the one delegated (to murder him,) "You are the one who wants to kill me by poisoning, aren't you?" But the physician denied this allegation. Don Pedro then advised him that denial was useless because he *knew* that he carried a bottle of poison under his coat. "Give me what you carry then," Don Pedro told the physician, "because it

---

[18] See Chapter 2, this volume.

[19] For additional materials on Don Pedro Jaramillo, see the collection of tales by Ruth Dodson which appears in *The Healer of Los Olmos and Other Mexican Lore*, Wilson M. Hudson (editor). Dr. Octavio Romano has collected an extensive body of material which relates to Don Pedro's healing powers.

cannot harm me! I cure with a gift from God, and I represent Him here!" With that, Don Pedro drank down the lethal contents of the bottle and said to the other that what had been intended for him would instead affect the other. At those very words, the physician began to suffer severe diarrhea, an attack so beyond his control that he dirtied himself as if he was once again a small boy. Then the revered curandero offered his opponent a glass of water, advising him that if he drank the water he would be cured of his attack. This gesture came about because Don Pedro was not here on earth to cause harm to come to others, not even to those who intended his own death. Instead, Don Pedrito's purpose on earth was to alleviate the miseries of others. When the ill physician recovered, he and the others were convinced of Don Pedro Jaramillo's powers and returned to their homes.

Other parables about Don Pedro Jaramillo describe how the healer demonstrated his awesome power to those skeptics who existed even among his own chicanos. Typical is one which describes a man who was on his way to Don Pedro's shack at Los Olmos in order to request the curer's assistance. On the road the patient passed another who asked him his destination. When the traveler responded that he was sick and on his way to ask Don Pedrito's assistance, the bystander began to laugh uproariously and told the wayfarer that Don Pedrito was a fake and that the stories of his prowess were hokum. "If Don Pedro is so powerful, tell him to send me a *vara*," said the skeptic.[20] The patient then continued on his way to Los Olmos, where Don Pedro diagnosed his condition and prescribed an herbal tea, after which he looked at his patient and asked: "Well, what is it?" "What do you mean?" asked the other. "Someone told you to tell me something," said the curandero. The inquiry embarrassed the visitor who had been too bashful even to repeat the story of his encounter with the skeptic. Finally, however, he was induced to tell what had happened, after which Don Pedro advised him not to worry about the skeptic's request any longer because he had already sent him a *vara*. The patient then bade goodby to the wise old man and rode home.

In accordance with instructions, on the following day the patient returned to Don Pedro's. Alongside the road he met a stranger who

[20] *Vara* refers to a wooden stick or branch, and may also be a lineal measurement of approximately three feet.

advised him that a sick man, residing in a house nearby, wished a word with him. When the traveler entered the house, he discovered the scoffer of the previous day; this time, however, the latter was most unhappy because his intestines extruded three feet beyond his anus. "Tell Don Pedrito," said the discontented skeptic, "that I have my *vara* now, and I no longer want it! Tell him that I now believe in his power!" The traveler continued on his way to the curandero, to whom he delivered the message.

The two important themes of the above parables are that Anglo physicians and chicano curanderos are in competition and, second, that the more powerful curanderos will brook neither ridicule nor skepticism from more ordinary men, be they Anglos or chicanos. It follows that those who fail to believe in their powers must expect to be smitten with one discomfort or another.

Another very prominent male curandero in this region, El Niño Fidencio, was Pedro Jaramillo's contemporary, but folk tales which acclaim him seem not to have survived. Nevertheless, and in spite of the distance between El Niño's home in Mexico and Mexiquito in Texas, many residents of the latter locality recall undertaking the long trip in order to benefit from El Niño's healing powers. Then, as now, the international border between the two nations was no hindrance to those in search of relief from illness.

Today, the chicanos of Mexiquito depend on assistance from several curanderos, who have adopted the names of Don Pedro Jaramillo and El Niño Fidencio. The relationship which obtains between contemporary curanderos and their revered predecessors illuminates the unusual character of these charismatic personages of yesterday and today.

Unlike either those housewives who have learned a limited number of prescriptions and prayers for the proper protection of the members of their households, or the more versatile and experienced healers and midwives with neighborhood clienteles, the charismatic curanderos of this region heal by virtue of a special gift (*don*) from God. Certification that an individual is a recipient of such a divine gift takes the form of repeated dreams in which there appears a personage known to have the power to intercede with the supernatural. Not all persons, however, have access to this form of certification; dreams are necessary but not in themselves sufficient criteria for validation of a person's divine election as a curandero. Such dreams are preceded by recognition of unusual personality characteristics, which separate the potential curandero from his or her peers. The combination of these two validating devices—dreaming of power figures who mediate between man and the supernatural, and deviant personality characteristics—liken the curanderos of the lower Rio Grande Valley to the classic shamans of Siberia.

In recent years, three curanderos have attained great renown in the lower Rio Grande Valley and adjacent areas. Two of these personages are personally known to me; the third description is based on information from one of Mexiquito's young men, who has often sought help from that young woman.

The first vignette is that of the young woman curandera with whom I do not have personal acquaintance. She lives with her parents on a small ranch, which is almost inaccessible to motor vehicles. As a child, the girl suffered from a series of seizures during which trembling and fainting played prominent parts. As she approached maidenhood her seizures continued and, in addition, she commenced to receive visions of the Virgin of Guadalupe, patroness of Mexico. The Virgin always reappeared in the thorn forest close to this girl's ranch home.

News of her miraculous experiences brought nearby ranchers to the scene in hopes of ameliorating illness and other problems which troubled them. In time, her fame spread far enough to attract large numbers of people from Mexico north of Monterrey and from such Texas localities as Mexiquito. From reports by informants who have undertaken the journey, the trip to the ranch house was arduous, indeed, and the time consumed in awaiting the curandera's assistance required a great amount of suffering patience. The long wait was to a large extent a function of the curandera's practice to retire to the scrub forest in order to consult with the Virgin on each of her cases.

It seems, however, that this curandera's attraction was short-lived; her original promise as a miraculous healer failed to bear fruit, and the crowds of hopefuls rapidly diminished. Today, it is said, the ranch is as isolated from the outside world as it was before the Virgin of Guadalupe made her appearance.

Another woman who has acquired fame for her prowess as a gifted curandera is El Niño Fidencio, who practices at a locale between Reynosa and Monterrey in northern Mexico. The contemporary El Niño Fidencio derives her name from her celebrated male predecessor.[21] Although the custom is at times confusing, it is by no means unusual to discover a female (as in this instance) who practices the healing arts under a man's name. Furthermore, because of the importance of being associated with the spirit of a renowned predecessor, several curanderos practicing contemporaneously may be known by the same name. For example, today there are several Pedro Jaramillos practicing in South Texas and on the Mexican side of the border.

But now to return to the story of the current El Niño Fidencio, a woman now in her fourth or fifth decade. As a girl, this unusual woman found herself unlike others her own age. Her most striking distinction was that she repeatedly dreamed of a large stone, which seemed to her a marker of some kind. Once, when she and her family traveled about northern Mexico near the city of Saltillo, they chanced upon a monument erected to the memory of a renowned curandero, the deceased El Niño Fidencio. The young woman was immediately struck by the resemblance between the monument and the large stone which recurred so often in her dreams. This perceived correspondence led her to recognize her calling as a curandera, and she began to practice healing with the assistance of El Niño's spirit. At that time she adopted the name of El Niño Fidencio and began to dispense diagnoses, prognoses, and healing regimens in an adobe hut with a thatch roof, in which she still practices today. As her renown spread, individuals in ever increasing numbers came from both sides of the international boundary to seek her aid and comfort.

Today the compound in which El Niño Fidencio attends the large numbers of persons who visit her consists of an adobe hut in which the actual curing takes place, and several auxiliary buildings. Outside of her healing hut an arbor of branches shields the waiting patients from the sun. To one side of the first hut is another, in which the practitioner's mother and other female relatives prepare meals for the family. On another side of the compound is a hut to accommodate those who must remain overnight. In the center of this clus-

---

[21] The individual who supplied biographical data on the current El Niño Fidencio and who claims to be her brother, refers to her as "him" or "he" during conversations. Moreover, the brother lists the curandera's age as "eight," supposedly the length of time she has practiced with the spirit of El Niño Fidencio.

ter of buildings there is an open well, from which the waiting patients scoop drinking water from time to time.

On my arrival at the curer's establishment thirty-two persons
awaited her attention, and others came throughout the remainder of
the day. Most sat under the arbor, but those others whose turn was
close stood outside the curtained doorway of the curing hut, while
still others waited within. Inside the two-room hut the walls were
banked with flowers brought by patients, while letters which attested to El Niño's successes were fastened to nails for all to see and read.
Those who awaited their turn within stood hushed, lined up against
the walls, and all eyes were fastened upon the curiously masculine
face and figure of the woman, El Niño Fidencio. Her greying hair
was drawn back severely from the forehead and tied tightly in a bun
at the back of her head. The features of her face appeared massive,
but her arms and fingers were short and stubby. A white habit,
which covered her body and reached to the ankles, almost completely obliterated the outlines of her bust. In truth, if this last indice
of femininity had been completely hidden from sight, it would have
been most difficult to decide the curer's sex.

As each of the waiting patients approached El Niño, the curandera quietly asked the nature of the complaint. Sometimes the problem was in the form of a generalized ache or pain, in other instances
it was a clubfoot or a persistent cough; still other visitors sought
news from a loved one who was either deceased or traveling in some
far place; moreover, there were two children who had evidenced
mental retardation from the time of their birth. During each of these
brief preliminary exchanges, one of the curandera's bare feet rested
against the bare foot or, in some cases, the shoe of her patient; moreover, when an ache or pain was specifically localized by the patient,
the healer's hands found their way there, touching the body and
passing back and forth over the site. Then the patient was counseled
as to the best medicinals to be taken for his particular problem and,
in some instances, herbs were given him by his benefactress. Finally, as each encounter was brought to an end, the patient was
passed on with a blessing, leaving a gratuity in a receptacle which
was placed near the doorway. Those who left the hut appeared ex-
hilarated. Their demeanor was in marked contrast to those solemn
others who waited their turn outside.

On the other, Texas, side of the border Don Ramón is a counterpart of El Niño Fidencio. The two are similar in a number of ways.

Don Ramón was born and raised in a Texas town close to Mexiquito. Early during his childhood several remarkable happenings fore-warned an unusual life to come. The first sign of his calling came when the boy was eight years old. At that time he was wont to talk, to sing, and to walk in his sleep. Furthermore, when the boy walked in his sleep, he wandered unwittingly through the thornbrush for-est without suffering serious consequences. Still later, during the course of his Catholic parochial-school training, Ramón perceived himself, and was perceived by others, as a deviant because of his questioning attitudes on the nature of God and the saints, attitudes which his teachers thought blasphemous.

At the age of ten Ramón began to enter trancelike states, a condi-tion to which he was prone for many years afterward. Once, while Ramón was in such a trance, a bearded old man arrived at the ranch accompanied by another stranger. These strangers advised the fam-ily that they were in search of treasure, which they had reason to believe was buried on the grounds. After receiving permission from Ramón's father to dig near the ranch house, the work commenced. While the two men dug their holes, Ramón (deep in trance) and his father watched. At one point the old treasure seeker stopped his work to ask the identity of the boy in a trance. After his question was answered, the stranger announced that the boy was destined to become a great medium because powerful forces could be dis-cerned swirling and playing about him.

Although Ramón now says that he had always foreseen an un-usual life for himself because of the signs listed above, it had never struck him so forcibly as when he began to dream of a white-bearded old gentleman. The dreams in which an unidentified man reap-peared were a regular part of the youth's sleeping hours. It was not until he was fifteen that he recognized the man in his dreams, a discovery which made clear once and for all time that Ramón's calling was that of a curandero. The recognition occurred in the following manner. A rancher brought news to the boy and his father that the latter's brother lay dying on an isolated ranch near La Re-forma, Texas. Father and son drove to this ranch, and upon their arrival discovered the old uncle in a moribund condition. At the same time, youthful Ramón noted a photograph on the wall depict-ing a white-bearded old gentleman, the man in his dreams. Ramón stared fascinatedly at the photograph while he reiterated aloud: "That's the man! That's the man I keep dreaming of all of the time!"

His father, thinking it was the uncle to whom Ramón made reference, paid the ranting youth little attention. After they succeeded in trundling the ill man into their small automobile, Ramón explained to his father that the photograph depicted the man who recurred in his dreams. Their ill passenger then explained that the photograph was of Don Pedro Jaramillo, the healer of Los Olmos. When they arrived back home, Ramón commenced to offer his assistance to those who complained of minor medical problems, and soon it became widely known that with the assistance of the spirit of Don Pedro Jaramillo, Ramón was able to perform great works. In fact, some now began to speak of him as Don Pedro.

Although Don Ramón derives his healing powers from a special relationship with the spirit of Don Pedro Jaramillo, he is not the first of his family to have won acclaim as a healer. The manner in which he distinguishes his own competencies from those of his relatives is instructive. Ramón's paternal grandmother was widely known as a healer of snake bites as well as for her skills as a midwife. She was said to have been so gifted that witnesses swore that "you could actually see the venom draining from the limbs" as she applied her skills. Nonetheless, Don Ramón denies that his grandmother's skills were by grace of a special divine gift or calling. Instead, he says that his grandmother's abilities came from *within* herself; hers was a competency gained as a result of experience and, as such, it was sharply in contrast to Ramón's gift from God through Don Pedro.

Today, an encounter with the renowned curandero, Don Ramón, reveals a pudgily built man of middle age, who tends to dress in loose-fitting shirts, often with the tails hanging outside the trousers in a skirtlike fashion. Some of Don Ramón's other personal characteristics are his effeminate gestures and postures, complemented by a nearly glabrous body. His success as a healer is attested by the handsome, expensive sandstone house in which he lives, and by the commodious chapel in which he performs healing rites.

The multiroomed house in which Don Ramón lives is located in the South Texas countryside. Elsewhere on the well-kept grounds is a chapel, the pews of which seat between 200 and 250 persons. On those nights of the week when services are held, an empty seat is a rarity. Moreover, on most afternoons of the week automobiles and pickup trucks pass in and out of the driveway as chicano families seek Don Ramón's assistance.

Evening services in the chapel begin shortly after eight, at which time its large doors are closed. The electric lights are extinguished, but the darkness is illuminated by the flickering of candles, as a tape recording of Christian hymns commences. Prayers are then said by the curandero, who is dressed in a white, loose-fitting habit which reaches below his knees. At times the congregation joins in refrains, in which are interspersed references to the Virgin Mary, the Holy Ghost, and Don Pedro Jaramillo. Then, by means of ventriloquistic skills, there appears little Coquito, a small boy with a high-pitched voice.[22] Coquito proves to be a mischievous diviner and fortuneteller. He quickly becomes engaged in rapid exchanges with members of the congregation who shout out their requests for information, which Coquito attempts to answer in a highly diverting way, one which those present enjoy immensely. The range of information which they request of Coquito is wide, indeed; inquiries include the whereabouts of lost, strayed, or deceased spouses, news of relatives in distant places, the locality of a pair of lost earrings, and several requests as to whether the date is propitious to undertake a long trip to northern harvests.

After all of these requests have been honored by Coquito, the public curing services commence. Once again the recorder plays music and all but a rare candle are extinguished. One by one the pews empty as the congregation moves in ordered procession to face the white-robed Don Ramón. As each person confronts the curandero he is asked whether he does not have some particular affliction which troubles him. The healer's hands pass rapidly over the front of the body and then the communicant is turned around and the curandero's hands move rapidly over the spinal and shoulder areas while he murmurs soothing prayers. Following this, each celebrant returns to his seat, and those of the next pew form in line to approach Don Ramón, who repeats the rites. These services terminate with prayers and chimes, and the participants depart from the chapel to the notes of a recording of "Onward Christian Soldiers," after depositing gratuities in several receptacles left for that purpose.

The vignettes of the three charismatic curanderos who have attracted most fame in Mexiquito during the past decade make salient several striking similarities. In the first place, all three are attributed

[22] The identity of the ventriloquist could not be ascertained under the circumstances, but presumably it was Don Ramón.

special healing competencies by virtue of their close association with the spirit of a renowned predecessor. Secondly, each perceives himself, or is perceived by others, as possessed of personal characteristics which markedly distinguish him or her from peers. In the first vignette, the young woman regularly suffered seizures which terminated with fainting, and as she entered her maiden years she received visitations from the Virgin of Guadalupe. In the case of El Niño Fidencio, her mentor was the famous curandero whose name she adopted, and it is with the aid of his spirit that she practices her art. According to her brother, in her early years she was quite different from other girls her own age. Moreover, her calling as a curandera was made clear when she discovered that the subject matter of recurrent dreams was a symbolic representation of her guide, already deceased.

Finally, in the case of Don Ramón, signs foretelling an unusual calling were received by him in childhood. Among those signs were somnambulistic activities, trances, and nonconforming inquiries about God and other religious matters. Validation of Don Ramón's calling arrived upon his identification of a recurrent figure in his dreams as Don Pedro Jaramillo. Ramón then began to heal with the assistance of his venerable mentor and, in time, dedicated a chapel to his name.

The culture of the residents of Mexiquito provides alternate roles, in particular those of charismatic curanderos, to persons who do not easily fit into more customary ways of life. A substantial literature in anthropology and psychiatry describes how in many societies with distinctive cultures there recurs this technique of allocating healers' roles to those who do not readily fit into other more usual role activities.[23] But it should be noted that curanderos from whom chicanos of Mexiquito seek assistance appear not to be gravely disturbed in their interpersonal relationships, or characterized by manifestly abnormal anxieties, or unable to sustain their viability in the larger society.[24] Surely, if the numbers of people from Mexiquito who frequent curanderos are an indication of the importance of the latter, then this class of healer continues as a major force to be contended with by professional medical personnel.

[23] Robert H. Lowie, *An Introduction to Cultural Anthropology* (revised ed.), pp. 310–312.

[24] John J. Honigmann, *The World of Man*, p. 638.

Physicians

The preceding section discussed the three classes of folk healers to whom chicanos of Mexiquito have recourse. This present section discusses a fourth class of curer—physicians—who provide essential resources to chicanos in time of illness or injury.Only one physician—himself a chicano—practices within the bounds of Mexiquito, but seven Anglo doctors have offices across the tracks.[25] Moreover, professionals in such Texas cities as McAllen, Corpus Christi, and Brownsville as well as in the Mexican cities of Reynosa, Matamoros, Montemorelos, Linares, and Monterrey, are consistently utilized by residents of Mexiquito. The quality of the relationships between chicano patients and their physicians is quite distinct from that which is characteristic between patients and any class of folk healer. The explanation of that difference is not hard to find. There are three major reasons, all of which may be subsumed under the rubric of social distance.[26]

Physicians, whether they are Anglos, chicanos, or Mexican nationals, are quite unlike the overwhelming majority of patients from Mexiquito. The former are members of a social stratum which overrides nationality and language; they share a professional culture. Furthermore, physicians are members of a social-class stratum which is characterized by high income gained in a prestigeful occupation, by a high level of educational achievement, and by an expensive residence with appropriate accoutrements. Moreover, physicians communicate by means of a professional vocabulary, one which the overwhelming majority of patients (chicano as well as Anglo) do not share with them.[27] The fact that only two physicians in this city are able to communicate with the chicanos or to elicit basic health-relevant information from them in the patient's primary language merely exacerbates an already grave problem. Phrased somewhat differently, a communication gap exists between all physicians in this area on the one hand and all patients on the other, but the problem is more pronounced between *non*-Spanish-speaking physicians and their Spanish-speaking patients.

A second reason why the relationship between chicanos and their

[25] Since the end of field work, this chicano physician has moved his office to the south side of the tracks.

[26] Compare with Schulman, "Rural Healthways."

[27] Cf. Julian Samora, et al., "Medical Vocabulary Knowledge among Hospital Patients," *Journal of Health and Human Behavior*, 2 (1961), 83–92.

physicians has about it a prominent quality of stiffness and mistrust is the fee-for-service arrangements. Undoubtedly, minimal fees of four and five dollars are high for a group of families most of whom consider themselves fortunate if the principal wage earner garners four dollars daily. (The financial hardships of high fees in this city, as in others, is tempered by a practice on the part of physicians to set fees based on sliding scales according to a patient's income.) However, it is noteworthy that most of the negative feelings which chicanos so often express about fees-for-service do *not* center on the amount of a fee but, instead, on the fee-setting practice itself. The two are different orders of phenomena.

In order to understand the reasons for the distaste chicanos display toward the arbitrary setting of fees by physicians, it is best to compare physicians with lay healers. An important feature which contrasts lay healers with physicians is that the former are traditionally recompensed for their services in the form of gratuities, while the latter exact fees.[28] To an important extent this distinction contributes to the widely held supposition that physicians on the one hand practice medicine to enrich themselves at the expense of their patients, whereas on the contrary, lay healers practice "to help the people" (*ayudar a la gente*). Furthermore, chicanos consider particularly galling the necessity to purchase expensive drugs, which their physicians prescribe. The combination of physicians' fee and charges for required prescription drugs are considered double penalties.[29] The chicanos invidiously contrast the additional charge for drugs with the practice by which lay healers either donate the necessary balms, roots, or herbs, or else prescribe items which are very inexpensive.

The third of the major reasons why chicanos lack confidence in their physicians is that the doctors prove ignorant of entire sectors of the health concepts to which their patients firmly hold. Mexican-Americans logically reason that if a physician customarily turns a deaf ear to a large number of the complaints which afflict his patients, it is foolish to continue to bring those complaints to this kind of practitioner.

Chicanos are always quick to point to cases which were diagnosed

[28] In none of Dodson's stories about Don Pedrito is a fee mentioned; in fact, the lore describes the curandero as opposed even to gratuities.

[29] In Laredo the attitudes of migrant agricultural labor families toward physicians' prescriptions were the same.

as a form of folk illness and which responded satisfactorily to a folk healer's ministrations. They accurately note the association between commencement of a folk cure and improvement of symptoms of illness. Conversely, chicanos fail to credit physicians for their successes unless a direct relationship can be established between a physician's efforts and improvement of the condition.[30] In general, in those cases in which a direct linkage can be established between application of a healing technique and improvement of a health condition, credit is given the healer and his techniques; the more acute and uncomfortable the condition and the more immediate and perceptible the relief, the higher and more dramatic the demonstration value of the technique and the more confidence generalized to that class of healer.[31] The problem herein lies in the fact that inasmuch as chicanos try several different classes of healer for serious or prolonged illness it is difficult for them to establish a correlation between relief of symptoms and the practitioner responsible.

If all other things were equal we should expect that in those instances in which chicanos sought relief of an illness from both physicians and lay healers, credit for success should be evenly distributed between the two categories of healers. Actually, all other relevant factors are not equal. It is these additional factors which help us to understand why each time a link is established between application of traditional folk cures and healing of illness, traditional healing techniques are acclaimed; conversely, when a similar link can be established between a physician's methods and amelioration of sickness no such response is forthcoming. The reason for this apparent logical inconsistency lies in the fact that systems of healing are as much an integral part of social life as are families, church membership, and the customary relationships between chicanos and Anglos. When viewed in this holistic context, the unusual acclaim awarded each victory of a traditional means of healing can be understood as an effort to validate the worth of the traditional culture in the face of constant and severe criticism by Anglos, especially in the area of health-related beliefs and behavior. Each victory of a traditional means of coping behavior is a validation of the worth of the Mexican-American way of life.

If the preceding paragraphs seem unduly critical of physicians

[30] Cf. Lyle Saunders, "The Spanish-Speaking Population of Texas," *Inter-American Education, Occasional Papers*, No. 5, p. 310.

[31] Erasmus, *Man Takes Control*, p. 78.

in their relationship with chicanos it should be remembered that
one purpose of this monograph is to present a chicano view of a
world in which physicians play important roles. What then of that
relationship from the perspective of the physicians? The following
paragraphs describe some of the problems faced by general practitioners in their dealings with chicanos. Because of the novelty of chicano physicians in this region, all of whom are quite young men
recently graduated from medical schools, attention is focussed on
the older Anglo physicians, most of whom have practiced in the
Valley for many years.

One of the prominent characteristics of those Anglo physicians
who have dedicated their professional lives to the care of the Valley's residents is the deep concern with which they originally set
about the task of changing traditional Mexican-American concepts
of health and illness. These doctors have perceived their functions
as, in part, providers of medical care services and, in part, teachers
and innovators.

All physicians with whom the matter of changes in traditional
medical-care patterns was discussed concurred in the observation
that they have witnessed extensive changes in traditional Mexican-
American health attitudes and behavior. Despite such extensive in-
novations, the practitioners manifest puzzlement, even dismay, because chicanos have not eagerly embraced the entire package of
modern preventive and curative care proposed by doctors. Recognition that all classes of chicano—educated and illiterate, rich and
poor—continue to utilize the services of lay healers as well as those
of physicians gives rise to considerable irritation on the part of the
latter group. Quite rightly, they feel that lay healers sometimes hinder the work to which physicians are dedicated.

The physicians' vexation is most salient on those occasions when
a patient's condition manifestly worsens as a consequence of delays
caused by visits to lay healers. In such instances physicians tend to
accuse those responsible of outright neglect. An illuminating instance of what sometimes transpires when a patient is taken from
one folk healer to another before being brought to the attention of a
physician follows. In this case a young impoverished mother carried
her infant son from one lay healer to another, some of whom practiced in neighboring towns, in search of a cure for her child. Finally,
one healer recognized the boy's grievous condition and urged his

mother to seek a physician's aid without delay. That very night the mother took her infant to a proprietary clinic in New Lots, only to discover that it was closed for the night. Throughout the night she remained in close attendance on the baby, constantly changing the meat patties on his stomach, by which means she intended to draw out the fever ravaging his body.

Early the following morning she arrived at the same clinic only to discover that services were not provided before nine. By now distraught, she rushed to the city's other private clinical facility but it, also, was closed. However, this one was equipped with a nightbell. A ring of the bell galvanized the nursing staff into action and they, in turn, called the attending physician from his home. Despite the alacrity with which the clinic staff responded to the mother's call, the prognosis was declared "hopeless." Nevertheless, the physician and his staff made herculean efforts in behalf of their patient. While intensive emergency care was taking place upstairs, the child's father was downstairs engaged in efforts to guarantee the clinic that its fees-for-service would be paid. This requirement was finally met by his employer's advancing a check against future wages. But, despite all the efforts expended in his behalf, the infant expired that same day.

Frustrated, the physician fulminated that the death was a consequence of outright parental neglect and stupidity. The disappointed practitioner remained unaware that the mother whom he was accusing of neglect had spent increasingly desperate days in attempts to ameliorate her child's condition. Characteristically, so long as the infirmity continued to be diagnosed as fallen fontanel and, later, *empacho*, the woman acted according to traditional usage. But, as the treatments logically called forth by those diagnoses failed to prove of help, the diagnosis was changed and the patient was referred to another class of healer—a physician. By then it was too late!

Finally, the doctor in this case was not the only aggrieved party. For several weeks after the loss of their son, the parents were curiously ambivalent about the clinical staff. On the one hand, they felt that the staff had spared no effort in the battle to save their child; on the other hand, the physician was accused of delaying emergency treatments until he was convinced that the family could afford the costs of his professional efforts in behalf of the moribund child. The financial assurance required by the physician firmly bolstered the parents' belief that efforts to save the child were motivated by the promise of the fees involved.

El Hábito

To a chicano, whichever the class of healer from whom he seeks assistance, success or failure of a curing venture is dependent in the final analysis upon the will of God through His intermediaries, the saints. ¡*Primero Dios*! (God first!) is an axiom which consistently and fervently accompanies discussion of illness or injury. Another aphorism notes that [even] saints may not cure if God proves unwilling (¡Santos no puede si Dios no quiere!). Fatalistic verbalizations such as these, however, in no way interfere with the notably action-oriented behavior of chicano families when an ill member is in need of aid. Unlike the fatalism reported of the Spanish-speaking people of New Mexico and Colorado, chicanos of Mexiquito leave no stone unturned in their search for healing success.[32] However, after all else has failed, when despite the assistance of neighborhood healers, curanderos, and physicians, disease continues its course unchecked, a patient may make a vow to a saint. Most often these are female patients in terminal stages of illness.

Although making a vow to a saint, "donning the habit," as it is called, is a last resort for chicanos following a series of efforts to ameliorate the condition, the procedure by which the rite is undertaken is a simple one. A patient makes a vow to a particular saint, the image of which is found in one of the churches important to local chicanos: perhaps to San Juan de los Lagos (Mexico), or to the virgin in the church of San Juan (Texas), or maybe to the Virgin of Guadalupe. When a patient undertakes this obligation she elects an individual to serve as sponsor of the habit (*madrina de hábito*). The *madrina* is required to purchase a dress of the same color as that worn by the image of the chosen saint and to present it to her new godchild after having had it blessed by the clergy. The patient then wears the habit until it finally disintegrates from constant use, if death does not eventuate earlier.

The solemnity with which a habit is worn cannot be exaggerated;

---

[32] Cf. Saunders, "Spanish-Speaking Population," p. 166; L. S. M. Curtin, *Healing Herbs of the Upper Rio Grande*; Florence R. Kluckhohn and Fred L. Strodtbeck, *Variations in Value Orientations*, p. 244. Conversely, Saunders notes that "Like people everywhere, the Spanish-speaking are motivated to do something about conditions which cause them discomfort or pain or which they define as illness" (p. 173).

the act itself is acknowledgment that all other *known* methods have proved of no avail. However, one would be quite incorrect if he were to derive from this the thought that a patient's family has placed all of its hopes in the hands of the supernatural, as it were. Even at this seemingly hopeless stage of illness the introduction of a previously unknown healing technique or medicine is eagerly seized upon. In health crises chicanos are never loathe to make one more effort, one additional attempt to turn the course of illness. Truly, in Mexiquito, God, Himself, is final arbiter of sickness and health, life and death, but a patient's family never relaxes its pragmatic efforts in his or her behalf.[33] Verbal acknowledgment of God's will on the one hand and unstinting pragmatic activities to secure a cure for illness on the other, need not be mutually exclusive. In Mexiquito they are not.

Summary

In Mexiquito a remarkable amount of attention and concern is paid to the matter of sickness and health. Sickness constitutes one member of a class of misfortunes to which any individual is susceptible. Thus, illness, and such other misfortunes as barrenness, an automobile accident, bickering between spouses, and loss of a breadwinner's job are all members of a general class of misfortune, which, according to chicanos, may simply be natural events, something which might have happened to anyone. On the contrary, an instance of one of the above misfortunes may be a consequence of unnatural causes, a manifestation of the harm which someone else is directing against one's self or members of one's small family unit. The discovery of the precipitating causes of a condition plays an important part in the social life of this neighborhood. In Mexiquito, illness is assumed to be as much a product of dysfunctional social relations as it is a consequence of the improper functioning of one's body, or of those unseen forces which a physician refers to as germs.

Traditional diagnostic techniques are utilized by chicanos to arrive at the nature of a condition, its causes, and the appropriate healing techniques. When a condition fails to respond favorably to the technique a diagnosis calls for, it is assumed that either the diagnosis is faulty or that a more competent healer is required. In any case, when a condition of illness becomes chronic or when an individual or others of his family are smitten by several misfortunes

[33] Cf. Saunders, "Spanish-Speaking Population," p. 166.

within a short space of time, it is probable that the condition will eventually be attributed to unnatural causes—witchcraft. In the final analysis, a diagnosis is validated by the favorable response a patient makes to the healing techniques the diagnosis demands. In Mexiquito, as elsewhere, the proof of the diagnosis is in the healing.

Among the illnesses which are common in Mexiquito, but absent on the other side of the tracks, are evil eye, soul loss, *empacho*, and witchcraft. Quite in accord with the finding that the proof of the diagnosis is in the healing, these chicanos prove to be peripatetic shoppers, selecting from the diverse skills of a variety of healers.

In time of illness the chicanos seek assistance from four categories of healers, of which the least specialized is comprised of housewives, whose usual responsibilities include home cures for members of their own families. More highly thought of is the second category, neighborhood healers with more experience in the field, who serve a neighborhood clientele, and who expect a gratuity for services rendered; included in the latter category are Mexiquito's seven midwives. The most highly revered of all categories of healers, the curandero, is unlike any other. This category is comprised of both men and women, all of whom cure by virtue of personal characteristics which serve to validate their calling. Among others is a consistent dreaming about a deceased curandero of renown, whose spirit serves as a mentor and whose name the contemporary healer adopts as his or her own. Moreover, unlike others, curanderos cure by virtue of a special gift (*don*) from God. Finally, there is a category which consists of certified physicians—chicano and Anglo alike—whose technical skills and knowledge are accorded considerable respect by chicanos.

In those cases in which it seems that all healing resources have been exhausted, a patient will don a habit which is a replica of a gown worn by one of the images in the church; this costume will be worn until it becomes completely worn out, or until the patient either expires or recovers.

Nevertheless, even when a terminal stage of illness has been reached, when all hope has seemingly been discarded, the patient's family remains alert to any new possibility which might change the course of illness. Although chicanos verbalize a fatalistic dependence upon God's benevolence, especially in time of sickness, a family never relaxes its pragmatic efforts on the patient's behalf.

Part III

COMPARISONS AND CONCLUSION

8. PERCEPTIONS OF SOCIAL RELATIONS: A COMPARATIVE ANALYSIS

In preceding chapters are described the ways in which a chicano of Mexiquito relates to those others who comprise his society, and how he perceives those relationships. This chapter addresses itself to the third and final aim we set for ourselves in the introduction: an explanation of why the chicanos, themselves, attach qualities of anxiety and disaffection to their perceptions of social relations.

From the very beginning of this book—the biblical account of genesis in which chicanos depict themselves as generically disputatious, followed by the parable about the Mexican shepherd who astutely discovers the principle of the steam engine only to meet death at the hands of his envious neighbors—recurs the theme that chicanos cannot get along with one another, that neighbors are against one. This theme appears most clearly in the various chapters which constitute Part II (Social Relations), where it is expressed in a number of diverse ways ranging from accusations that chicanos don't want others to succeed in school or business to a fear of neighbors and strangers as agents of such dangerous illnesses as *mal de ojo* and *mal puesto*. The relevant data have been presented. Now what do they mean?

No attempt is made here to evaluate the truth of the deposition by chicanos to the effect that they are more disputatious than other peoples, or that a chicano cannot in fact maintain a viable partnership or work crew with one or more other chicanos, or that any success

on the part of an individual incurs negative sanctions from his
friends and neighbors. (For the record, I found these chicanos a
thoroughly likeable, friendly group of individuals.) Those are problems which lend themselves to the experimental techniques of the
social psychologist, not to the methodology which was employed in
this study. My effort here is to provide an anthropological explanation of why these chicanos perceive social relations in a framework where anxiety and disaffection are prominent features. Finally, no claim is advanced that the following interpretation is definitive. The ethnographic data remain ready at hand for colleagues
who find another explanation more cogent and economical.

To begin, the distributional patterns of anxiety and disaffection
have several interesting facets. In the first place, they appear in association with relationships between an individual and persons who
are not members of his nuclear family, but not between family
members. Two illustrations of this skewed distribution adequately
demonstrate this fact. In the preceding chapter it was determined
that although anyone, inclusive of members of the same household,
is believed capable of inflicting *mal de ojo* on another, there appears
not a single instance in which victim and agent are members of the
same household. The same can be said of the data on *mal puesto*,
from which it is learned that whereas the relevant belief system assumes that every chicano individual is considered capable of deliberately causing harm to another by means of witchcraft, in actual
fact none of the case histories include an accusation by one member
of a nuclear family against another. Anxieties associated with con-
ceptions of these two folk illnesses seem clearly to demarcate the
nuclear family as an individual's basic security unit, from which he
peers out at an unpredictable world.

Secondly, individualistic anxiety and disaffection are never attached to chicano-Anglo relationships. A chicano never presumes an
Anglo to have inflicted *mal de ojo* or *mal puesto* on himself, or a
member of his household. Nor does a chicano aver that in the very
nature of things a chicano cannot maintain a viable working relationship with an Anglo or that "Anglos are against *one*." When dis-
cord arises between an Anglo and a chicano the latter attributes it to
the nature of intergroup relations which obtain in this region. For
example, a chicano employee fired from his job by a chicano supervisor perceives the action as simply one more example of the inability of chicanos to work together, one additional bit of evidence

that in the very nature of things chicanos are pitted against one another. If the very same man were to be discharged by an Anglo supervisor, he would interpret it as proof of the thesis that the Anglo group has its foot "on our necks," in other words the Anglos as a group are perceived as intent on maintaining the chicano group in a subordinate role.

In either instance, the end result is that a chicano's perception of his nuclear family household as a place of security is strengthened and, to the same degree, his understanding of the larger society as threatening receives support. The depiction by chicanos of the nuclear family household as a place of security and, contrarywise, an observed prominence of anxiety and disaffection which attaches to extrafamilial relationships suggests the utility of assuming an association between the type of social system which orders behavior in Mexiquito and the prominence of the emotional qualities now being discussed. Accordingly, a brief summary of the important organizing features of this social system follows.

Briefly, the social system may be described in terms of three major organizing features. First, a chicano thinks of his nuclear family as the only formally organized unit in terms of which he should pursue economic and social ends. Outside the family the male chicano has his palomilla, but this aggregation serves emotional rather than instrumental ends. The activities in which a palomilla engages and the information communicated between participants are not such that assist an individual in earning a living, acquiring a wife, or caring for his family.

A palomilla is best conceptualized as a network of informal dyadic relationships, some of which may be formalized by initiation of ritual kinship (compadrazgo) bonds. Thus, the second major organizing principle of this social system is that relationships beyond the range of the family are between one individual and another, rather than between an individual and a *group* of others.[1]

Third, relationships between a chicano and others are characterized by a high degree of personalism. Probably, if one were to seek one single principle by which to contrast most markedly the chicano social system and its Anglo counterpart it would be the extent to

[1] George M. Foster, "The Dyadic Contract: A Model for the Social Structure of a Mexican Peasant Village," *American Anthropologist*, LXIII, 6 (December, 1961), 1173–1193; "The Dyadic Contract in Tzintzuntzan, II: Patron-Client Relationship," *American Anthropologist*, 65, No. 6 (December, 1963), 1280–1294.

which the former seeks to invest his social activities with personal characteristics and the opposite tendency by those who live south of the tracks.

The above sketch of Mexiquito's social system suggests that it evolved over a period of time to function most efficiently under circumstances in which members of the society knew personally most of those with whom they came into contact, and nuclear families were self-sufficing and independent—economically, socially, and spatially. Needless to add, the densely populated neighborhood of Mexiquito and the fact that every chicano inhabitant is required to work for or with others in pursuit of a livelihood makes this kind of system maladaptive and dysfunctional.

Moreover, the presence of a very considerable populace of Anglo-Americans, who control economic, political, and social resources for which chicanos strive, and whose own social system contrasts sharply with the one described above, exacerbates the difficulty encountered by chicanos as they attempt to secure valued goals by means of social techniques which are maladaptive.

Because most Anglo-Americans in the city and the lower Rio Grande Valley are members of Protestant Churches, they are not amenable to the establishment of formal godparental relationships, an instrumental technique so important a part of the chicano's society. And, the ability of chicanos to control their social environment in strategic ways is even further diminished by the almost total prohibition by the dominant Anglos of intergroup marriages.

Finally, there is the question of whether chicanos may join Anglo social groups and thereby manipulate the behavior of them to their own satisfaction. In fact, many religious, secular, and fraternal groups in New Lots' Anglo society remain closed to chicanos. In a total of more than fifty secular groups, five have small proportions of chicano members, none of whom hold leadership positions.

The tendency of Anglos to form organized groups in order to carry out tasks for common needs, their essentially impersonal approach to social relations, and their unresponsiveness to the social techniques which derive from kinship and personal relationships of the chicanos make extremely difficult any efforts of the latter to gain from the former the social and economic goals to which they strive.

It is now hypothesized that the anxious and disaffective qualities which are so apparent in Mexiquito may be understood as a function of the incongruity which obtains between the atomistic social system for which the chicanos are socialized and the wider and far more complex society with which they must *really* contend. That is, during the course of growing up a chicano is taught to act as if there were no solidary ties required between his family unit and the remainder of the society. It is as if one were trained to interact only with close relatives and yet, realistically, social circumstances require individuals and their families to adapt their needs to those of other individuals and groups not members of their own family unit. The hypothesis argues that the incongruity between their expectations and the reality with which they must cope gives rise to anxiety and disaffection. Moreover, as the materials which follow indicate, the hypothesized relationship between an atomistic social system and a prominence of anxiety and disaffection may be extended to other Mexican-American societies in the lower Rio Grande Valley, as well as to some societies which are historically unrelated to Mexiquito.

Because social systems remarkably like Mexiquito's exist in societies otherwise unrelated to this neighborhood, and inasmuch as they recur in association with a prominence of anxiety and disaffection, I am prompted to write of a type of society which is atomistic. An atomistic-type society is here defined as one in which the social system is characterized by an absence of cooperation between nuclear families; in which qualities of contention, invidiousness, and wariness are paramount in the perceptions which nuclear families hold of one another; and in which such social behavior and emotional qualities are consonant with normative expectations.[2]

In construction of such a cross-cultural type of society, reference is made to three criteria:

1. A cross-cultural type is characterized by selected features rather than by its total element content.[3] Since no two cultures are quite alike in their element totality, it is necessary to select special constellations of causally interrelated features which are found among two or more cultures, but not necessarily among all.

2. The selection of diagnostic features must be determined by the

---

[2] This represents a slight revision of a definition provided in "The Atomistic-Type Society," by Arthur J. Rubel and Harriet J. Kupferer.

[3] In the following discussion the influence of Julian H. Steward's *Theory of Cultural Change* will be readily apparent.

problem and the frame of reference. Conceivably, any aspect of culture may be attributed taxonomic importance.

3. The selected features are presumed to have the same functional interrelationships with one another in each case.[4]

Unlike Steward, however, I do not conceive of these interrelationships as of a cause-and-effect nature, but, rather, as correlates of one another, or "adhesions" as E. B. Tylor phrased it.[5] Neither need one follow Steward in stressing economic factors as necessarily possessing the status of independent variables in such correlations. As they are used here, functional interrelationships imply only a recurrent association of two or more variables, for example, a kind of social system and the prominence of anxiety and disaffection in several societies, which are not otherwise related to one another.

In order to avoid a major pitfall of comparative research, one recently described as "Galton's Problem," I selected several societies which share with Mexiquito a prominence of anxiety and disaffection, but which do not share history, economic base, or acculturation pressures with this South Texas neighborhood.[6] For purposes of cross-cultural comparison, South Italy society, exclusive of Sardinia and Siciliy, and settlements of Algonkian-speaking Ojibwa (or Chippewa) Indians of northern North America have been selected.

However, rather than attempt to compare a single settlement of Mexican-Americans with such broad spectrums of Italian and Algonkian ways of life, it will first be shown that the fundamental features of social life in Mexiquito recur in other Mexican-American settlements. Furthermore, studies of several towns in widely separated areas of Latin America are utilized to show that the covariance of the type of social system characteristic of Mexiquito and a prominence of anxiety and disaffection is not restricted to the United States-Mexico border regions. Quite the contrary.

Other Mexican-American Settlements

Frontera

While I was doing field work in New Lots, another anthropologist, Dr. Octavio Romano, was studying the people of Frontera,

---

[4] *Ibid.*, p. 23.

[5] E. B. Tylor, "On a Method of Investigating the Development of Institutions Applied to the Laws of Marriage and Descent," *Journal of the Royal Anthropological Institute*, 18 (1889), 272.

[6] Raoul Naroll and Roy G. D'Andrade, "Two Further Solutions to Galton's Problem," *American Anthropologist*, 65 (October, 1963), 1053–1067.

Texas.[7] This village is located approximately twenty-five miles west of New Lots, and the two settlements have a great deal in common.

Frontera was founded early in this century by refugees from the unsettled, revolution-torn states of Nuevo León and Tamaulipas in northeastern Mexico. A few were native-born citizens of the United States. The refugees were attracted to Frontera by employment opportunities for unskilled workers in construction and land-clearing operations. Those who settled Frontera were Spanish-speaking and Roman Catholic. Thus, the historical and cultural roots of Frontera and Mexiquito are similar.

In some other aspects, though, Frontera is unlike Mexiquito. In the former live several hundred Mexican-Americans. Immediately adjacent to the unincorporated village is the home of an Anglo family. By contrast, Mexiquito's population comprises more than nine thousand chicanos who live in an incorporated municipalitiy, which is also home for six thousand Anglos. Despite the demographic dissimilarities, the relations of each chicano populace to Anglos is similar. In Frontera the Anglo family owns and manages the principal source of chicano employment, and in Mexiquito all major sources of employment are controlled by Anglos. In each settlement chicano society is therefore dominated by its Anglo counterpart.

Romano's description of social behavior in Frontera is in substantial accord with my findings in Mexiquito. There, also, a chicano finds security only within his immediate family; he withdraws from interaction with others. Romano finds recurrent the isolation of individuals from nonkindred and, with a single exception, the absence of groups larger than the isolated nuclear family. A mutual benefit society includes a number of adult males, but its meetings and procedures are consistently rent by dispute and disaffection. The life history of an average chicano of Frontera shows an employment record notable for its inconstancy. According to Romano, its unusually high labor turnover is caused by distrust of the employer and a fear that the latter is taking advantage of his employee.

The social system of Frontera includes only one intense, consensual bond, that of the *amigo de confianza*, but even then, it is said: "Your friend today may be your enemy tomorrow."[8]

A great amount of verbal communication is devoted to duelling,

[7] Octavio Ignacio Romano V, "Donship in a Mexican-American Community in Texas," *American Anthropologist*, LXII (December, 1960), 966–976.
[8] *Ibid.*, p. 972.

and the most innocent conversation in Frontera is feared; it may contain innuendos designed to cast doubt on the virility or social competencies of the other.

The quality of social relations, aside from those binding close kin, is characterized by features of threat and anxiety. Outside the kindred "... the most basic premise which governs behavior holds that the world is fickle and undependable."[9] Human relations are acted out in an ambient of generalized distrust and defensiveness. For example, in a rare moment of cooperation, funds were collected among residents for construction of a Frontera church. To guard against pilferage and misappropriation, three treasurers were appointed. So regnant was mistrust of others, that the designation of three guardians was not enough to prevent quick dissolution of the movement.[10]

The socioculturally mobile in Frontera are beset by a concern for the opinion of others; a fear of invidious sanction pervades the atmosphere.[11] More severe invidiousness is presumed to be transformed into witchcraft, which is considered to be an instrumentality of the envious. Similar attitudes are recorded in Mexiquito.

Border City

Ozzie Simmons describes social life in another chicano society of Hidalgo County, focusing his attention on the relationship between a dominant Anglo group and subordinate chicanos.[12] Simmons' material includes valuable observations of the social system and ethos of chicanos in Border City. The chicanos he describes form the majority of the population of a city of approximately twenty thousand people, chicanos and Anglos.

The history of Border City is very much like that of New Lots; each was founded on a site hacked out of a thornbrush forest. The cities were constructed to service irrigated Anglo farms which were developed at the turn of the century. Each locality was settled by Mexican-Americans and by Anglo-Americans. The former were attracted to the new cities by opportunities of employment as unskilled laborers. Most were emigrants from the northern Mexican states of Tamaulipas and Nuevo León seeking refuge from the in-

---

[9] *Ibid.*, p. 971.
[10] *Ibid.*, p. 973.
[11] *Ibid.*
[12] Ozzie G. Simmons, "Anglo-Americans and Mexican-Americans in South Texas"; "The Mutual Images and Expectations of Anglo-Americans and Mexican-Americans," *Daedalus* (Spring, 1961), pp. 286–299.

securities of a region beset by furies of revolution and drouth. The Anglo population was composed mostly of Americans and Canadians induced by salesmen to purchase lands in the newly developed tracts. With very few exceptions, the Anglos did not speak Spanish, nor were the laborers competent in English. The former were members of Protestant churches, the latter Roman Catholics.

Today the situation in Border City remains basically the same, although a large proportion of the Mexican-American population is bilingual, and many of the chicanos are engaged as professionals in medicine, the ministry, and education. Another sector of the contemporary chicano population is successful in commerce. Despite the fact that Border City's occupational status hierarchy is relatively open, and many chicanos are socially mobile, personal interaction between members of the two ethnic groups is limited. For example, intergroup courtship or marriage is rare, and they are discouraged.

Simmons describes the chicano society as home-centered. The father-husband dominates the household, presenting a rigid, gruff, and authoritative figure to the others. The mother is idealized as a nurturant and self-effacing person. The world of the Border City chicanos is described as extremely personal, where egos are easily hurt by the slightest criticism, and insults are remembered forever. Simmons also writes that extrakin relations are brittle and easily broken.

The more perduring social relationships, other than those produced by ascribed kinship, are instrumentally achieved by strategies of marriage, ritual kinship, and the formation of a bond between a patrón and his clients. But, as is true in Mexiquito, the Protestant affiliations of the overwhelming proportion of Anglos in Border City bar chicanos from establishing *compadrazgo* ties with superordinate counterparts. In Mexiquito, attempts by chicanos to create patrón-client bonds have also been frustrated. On the other hand, although in Frontera the Anglo employer is inaccessible as a *compadre* because of his religion, he has proved quite willing to act in the role of *patrón*. The bond between the Anglo protector and those who solicit his protection plays a major role in the social system of Frontera.[13] Although each of the three settlements differs somewhat from the others, descriptions of the social systems and ethos are remarkably accordant.

[13] *Ibid.*, Romano, "Donship," pp. 969–970.

Demographic features in Frontera on the one hand, Mexiquito and Border City on the other, are dissimilar. Moreover, the inaccessibility of powerful Anglos in the larger towns contrasts with the situation in Frontera. Nevertheless, social life in the societies seem quite uniform. The recurrence of behavior patterns and themes permits one to make some general statements about social life of chicanos in the lower Rio Grande Valley.

In chicano society individuals are ranked, some higher than others. No matter how highly ranked a chicano, he is subordinate to Anglos. In Mexiquito, members of the formerly prestigious, landed families are referred to sardonically as *los tuvos*—those who once had. Elsewhere, as well, the ranking system of the Mexican-Americans is overshadowed by the dominance of the Anglo-Americans.

Until 1940 the great majority of Mexican-Americans were occupied as unskilled and semiskilled workers. They worked in fields of produce or citrus, in canning and processing plants, and in heavy construction. Occupation is today emerging as an important criterion which ranks intragroup and intergroup status. An increasing number of younger chicanos in Mexiquito and Border City are employed in professional and white-collar tasks. The pattern is emergent in Frontera to a lesser extent.

In the two larger settlements achieved occupational status with its requisite antecedents—formal education and English-language skills—emerges as an ascendant criterion in the social-status system. In Frontera, ascribed status based on sex, age, and the power to dispense favors, remains unquestionably paramount.

In spite of the apparently immutable restrictions on intergroup marriage, and the barring of chicanos from membership in a number of fraternal and religious organizations, the social system of the region, or any one of its component towns, remains relatively open. The next few years will determine whether, in fact, equivalence of income, occupation, and English-language competencies generate a true open-class system, or whether ascribed ethnic characteristics will remain ascendant criteria of social rank. If the latter condition prevails, one foresees a nativistic response by upwardly mobile chicanos. If the former condition emerges as the dominant criterion, chicano energies will be devoted to attainment of superior status in the system of social stratification.

No settlement in the Valley exists as a unit isolated from the total society. Residents are attached to others outside of the settlements;

together with all other chicanos they comprise the *chicanazgo*. The *chicanazgo* perceives itself a solidary unit vis-à-vis Anglos. But, the chicano residents of any specified settlement such as Mexiquito, for example, do *not* perceive themselves as an unique unit vis-à-vis chicanos of other towns, Border City, for example. Absent is any indication that chicanos of Border City, Mexiquito, or Frontera feel allegiance or loyalty to the town in which they reside. In each town the presence of a superordinate Anglo society creates a sense of solidarity among the Mexican-American residents, where none would have existed otherwise. Anglo-chicano conflict erects boundary-maintenance devices around the chicano villages and quarters. Remove the Anglos from the region and the chicanos' sense of in-group solidarity would disappear. The perception of a community as deserving of allegiance or loyalty is alien to the Mexican-Americans. The chicano confines his loyalties to his narrow and shallow kin group.

In chicano society the nuclear family stands forth clearly and distinctly. The loyalties of the chicanos are home-centered. Ties which bind him to his nuclear family also bind him to its locality. The husband-father is the personage in whom decision-making rests, but in actuality, many of the day-to-day minor decisions are made by the household's wife-mother. Nevertheless, all decisions are subject to the approval of the male head of the household. Among chicanos, "The older order the younger and the men the women."

Social life at home is marked by clearly defined patterns of deference. A father represents stern but, ideally, just authority. In a household in which a father-husband is absent, the oldest son substitutes. The mother represents the nurturant aspects of family life. Early in life the children commence to learn their sex-typed roles.

In both Mexiquito and Frontera the palomilla engages much of the time of a virile member of society, but none of his loyalties. Palomillas are a logical product of complementary congeries of values, which provide behavioral expectations for young men. Values which govern behavior in the home proscribe frivolous activities such as dancing, smoking, drinking, and levity. Verbal expression of those behaviors are frowned on. Yet other values direct a youth to validate his manhood at every opportunity; virility and its proper expression are extolled. The participation in palomillas of youthful males enables such validation while preserving the sanctity of the home. No matter what the extent of his interaction with a palomilla, a young husband retains and exercises effective control of family affairs. At approximately forty years of age a chicano diminishes the frequency of his interaction with a palomilla, and engages more actively in the management of household affairs.

In Romano's description of Frontera, social life is depicted as remarkably similar to that of Mexiquito. Likewise, Simmons' observations of chicano life in Border City contribute to a generalization: Social behavior of Mexican-Americans in the lower Rio Grande Valley is organized in small units, of which the nuclear family is of overwhelming importance, and relationships outside the family are arranged by means of dyadic relations based on personal esteem of the parties involved. Interaction between adults is characterized by a high evaluation of the autonomy of the individual, a factor associated with the reported brittleness of nonfamilial social relations.

Each case reports anxious feelings attached to relations between chicanos not members of the same household; in Frontera and Mexiquito there is reported to be an important quality of disaffection. From Border City, Simmons reports a tendency to withdraw from interpersonal relations and to seek safety in the haven of the home, but one does not receive an impression of the degree of threat and danger impinging the chicanos of Border City as is reported from Frontera and Mexiquito.

It has been suggested that in a society whose members strive to achieve valued goals by means of incongruous instrumental behavior, qualities of disaffection and anxiety will be prominent. More specifically it was suggested that such qualities appear in association with participation by individuals who have been socialized in an atomistic social system but who are seeking to achieve highly evaluated goals, which are controlled by individuals not members of the nuclear family.

Simmons proposes an alternative explanation, offering distrust generated in a fragile ego as an antecedent variable. He hypothesizes that in Border City the ease and regularity with which social relations are fractured depends on the sensitivity of the adult ego. In Border City, writes Simmons, adult egos are hurt quickly by the slightest criticism, and insults are remembered forever. He postulates that brittleness of relationships is a consequence of fragile egos which, in turn, are caused by discontinuity during socialization. In infancy and early childhood a youngster is the center of attention in a chicano home in Border City, and Simmons describes those places as infant-centered. After the first years of childhood a father's relations with his child changes from warm affection to brusqueness and coolness. A similar developmental sequence is noted in Mexiquito. If Simmons' explanation of the connection between the ethos and the social system characteristic of Border City is acceptable, then it also serves to explain the connection between the two in Mexiquito.

First, Simmons' post-factum explanation is reasonable and credible, although it contains several difficulties. One of these lies in his contention of a discontinuity in the relationship between a father and his children in Border City; I have noted the same phenomenon in Mexiquito, but there discontinuity is confined to the bond between the father and his child, and does not seem to extend to others of the family. Furthermore, quite unlike her brother, a girl is not thrust into a presumably hostile world outside the home where she would be expected to fend for herself; just the reverse. In each of the respective populations, relations between a child and its mother, or its female siblings, is *not* characterized by discontinuity. Indeed, Simmons describes chicano children in Border City as carried everywhere by their mother or older sisters. The warmth of the relationship between a mother and her children is readily observed and perdures over many years. Although there is no quarrel with Simmons' observations of the relationship obtaining between a father and his child, the observed *continuity* in the socialization of a child by its mother and sisters makes difficult a conclusion that discontinuity in socialization gives rise to generalized disaffection and a sense of unpredictability in social life.

Although it is possible to some extent to factor out what Simmons discerns as the cause of a fragile ego in Border City, there may well be other causes which contribute to frail egos among the chicanos of that city and, by extension, those of New Lots. Because there are no primary psychological data available it is presently impossible either to accept or to disregard Simmons' hypothesis, which seeks to explain a connection between brittle social relationships beyond the family and a perception of the social environment as a dangerous and threatening field of relationships. Simmons' hypothesis provides an alternative explanation.

Latin American Areas

Tzintzuntzan

The similarities between Mexiquito and Tzintzuntzan, a peasant village in central Mexico, are striking. In Tzintzuntzan the essential social units are nuclear families; beyond those minimal units social relationships are organized by means of dyadic contracts. Personalism is a salient characteristic of such two-person relationships in Tzintzuntzan.

George M. Foster, whose research has elucidated Tzintzuntzan's social system, writes that a neolocal nuclear family represents the ideal, as well as being in fact the most common form of residence group. Following their marriage, newlyweds often reside in the home of either of their parents until the birth of a child, after which event the younger couple establishes its own separate domicile. Although the site on which they construct their residence may prove to be adjacent to that of the parents, each nuclear family household represents a "social isolate."[14] Furthermore, the village contains no social classes, lineages, functional extended families, or voluntary associations. All of these are notable by their absence.[15] Moreover, "People consistently are reluctant to work with others toward group goals."[16]

As Foster so keenly observes, the preceding description need not imply that the residents of this village do not have *any* means whereby to organize behavior to achieve social and other goals. Indeed, it is Foster's unique contribution to offer a model to explain an alternate system of organizational behavior which he finds to be characteristic of Tzintzuntzan social life. The alternative has as its major social characteristics the following:

1. Contracts between persons are dyadic in that they involve two people, no more.

2. Such "contracts are non-corporate since social units such as villages, barrios, or extended families are never bound" as entities to one another.

3. Contracts are informal and depend upon neither ritual nor legal bases.

4. As a consequence of the preceding, contracts continue viable only at the pleasure of the contractants.[17]

Tzintzuntzan's atomistic social system is found to be associated with a very narrow range of persons (kin as well as nonkin), on whom an individual feels he can depend and to whom he feels a sense of obligation. As the author notes:

---

[14] Foster, "Dyadic Contract: Mexican Peasant Village," p. 1180.
[15] *Ibid.*, pp. 1176, 1177.
[16] *Ibid.*, p. 1190.   [17] *Ibid.*, p. 1174.

Except for obligations toward elderly parents, married couples feel little economic responsibility beyond the nuclear family toward relatives simply because they are relatives. Rather, beyond the nuclear family, the outer world, including relatives, is viewed with great reserve. Villagers . . . tend to distrust their neighbors, be suspicious of each other's motives, speak ill of one another, engage in back-biting and petty bickering, try to tear down those who get ahead, and be reluctant to join in co-operative enterprises of any kind.[18]

Even the closest of friends do not accept one another without reservations.[19] The closeness of fit between Tzintzuntzan's social system, in which nuclear families and personalistic dyadic rather than corporate relationships are predominant characteristics, and salient qualities of anxiety and disaffection are remarkably similar to that which obtains in the lower Rio Grande Valley settlements. The similarity between these societies and still others is equally striking.

Aritama

Similar to the Mexican-American and Tzintzuntzano societies, Aritama, a town in the Colombian highlands, suggests itself for comparison.[20]

As in the preceding instances, households in Aritama are composed of narrow and shallow kin groups. However, unlike the previously described ways of life, in Aritama matrifocality and a high incidence of polygamous relationships are important features of social life. The combination of these two additional factors contributes to differential participation of males and females in Aritama society.

Cooperation within the female line of a kin-group is much stronger than in the male line. A woman can practically always count on the active help of her mother, grandmother, sisters, or daughters and finds in this group a kind of security that is almost completely lacking in the situation of the male. A man . . . is an isolated individual and finds little or no support in his family of orientation and his kin-group. His economic and social security lies in his work, not in the combined labor effort of a group.[21]

Recently, however, the isolation of young men has lessened due to the formation of very loosely organized neighborhood cliques (pandillas), in which are found neither rites of initiation nor rules of

---

[18] *Ibid.*, p. 1180.   [19] *Ibid.*, p. 1184.
[20] Gerardo and Alicia Reichel-Dolmatoff, *The People of Aritama.*
[21] *Ibid.*, pp. 157–158.

conduct. As a matter of fact, "adults pay little attention to the activities of these gangs, and even for the boys themselves they are not of great importance. Loyalties change easily and membership fluctuates greatly."[22]

Although the people of Aritama do, in fact, arrange themselves into hierarchic strata based on differential attribution of status and influence, their criteria are so particularistic as to defy interpretation of strata as socio-economic "classes" in the usual sense of the term. For example, attribution of status is dependent on the following particularistic traits: phenotype, legitimacy of birth, extent of participation in community affairs, social and religious conduct, amount of formal education, location of domicile, traditions associated with subject's surname, and whether his marriage has been sanctified by the church. Moreover, the place in the system of stratification which is accorded one individual by another varies in relation to the personal esteem in which the former is held by the latter. "Envy, prestige behavior, traditional attitudes toward certain families, and the marked intrasocial hostility which characterize all inter-personal relations within the community are all factors which contribute to the interpretation and application of these criteria."[23] The emphasis on particularistic as opposed to universalistic criteria for the assignment of status is clearly stated by the authors when they note that "Even within the same nuclear family not all members occupy the same class-status."[24] "Finally people will say that each individual represents 'a class apart,' a unique phenomenon that cannot be grouped with others."[25] Here, as in other aspects of Aritama social organization, personalism overrides more objective considerations.

The people of Aritama cannot be said not to organize themselves into instrumental groups; two lay Catholic groups, the Daughters of Mary and a male counterpart, Brethren of the Sacred Heart, are present—but their memberships are inconsiderable.[26] There are also spasmodic cooperative work groups, but these small combinations are, in general, based on kinship ties. Exceptions to that generaliza-

---

[22] *Ibid.*, pp. 200–201.   [23] *Ibid.*, pp. 136–137.   [24] *Ibid.*, p. 136.

[25] *Ibid.*, p. 137. A specific finding, which accords with John Gillin's earlier generalizations about Latin American ethos components in "Ethos Components in Modern Latin American Culture" (*American Anthropologist*, LVII [June, 1955], 488–500).

[26] Reichel-Dolmatoff, *People of Aritama*, p. 343.

tion are groups formed for the purpose of exploiting a fishing site, for clearing lands for cultivation, and, less often, for the construction and clearing of paths and roads. Such extrakin groups are formed to achieve immediate goals; they disintegrate as soon as the specific task has been accomplished, if not before.[27]

The ephemeral nature of cooperative work groups in Aritama is consonant with the general absence of corporate group formations in this society. It remains but to note that Colombian peasants fail to conceive of their settlement as a community in the sense of a group of neighbors who value their interdependence. "The concept of forming a community, of all being *aritameros*, is rarely openly expressed and, when suggested is not found desirable."[28] Except on those occasions when an individual finds himself under attack by an outsider, it is rare, indeed, for one of Aritama to "generalize as far as to say, 'we' of 'our village'."[29] Needless to say, there is no evidence of organized activities in which the entire village or any substantial sector of it works together toward common goals.

As in preceding cases, associated with such a social system is a prominence of interpersonal hostility, suspiciousness, and invidiousness. Those qualities are distinctly present in the form of overt gossip, but they are even more dramatically demonstrated during discussions of health and illness. In Aritama, as in Mexiquito, the linkage between illness and other aspects of social behavior cannot be underestimated.

Disease continuously menaces the aritameros and:

. . . falling ill is always interpreted as the result of sorcery, as a vengeance, or as a punishment meted out by God but more often by ancestral spirits which use human agency. Disease is, therefore, an instrument that is used by others to vex or destroy a chosen victim. Even the slightest indisposition is thought to be caused in this manner, and disease or death are always attributed to the malevolence of others. The common saying is: 'no one dies without having been made to.'[30]

In this suspicious-ridden atmosphere any calamity is immediately attributed to the magic of an enemy who, through ill-will and envy, caused the trouble. Only a very small circle of close relatives are excluded from magical aggression . . . and *beyond the elementary family anybody is suspect.*[31]

27 *Ibid.*, pp. 211, 230, 257–258.
28 *Ibid.*, p. 137.
29 *Ibid.*, p. 258.   30 *Ibid.*, p. 278.
31 *Ibid.*, pp. 403–404 (emphasis added).

Space does not permit citation of the abundance of data which is provided by the Reichel-Dolmatoffs to support the argument that hostility, suspicion, and invidiousness are prominent qualities of social life in Aritama. The authors very clearly demonstrate the numerous mechanisms—inclusive of concepts of illness—whereby hostility and suspicion are projected by members of this society and, secondly, how those cultural vehicles separate out the elementary family as a basic security system from the remainder of the social environment.

The South Italians

In recent years anthropologists, sociologists, and others have interested themselves in southern Italy's villages and towns. Out of that interest much thought-provoking discussion has arisen. In a number of significant ways societies characteristic of South Italy are remarkably similar to Mexiquito. But, unlike Frontera and Border City, village society in southern Italy shares neither history nor tradition with Mexiquito.

South Italy is one of the world's underdeveloped and overpopulated regions; it suffers from high pressures of population on land resources and low standards of living. The area, known popularly as *Mezzogiorno*, comprises the following regions from north to south: Abruzzi e Molise, Campania, Apulia, Basilicata (Lucania), Calabria. Although Sicily and Sardinia are geographically a part of the South, their history and traditions distinguish them from the five regions. Consequently, Sicily and Sardinia are excluded from this investigation.

In this section three independent studies of village life in southern Italy are considered; the first is by a sociologist, the others by anthropologists. The villages are Montegrano in Lucania, Cortina d'Aglio in Abruzzi e Molise, and Avellino in Campania.[32] Reference will also be made to understandings attained of the region by prominent

---

[32] Edward C. Banfield (with the assistance of Laura Fasano Banfield), *The Moral Basis of a Backward Society;* Leonard W. Moss and Stephen C. Cappanari, "Patterns of Kinship, Comparaggio and Community in a South Italian Village," *Anthropological Quarterly*, XXXIII (January, 1960), 24–32; Frank Cancian, "The Southern Italian Peasant: World View and Political Behavior," *Anthropological Quarterly*, XXXIV (January, 1961), 1–18.

novelists and a philosopher; the latter views are substantially in accord with the others.[33]

In this region, conditions of an inadequate, impoverished land-base associated with an insufficient technological knowledge by which to effectively exploit the available resources, make the populace one of the poorest in the Western World. It is estimated, for example, that average income in the South falls 60 per cent below the average of rural Italy. Like the rest of this area, the regions in which are located the three villages studied are characterized by economies based on agriculture. It is estimated that more than 74 per cent, 75 per cent, and 47 per cent of the populations of Abruzzi e Molise, Lucania, and Campania, respectively, are engaged in agriculture.[34] (The relatively low percentage of agriculturally employed in Campania is accounted for by the fact that this region includes Naples, a city with a population estimated at one million.) Furthermore, the three villages are located in the interior, away from the coast; consequently there are available few alternatives to sufficiency agriculture as the basis of livelihood. The peasant farmers in the South live in compact settlements, a demographic pattern quite unlike the isolated family farm (*podere*) of Central Italy. Landholdings in the South tend to be quite small, 38 per cent of the holdings are under five hectares, according to Dickinson's calculations.[35]

Probably the most striking social phenomenon in the region is a stratification into two groups: those who own land and those who do not; ownership of land overrides the question of whether the quality or size of the holding permits it to be exploited for anything other than sufficiency cultivation. Objective observers are in agreement that ownership of land is of far greater significance as a symbol of social status than is the real economic worth of the holdings.[36] A wide schism exists between those who labor with their hands on the land and those who are occupied in any other form of employment;

[33] See L. W. Moss and W. H. Thomson, "The South Italian Peasant: Literature and Observation," *Human Organization*, XVIII (Spring, 1959), 35–42; F. G. Friedman, "The World of 'La Miseria'," *Partisan Review*, XX (March–April, 1953), 218–231.

[34] Robert E. Dickinson, *The Population Problem in Southern Italy: An Essay in Social Geography*, p. 13, Table II.

[35] *Ibid.*, p. 28.

[36] *Ibid.*, p. 42; Banfield, *Moral Basis*, p. 69; Friedman, "World of 'La Miseria'," p. 223.

the distinction is a cardinal feature of the social system. Those who are at the lowest level of the ranking system work with their hands, whereas those who belong to the "better classes" prove it by disdaining manual labor.[37] Moreover, the class system is "closed" rather than "open." Mobility from the social class which labors on land to more prestigious strata is effectively closed to all but a rare exception. To all intents and purposes an individual born into a family of laborers will die a member of the same social class; his or her fortune is predetermined by an inability to earn a livelihood sufficient to achieve the cultural symbols pertinent to upward mobility. Because the only alternative to farming in this depressed region is commerce or the professions, both of which require some amount of schooling, there is little opportunity for someone ambitious to advance his status. To enhance one's social-class standing, achievement of appropriate education, clothing, private land, or other source of nonlaboring income are prerequisites. Absence of the means to acquire those symbols of status places an effective ceiling on the upwardly mobile. That ceiling blocks aspirations for enhanced prestige throughout the rural areas of southern Italy.

Since all the lands are worked by persons other than those who own them, it is pertinent to examine the nature of the relationship which obtains between the landowner and those he employs as laborers, share croppers, and tenants. The practice of renting or cropping landholdings is known as *colonia parziaria,* or *compartecipazione.* Agreements between owner and tenant, laborer, or cropper are verbal and impermanent; continuity of an agreement depends on the mutual esteem in which each of the parties continues to hold the other. Dickinson notes that in so precarious a world "Only the peasant is permanent."[38] Relations between tenant and owner, or farm laborer and those for whom he farms, are characterized by unpredictability, brittleness, inconstancy. Those who perform the work are permitted to do so only as long as their personal relationship with the owner justifies their employment. In short, contracts which determine one's livelihood are controlled by consensual bonds, rather than structured agreements. Unlike other sections of Italy the South

[37] Friedman, "World of 'La Miseria'." See also Donald S. Pitkin's observations of the little regard peasants hold for their lands in another southern village ("A Consideration of Asymetry in the Peasant-City Relationship," *Anthropological Quarterly,* XXXII [October, 1959], 164).

[38] Dickinson, *Population Problem,* p. 47.

was never a region in which classic feudal relations reigned, and as a consequence patterns of responsibility between owners and those who labor on the land are absent. As one observer notes, "The laborer may be able to get help from one of his employers in an emergency, but he cannot depend on it."[39] Those peasants who wish to leave the land in order to seek employment in northern urban centers are prevented from doing so because of a national law which stipulates that "the call" to work must be initiated by an employer.[40] Now to an examination of features of the social life in each of the representative southern villages.

Montegrano

In Montegrano one-fourth of all family heads are farm laborers, whose employment hinges on verbal agreements between themselves and the owners or tenants of holdings. One-half of all heads of families are owners or tenants of farms, most of whom hire others to work the land. On the other hand, many of the holdings are so small that the owners must work on somebody else's land to produce enough for their families to subsist. Unlike circumstances in some other villages, in Montegrano a share cropper tends to work the land with relatively long-term security; he "usually has a written two-year contract."[41] But, in spite of better security, "with few exceptions, the peasant loathes the land."[42] Unfortunately, comparative estimates from Avellino (Campania) are unavailable.

Behavior and interpersonal relations in Montegrano are described in very general terms. Here as elsewhere in the region, specific observations of interpersonal behavior are unfortunately rare.[43] Banfield's observations lead him to state that individuals in Montegrano are so much a part of their nuclear family that they cannot be viewed apart from it. A person's obligations are confined to a narrow and shallow social group: his nuclear family. The bounds of his social responsibilities are circumscribed by the *interesse* or advantage of his nuclear family.[44] Indeed, so clearly does that elemental

---

[39] Banfield, *Moral Basis*, p. 57.

[40] Ignacio Silone writes tellingly of two peasants who break the law in order to seek work in an urban center, and the misery they encounter (*Fontamara* [rev. ed.], Chapter 8).

[41] Banfield, *Moral Basis*, p. 51.

[42] *Ibid.*, p. 37.

[43] An exception is Joseph Lopreata's "Interpersonal Relations: The Peasant's View," *Human Organization*, 21, No. 1 (1962).

[44] Banfield, *Moral Basis*, p. 115.

social unit stand forth from all others that Banfield writes: "In the Montegrano mind, any advantage that may be given to another is necessarily at the expense of one's own family.[45] Those who are not members of the family group are potential enemies to be regarded with suspicion. In Montegrano one may understand social behavior by postulating that the villagers act as if they were following this rule: "Maximize the material short-run advantage of the nuclear family; assume that all others will do likewise."[46] Banfield carries his analysis of the relationship between the family as an institution and the remainder of the social system further: He writes that Italians whose behavior is predicated on the above rule act amorally with persons outside the family circle, but they act in a different fashion, that is, morally, with those within the small familial circle. The significant family unit is narrow and shallow, consisting of a father, a mother, and their unmarried children. "In so fearful a world, a parent must do all he can to protect his family. He must preoccupy himself exclusively with its *interesse*. The *interesse* of the family is its material, short-run advantage."[47] Those who are not in the family circle are regarded with fear and hostility; to do otherwise would be to lay one's self and family open to attack. Aside from his obligations to enhance his own aspirations, the Montegranesi's responsibilities are to the elemental family unit.

Given the small size of the family unit and the intensity of an individual's interaction within it, one might presume that acquaintanceships and friendships would provide supplementary social comforts, but "Friends are luxuries the Montegranesi feel they cannot afford." According to villagers one has more to fear from friends and neighbors than others because they know more of your personal life, and they are more likely to engage in invidious emulation. One does, however, extend his family by creation of godparental ties with others. Such bonds in principle are close and immutable; but one forges few such ties, because each of these bonds permits one more person access to the household, there to seduce the womenfolk, so it is feared. Cousins and godfathers, it is said, are to be watched most carefully of all!

The central theme of Montegranesi existence is the family of procreation. "Goodness and badness exist for him mainly in connection

---

[45] *Ibid.*
[46] *Ibid.*, p. 85.
[47] *Ibid.*, p. 115.

with two statuses, that of 'parent' and that of 'outsider-who-may-affect-the-family'."[48] The only way in which a person may enter the latter category is to conduct himself in such a way that his presence poses no threat, real or imaginary, to one's family of procreation.

In Montegrano there is no one to take responsibility for works which aim to enhance the common welfare; in fact, to some, the concept of a commonweal is incomprehensible. Nor is there such a concept as "leadership" used in the sense of an individual acting in such a manner as to guide others toward a common goal. Banfield finds the "nearest approximation to leadership is the patron-client relationship." By dispensing favors small or large a well-to-do Montegranesi accumulates a clientele of those who owe him favors. "Such clients constitute a 'following,' perhaps, but the patron is not a 'leader' in any significant sense."[49] The absence of that concept is the more noteworthy in that a number of situations exist which seem to call for a leader, for example, work gangs. As a matter of fact, anyone who accepts a leadership task is assumed to be exploiting the others to his own advantage. If a Montegranesi were to volunteer his services in a leadership capacity, the others would reject him out of mistrust.

In Montegrano, social relationships are hierarchized and asymetric; there are those who control power and others who solicit from them protection and assistance. The former may be comprised of persons whose landholdings permit them to offer work and livelihood to others, but it also includes individuals who as merchants or professionals are called on to extend credit or make cash loans. A physician is asked to provide the services for which he is trained without immediate recompense, for example, or a lawyer to advance a small loan. Favors are dispensed benevolently at the discretion of the powerholder since there is no technique by which such protection or assistance may be demanded by dint of application of pressures (Montegranesi seek to forge bonds of godparenthood with those they are least likely to have dealings with in business). In a village in which all laborers and artisans, as well as most tenants and petty landowners, live at a subsistence level, crises forever threaten.[50] In such emergencies the victim is dependent on the "kindness" of an employer or other benefactor, "but he cannot

[48] *Ibid.,* p. 132.
[49] *Ibid.,* p. 100.
[50] *Ibid.,* pp. 71, 74.

depend on it."[51] Remaining on friendly terms with those who dispense such benevolence is the only assurance available to those who must solicit assistance. "The peasant wants to be polite and amiable (*civile*) and he knows that a time will come when the gentleman can give or withhold a favor or an injury."[52] To cite Friedmann's felicitous phrase, "one does not so much 'achieve' anything as 'obtain' something," in South Italy.[53]

Only one voluntary association in Montegrano exists, a "circle" of twenty-five card-playing upper-class men, who come together to pass the time of day. Political parties exist in the village, but they are of little consequence. Voters and party officials shift their allegiances from party to party for personal reasons, rather than because of relative attractiveness of party platforms. Until termination of the Second World War political parties did not even exist in the village. (The obvious exception was the Fascist Party in which membership was mandatory, but participation negligible.) The church and its organized associations are given short shrift by the men, and not even many of the women participate in church services. Banfield estimates that Sunday mass is attended by 350 people out of a total population of almost 3,500, and most of those attending are females. In church the Montegranesi asks and hopes for protection which God and the saints may dispense, but there is not any way in which such assistance may be demanded, nor may he be assured help will be offered. God, like man, is motivated whimsically; and "Like God, the saints are capricious and demanding, however devotedly one serves them, one cannot be sure of their favor."[54] Montegranesi act as if their behavior was predicated on a comprehension of the world as composed of more and less powerful figures, inclusive of God, saints, and man. An individual neither achieves nor demands, but seeks to guide in his direction some of the benevolences that others control. The social behavior which Banfield finds in Montegrano typifies those found elsewhere in southern Italy.

Avellino

Cancian, working in Avellino, discovers, for example, that an individual may only *hope* that others more powerful will prove them-

---

[51] *Ibid.*, p. 57.
[52] *Ibid.*, pp. 76–77.
[53] Friedmann, "The World of 'La Miseria'," p. 226.
[54] Banfield, *Moral Basis*, p. 313.

selves benevolent.[55] The residents of Avellino act as if their world was structured hierarchally into more and less powerful personages, and members of each such aggregation are treated accordingly. Congruent with such a world is the glaring absence of concepts like "leader" and "community." Indeed, Cancian finds no word at all in Italian which is equivalent to our English "leader" or "community." He suggests that the Italian words which are most similar to the concept rendered in English as "leadership" all suggest someone who commands, one with *autorita*, for example, *capo, comandante,* or *duce*. And, in Avellino, "The peasant, lacking confidence to do for himself and lacking any expectation of leadership, awaits benevolent *autorita*, not leadership."[56] In Avellino, Cancian finds it difficult even to discuss with natives the village or all of its residents in some unitary sense, for there are no words to describe such holism.[57] The village is perceived as an aggregation of small family units, and social interaction is seen in terms of the behavior of individuals. Friedman provides a label for this way of understanding one's social universe: *personalismo*.[58]

Bagnoli del Trigno

Located in the province of Campobasso, Bagnoli del Trigno boasts a population of 3,200.[59] As is true in the remainder of the region most of its residents are dependent on agriculture for their livelihood. The settlement pattern is that of a compact village, from which farmers disperse each day to the lands that they cultivate. Large landholdings are unimportant in this sector of the Mezzogiorno; most tracts are small, and they are rented or cropped by fellow villagers. As is elsewhere true, contractual agreements between those who cultivate the land and those by whom they are employed tend to be temporary and brittle; the agreements rest precariously on continuance of the goodwill each party feels for the other.

The authors find that Bagnoli del Trigno's social system hinges on the nuclear families of which it is composed. The importance of the nuclear family far exceeds that of any other social unit in the village. Unlike others who describe village life in this region, Moss and Thomson describe the concept of family as subsuming two institu-

---

[55] Cancian, "The Southern Italian Peasant," p. 10.
[56] *Ibid.*, p. 13.
[57] *Ibid.*
[58] Friedmann, "The World of 'La Miseria'," p. 225.
[59] Moss and Thomson, "The South Italian Peasant."

tions. The more important of the two—*il nucleo centrale* of the social system—has reference to the families of procreation. The larger
and less important of the two units—*la famiglia*—refers to one's
consanguineal family as well as those to whom one is related through
marriage. The more important unit, *il nucleo centrale*, includes
one's spouse and children, as well as the few godparents contracted
during one's life cycle. It is described as "father-dominated but
mother-oriented."[60] To those few persons are restricted one's obligations, and persons outside that small circle of relations are not
even permitted access to the home.[61] Beyond that narrow and shallow unit, an attitude of cooperative effort "as a value in *any* terms,
does not exist. . . . Moreover, no value of cooperation exists for the
formation of voluntary associations which might lead to group action and/or group solutions to mutual problems."[62]

Cortina d'Aglio

Leonard Moss also did field work in another of Italy's southern
villages, continuing a study commenced by Stephen Cappannari.[63]
This village, Cortina d'Aglio, resembles "hundreds of villages" in
the region.[64] We find that 86 per cent of its work force is agriculturally employed and 81 per cent of the total population resides in the
village proper.[65] But Cortina d'Aglio differs in one important respect
from Montegrano: individual, private landholdings predominate in
the former, although the tracts seldom exceed five to seven acres.[66]
The landholdings are so fragmented that they are adequate only for
sufficiency cultivation.

As is true throughout the southland, the essential feature of the
social system is the nuclear family. This *nucleo centrale* is tightly
knit and headed by the oldest surviving male. It is a social group
with centrifugal tendencies; at marriage children establish new
households apart from either set of parents. Closely associated with
each nuclear family are first cousins (*fratello-cugino*) and godparents of each of the members.[67] Godparental ties are forged at the

[60] *Ibid.*, p. 38.
[61] *Ibid.*, p. 39.
[62] *Ibid.*
[63] Moss and Cappannari, "Patterns of Kinship."
[64] *Ibid.*, p. 24.
[65] *Ibid.*
[66] *Ibid.*
[67] *Ibid.*, p. 29.

time of baptism, confirmation, and marriage. The godparent is, ideally, treated with deference. His or her specific obligation to a godchild is to set a moral example. The godparent "is the only one outside the family circle in whom the child may confide."[68] In Cortina d'Aglio the investigators find the allegiance that one holds to the *nucleo centrale* so overwhelming as to depreciate all other interests and bonds. So powerful a force is the nuclear family that it actually stifles the growth of voluntary associations in this village and elsewhere, according to the authors.[69] In Cortina, associations between persons not bound by structural ties of family or godparenthood are extremely brittle. The local "political party, as an example of a voluntary association, is, at best, an unstable compromise of highly individualistic attitudes."[70] Another type of voluntary association once existed but is now extinct: "At one time, a joint confraternity composed of members of both parishes arranged the religious celebrations but, like most voluntary associations, fell apart because of inter-parish and inter-familial rivalries."[71] A veterans' organization still exists, "but there is no active membership." What little identification exists between the settlement and its residents is associated with the belief that one may distrust less those near whom one resides, than persons from other villages.[72] On the other hand, "it cannot be said that this identification necessarily leads to community participations and community responsibility."[73] Like those in Montegrano, the villagers of Cortina d'Aglio cope with problems as individuals, not as organized groups.

Villages in Calabria and Lucania

In another work, one which focuses on village life in the provinces of Calabria and Lucania, Friedmann finds social behavior and ethos similar to that already described. Sections of Calabria and Lucania with which Friedmann is particularly familiar demonstrate economic conditions characterized by a poor soil, which has been exploited for centuries without care or enrichment. Landholdings tend to be very small, the tracts averaging between six and eight acres.[74] The most significant feature of the social life is a stratification of so-

---

[68] *Ibid.*, pp. 29, 31.
[69] *Ibid.*, pp. 28, 29, 31; Moss and Thomson, "The South Italian Peasant, p. 40.
[70] Moss and Cappannari, "Patterns of Kinship," p. 27.
[71] *Ibid.*, p. 28.
[72] *Ibid.*, p. 25.
[73] *Ibid.*, p. 31.
[74] Friedmann, "World of 'La Miseria'," p. 218.

ciety into those who work with their hands and the others who disdain manual labor. Peasants perceive landed nobility and governmental officials with "almost pathological distrust."[75]

According to Friedmann the villagers he knows are incapable of cooperating "in the solution of the most insignificant problem of daily life . . ."[76] Indeed, in such a village, he writes, to love one's neighbor is to drop one's guard, and to drop one's guard in such a world is equivalent to committing suicide, according to the existential point of view. The barriers between nonkin are quite congruent with an incapability to cooperate in nonkin groups, but, as Banfield previously cautioned, an inability to organize and concert one's behavior with others is not indicative of a fatalistic way of life; the South Italian *does* show concern over issues which affect him vitally, or the well-being of his immediate family, and he *does* cope with problems in realistic fashion. Indeed, "There is reason to believe that the southerner's pessimism exists where social rather than individualistic action is called for; he is, then, realistic but not necessarily fatalistic."[77]

Just as southern Italy's social behavior may be portrayed in sweeping terms, so are other generalizations widely applicable. Probably the best description of South Italian ethos is to be found in Banfield's volume. In that work the human condition is painted in terms of a world at war, all against all, in which man is at the mercy of other men, subject to a capricious God and whimsical saints. Banfield and others write that each villager participates in social life as if he were thinking of no one but himself, or, at most, of the advantage to be gained for his family of procreation—*il nucleo centrale*.[78] They describe a world of *la miseria* in which villagers are overwhelmed by *preoccupaziones*: a state of mingled worry, fear, anxiety, and foreboding.

In Cortina d'Aglio there exists a continuum of distrust: "Through bitter experience the villager has learned to trust, or distrust least, those who live within the sound of the local church bell (*campanalismo*)," and "if one *must* deal with someone outside the circle of kin, better a *paesano* (fellow-villager) than a stranger."[79] From these accounts one might surmise that villagers' antagonisms are

[75] *Ibid.*, p. 221.   [76] *Ibid.*, p. 225.
[77] Banfield, *Moral Basis*, p. 40.
[78] *Ibid.*, p. 173.
[79] Moss and Cappannari, "Patterns of Kinship," p. 25 . . (emphasis added).

projected away from their intimate associations, and that the more socially distant the individual the more likelihood that he will serve as a target. But disquieting accounts from other villages in the same region suggest this to be far too simple a surmise. Banfield, for example, finds that members of different social strata do not project their hostilities against one another as members of other strata. "In Montegrano there is not this sense of opposed identities whether in politics or in other spheres."[80] On the other hand, Friedmann comments that in Calabria and Lucania, "The bitterest antagonism . . . exists between two groups which do manual labor, the peasants and artisans . . ." and political behavior *does* reflect opposed identities between occupational groups.[81] Some other observers contend that the greater access an individual has to one's home the more of a threat he represents. "One can protect one's family from the envy of friends by not having any. But one cannot avoid having neighbors."[82]

Furthermore, Friedmann notes that the world of *la miseria* is by no means confined to poverty-stricken farm laborers, artisans, or tenant farmers. It is "an outlook not limited to the landless peasants," he writes, "but equally influential with the artisans, the professional men, and even the land owners—a point of view with which Banfield is in accord.[83]

In startling contrast to the prominence of anxiety and disaffection in extrafamilial social relationships is the world of the nuclear-family household, which is described as an environment in which predictability and mutual trust reign supreme. This skewed distribution of anxiety and disaffection, a relative absence within the nuclear-family household and a remarkable salience outside of it, demonstrates the comparability between these South Italian villages, the border settlements of the lower Rio Grande Valley, and Tzintzuntzan and Aritama as well. Moreover, the general distribution of this phenomenon among all strata of these populaces is of considerable interest inasmuch as the most current anthropological explanation of the qualities of interpersonal relations found in peasant, or

---

[80] Banfield, *Moral Basis*, p. 71.
[81] Friedmann, "World of 'La Miseria'," pp. 223, 224.
[82] Banfield, *Moral Basis*, p. 122.
[83] Friedmann, "World of 'La Miseria'," p. 220; Banfield, *Moral Basis*, pp. 125, 174. See also the many novels which describe South Italian life, among which are Ignacio Silone, *Fontamara*; Giuseppe Verga, *The House by the Medlar Tree*; and Roger Vailland, *The Law*.

formerly peasant, societies is that they are a function of a large number of individuals and families vying for an insubstantial amount of productive resources, land in particular.[84] Discovery that economically well-off gentry, government officials, physicians, and lawyers perceive social relations in very much the same way as agricultural laborers and other unskilled and lowpaid workers raises the query as to whether an alternative explanation might be more widely applicable.

One common factor among all strata of the societies under discussion is the overwhelming importance of the nuclear family and the failure of viable formal organizations other than the family to develop. Furthermore, there is the important role of the dyadic contract by means of which individuals engage with other individuals, even though they lack competence in organizing and maintaining viable groups for a common purpose. Finally, in each of the societies personalism very strongly colors all social relationships, whether they are between peers or between persons of different social strata. As an alternative to the explanation provided by Professor Foster, we advance the suggestion that persons in these settlements are socialized in such a way that they are enabled to effectively cope with a familial environment, but not with one which includes nonrelatives of considerable importance to them. Individuals act as if their social world were circumscribed by the nuclear family but, needless to add, they are required to rely on many others besides parents and siblings. The clustering of anxiety and disaffection around extrafamilial relations can be understood as a product of the incongruity between the instrumental social techniques they learn in order to manage others of their family and the social environment with which they really have to cope.

Unless one argues that the prominence of these qualities is somehow a built-in consequence of the relationships between these communities and the cosmopolitan cities on which they are dependent for market places and ideas, there is no reason to expect such prominence of anxiety and disaffection to be a constant element in all societies which are "peasant" by definition.[85] Neither need one expect to find this phenomenon restricted to peasant societies.[86]

[84] George M. Foster, "Interpersonal Relations in Peasant Society," *Human Organization*, 19, No. 4 (Winter, 1960–1961), 174–178.

[85] For current definitions of "peasant society," Alfred L. Kroeber, *Anthropology*, p. 284; Robert Redfield, *Peasant Society and Culture*.

[86] Compare with Foster, "Interpersonal Relations," p. 178.

The Ojibwa Indians

There are a number of anthropological studies of Ojibwa or Chippewa, Indians, some of which are historical, others contemporary. Aboriginally the Ojibwa gained their livelihood by means of hunting and gathering. Hunting grounds were owned and controlled by members of a nuclear family. Because food was obtained only with difficulty, hunger, even starvation, was a perennial problem.

In order to assure some modicum of control over his physical and social environment an Ojibwa had to seek assistance from powerful intercessor spirits, for without their aid a man was "powerless" or "empty," and his efforts to influence game were consequently impotent. But there was no assurance that an individual would secure that power or that, once secured, he could keep it.

Each winter the isolated nuclear family moved to its hunting grounds, where it remained alone until the spring thaw.[87] The difficulty of wresting a livelihood from a harsh environment demanded a distribution of a sparse population over a wide area. All observers concur that given the natural environment and available techniques of exploitation, isolation of each household was a logical consequence during the winter months. James, however, notes some evidence of larger Chippewa settlements during aboriginal periods.[88]

Ruth Landes' account of contemporary Ojibwa notes that dispersal of the population during winter months precluded interaction of nuclear families. But during summer and spring months some Ojibwa and Chippewa gather in large groups to exploit groves of sugar-producing trees; nevertheless, during those seasons of the year when the environment permits families to establish settlements there is "a remarkable perseverance of the winter habits. Individual families neighbor one another [in spring and summer] at fairly close quarters, and commonly two families live in one tent for the season. But each family, even when two families occupy one tent, works for itself as though isolated."[89] During those warmer months

---

[87] Ruth Landes, "The Personality of the Ojibwa," *Character and Personality*, VI (1, 1937–1938), 51–60; Victor Barnouw, *Acculturation and Personality among the Wisconsin Chippewa*, pp. 18, 71–72.

[88] Bernard J. James, "Some Critical Observations concerning Analyses of Chippewa 'Atomism' and Chippewa Personality," *American Anthropologist*, LVI (April, 1954), 283–286.

[89] Ruth Landes, *The Ojibwa Woman*, p. 1.

of the year settlements of Ojibwa are "only an aggregate of the families."[90] Landes notes that an Ojibwa

. . . never organizes comprehensive activities except in his personal name. If the village dances, it is because John gives a dance to which he issues personal invitations. There are no group hunts or fishing or berry-picking parties, but each person goes out by himself, never thinking of others except to wonder if they will get the jump on him.[91]

Landes finds striking the absence of a sense of responsibility for a group, and lack of identification with the summer settlement. She notes, also, that "It is as though the Ojibwa can never free himself from the wariness proper to winter, and at all times views the proximity of the Indians as a threat."[92] Moreover, even when Ojibwa find it necessary to associate with others for attainment of a mutually acceptable goal, "partnerships and teams often break up."[93] Furthermore, she observes that in spring and summer encampments children play games warily and suspiciously, something which does not occur when the games are played in the isolated family camp in winter.

Landes concludes that Ojibwa with whom she is familiar cannot cooperate with one another even under the best of circumstances. In that conclusion, others concur. Barnouw finds that "Even today, the average Chippewa household is a world in itself."[94] He finds Chippewa social life devoid of cooperative interaction beyond that which occurs between spouses. Barnouw contends that aboriginal Chippewa and Ojibwa did not associate in communal hunts, camp circles, councils of chiefs, or sodalities. Institutionalized leadership was notable by its absence. Even *symbols* of group integration were absent!

On today's reservations Wisconsin Chippewa evidence similar kinds of individualistic and nuclear-family-centered behavior. With the exception of attempts by a few men to coordinate rice-gathering activities and an instrumental group dedicated to promotion of a tourist "powwow," there are no signs of group activities among Chippewa familiar to Barnouw. Although organization of a tourist powwow is effective enough to reap a profit each year, most discus-

[90] Landes, "Personality of the Ojibwa," p. 53.
[91] *Ibid.*, p. 55.
[92] *Ibid.*
[93] *Ibid.*, p. 56.
[94] Barnouw, *Acculturation and Personality*, p. 16.

sions and decision-making in arrangements committees are accompanied by bickering and accusations of misappropriation of funds. Indeed, the honesty of the treasurer is usually suspected.[95]

Bernard James takes exception to Barnouw's reconstruction of aboriginal social life. James finds evidence suggesting that some Chippewa lived in settlements of several hundred residents. Moreover, James notes historical sources which describe large war parties marshalled by Chippewa. On the basis of such evidence he submits that Chippewa were quite able to coordinate activities of a large number of individuals; in other words, aboriginal Chippewa were less atomistic than once suspected. Landes agrees that Chippewa participated in large war parties, but she comments: "Even in a war party warriors refused to obey the traditional rules, violating the leader's orders with impunity."[96]

James' reconstruction of Chippewa social life leads him to offer an alternative explanation for Chippewa atomism.Here atomism appears to refer to a configuration comprised of individualistic exploitation of an environment, a psychological withdrawal of individuals from others, an absence of social cohesion, and an inability of Chippewa to engage in cooperative activities. Barnouw, however, hypothesizes that the prominence of the emotional qualities being discussed is produced by the persistence of an aboriginal atomistic social organization, which, in its turn, was brought about by the requisite individualistic exploitation of a very harsh environment. Another contributing factor to the Chippewa atomism was the inducement of a fear of sorcery during socialization. James reasons that aboriginal Chippewa were less atomistic than had been previously considered. He offers an hypothesis that the perception of social relations characteristic of the Lac Court Orielles Indians, among whom he did field work, is caused by ". . . the pauper economy and socially depressed conditions of the reservations today."[97] The ". . . persistent cultural 'atomism,' may in fact merely reflect situational factors which *emerged during* the reservation period."[98]

The crux of the difference between these rival explanations rests on reconstruction of aboriginal social life. For many years A. Irving Hallowell studied seventeenth- and eighteenth-century chronicles

[95] *Ibid.*, p. 17.
[96] Landes, "Personality of the Ojibwa," p. 58.
[97] James, "Some Critical Observations," p. 285.
[98] *Ibid.* (emphasis added).

of Chippewa and Ojibwa life. Hallowell has also had extensive personal experience with contemporary northern Ojibwa.

To Hallowell a paramount quality of Ojibwa and Chippewa social systems, both aboriginal and modern, is the absence of coherent groups other than small families. Indeed, he discovers a close connection to exist between the absence of cohering groups in these societies and a perception of others as "working against" one. In Hallowell's terms: "In other words, according to native theory one *should* be able to make a living unless something goes wrong, and, if something does go wrong, it is somebody's fault."[99] Hallowell utilizes the writings of missionaries and traders for their observations of aboriginal Indian life. He notes that Ojibwa of the seventeenth century were psychologically withdrawn and isolated from each other. Affect was replaced by pretended indifference produced by a wariness of others. Aboriginal Ojibwa life, as inferred by Hallowell, was rent by distrust, suspicion, and fear of sorcery.

Hallowell finds modern Saulteaux Ojibwa "almost identical" with descriptions rendered by Henry Schoolcraft a century ago. Schoolcraft, husband of an Ojibwa, wrote:

It became a prime object, in all classes, to suppress the exhibition of the feeling of nervousness, susceptibility, and emotion. He was originally a man of concealments. He always anticipated harm, never good. Fear and suspicion put double guards upon him. A look or a word might betray him, and he therefore often had not a look or a word to bestow.[100]

The seventeenth- and eighteenth-century chroniclers whom Hallowell cites portrayed Ojibwa as aggregations of individuals and nuclear families characterized by prominent qualities of threat and disaffection. The early chroniclers left no doubt that an atomistic ethos anteceded reservation life. Hallowell concludes "that in all probability the undercurrents of aggression . . . were even stronger in the past when native beliefs flourished in full strength and acculturative influence had not set in."[101] In fact he writes: ". . . I believe that it is reasonable to assert that the major factor which was at the root of the latent suspicion and distrust that colored the interpersonal

---

[99] A. Irving Hallowell, *Culture and Experience*, p. 145.

[100] Henry R. Schoolcraft, *Information Respecting the History, Conditions and Prospects of the Indian Tribes of the United States*, quoted in Hallowell, *Culture and Experience*, p. 143.

[101] *Ibid.*, p. 278.

relations of the Indians of earlier periods operates today."[102] That causal factor, according to Hallowell, is a fear of sorcery. "It is impossible for people to get together when their outlook is colored by the possibility of malevolence, particularly when there are no social institutions that demand a high degree of cooperation."[103] Hallowell's explanation appears to answer the question implicit in Landes' account: if isolation of the Ojibwa nuclear family is demanded by the sparse food supply during winter why do the "winter attitudes" persist in spring and summer?[104] Hallowell in effect answers that winter's attitudes persist in the villages of spring and summer *because* of a continuing pervasive fear of sorcery. The last hypothesis serves also to answer the issue of an incongruity which James finds between large settlements and the prominence of disaffection and anxiety. Hallowell implicitly contends that contiguity of residence does not necessarily give rise to community life if other variables intervene. On the basis of the ethnographic evidence from South Texas, Mexico, and South Italy, the present author lends that argument his hearty endorsement. In those societies people who live next to one another maintain their social distance and fail to enter cohering groups other than nuclear families. In all of the historically unrelated societies which have been compared with Mexiquito, an association is observed between an atomistically organized social system and the apparent importance of anxiety and disaffection which inhere in extrafamilial relationships but which are not found in relationships between members of the same elementary family. On the other hand, there come readily to mind other societies in which the norms outline a similar social system but in which those same emotional characteristics are of little importance. One thinks immediately, for example, of middle-class Parisian society.[105] Middle-class Parisians depict their household as clearly isolated from all except those of the immediate family. Despite those norms, however, neither anxiety nor disaffection are prominent in the perceptions which family members hold toward their neighbors.

A failure of anxiety and disaffection to assume prominence in the

[102] *Ibid.*, p. 147.
[103] *Ibid.*
[104] Landes, "Personality of the Ojibwa," p. 55.
[105] Rhoda Metraux and Margaret Mead, *Themes in French Culture: A Preface to a Study of French Community;* Jesse R. Pitts, "The Bourgeois Family and French Economic Retardation," and "The Family and Peer Groups," *A Modern Introduction to the Family*, Norman Bell and Ezra Vogel (eds.), pp. 266–286.

social relations of Parisian bourgeois in association with an atomistic social system as our formulation would lead us to expect, represents still another indication (if still others are required) of the hazards which inhere in the hypothesizing of universal correlations between social and cultural or emotional phenomena. Preferable are more modest—middle range—hypotheses which allow for the effect exercised by intervening variables, which, in particular instances, may very well modify the expected outcome. Inasmuch as the relevant literature in the case of Paris' middle class is not addressed to the same problems to which these pages are directed, it is difficult to identify features of social or economic life which may have worked against the expected association between an atomistic social system and a prominence of anxiety and disaffection. Such features would have to be factored out during the course of a, later, field investigation which would have as its intent the resolution of this particular problem.

By its very nature, the third of the problems posed in the introductory section cannot be answered in a definitive manner. Still, the regularity with which anxiety and disaffection are found to recur in association with social relationships outside the confines of the nuclear family in societies whose behavior is ordered by an atomistic social system suggests that additional cross-cultural studies with this problem in mind will justify the effort. As Fred Eggan has commented, "Generalizations do not have to be universal in order to be useful. If we can formulate the conditions under which social or cultural phenomena correlate or covary, such information will be exceedingly useful for the organization of further research."[106] Hopefully, the posing and discussion of the problem to which this chapter is addressed will stimulate colleagues to undertake additional research along this line.

Summary

Why do chicanos, themselves, attach qualities of anxiety and disaffection to their perceptions of social relations? An exploration and

---

[106] Fred Eggan, "Social Anthropology: Methods and Results," *Social Anthropology of North American Tribes*, Fred Eggan (ed.), p. 497.

explanation of this problem constitutes the third of the three aims
which were advanced in the Introduction.

It is discovered that although anxiety and disaffection are prominent features of perceptions of social relations, they are confined
to relations between an individual and persons not members of his
nuclear family. Consequently, a thesis is advanced that the anxiety
and disaffection which recur with such frequency when chicanos
discuss their relationships with nonfamily are a function of the incongruity which exists between the family-oriented social system
for which chicanos are socialized and the larger and far more
complex society with which they must contend. Because of the prominence of these emotional qualities in other societies in which the history, economic base, and social pressures are quite distinct from
Mexiquito's, but which are organized by a similar social system, it
is argued that the prominence of anxiety and disaffection is functionally interrelated with what is denoted as an atomistic social system, both together forming a configuration described as an atomistic-type society.

An atomistic-type society is one in which the social system is characterized by an absence of cooperation between nuclear families; in
which qualities of contention, invidiousness, and wariness are paramount in the perceptions which nuclear families hold of one another; and in which such behavior and emotional qualities are consonant with normative expectations.

Mexiquito is shown to be similar to the two other Mexican-American neighborhoods in the lower Rio Grande Valley. These three
communities are then compared with societies in Mexico, Colombia,
South Italy, and among the Ojibwa and Chippewa Indians—in all
of which a prominence of anxiety and disaffection covaries with nuclear family-oriented atomistic social systems.

Nevertheless, despite the suggestiveness of the above relationships,
the formulation proves not to be universally applicable. In another
society—among the Parisian bourgeoisie—a prominence of anxiety
and disaffection are not in evidence despite the presence of an atomistic social system, indicative of the presence of intervening variables
which are still unknown. Continued research on this problem will
enable researchers to factor out the particular intervening variables
which modify the expectation that, in general, an incongruity between socialization toward one kind of society and the necessity to

cope with very different circumstances, will be associated with a prominence of anxiety and disaffection.

It is hoped that this exploration of correlations between a specific kind of social system and the prominence of certain emotional qualities will stimulate interest in additional cross-cultural research with this type of problem in mind.

9. CONCLUSION AND SUMMARY

The preceding pages describe and analyze the social attitudes and behavior which characterize Mexican-Americans in a Texas city. The city of New Lots is young; its history dates only as far back as the period after the First World War. Throughout its brief history New Lots has been home for two groups of people, each of which traces its traditions to different sources. Those who are known as Anglos trace their heritage to the pioneering traditions of the United States and Canada, whereas those who live across the tracks from them in Mexiquito trace their historical roots to Mexico, and, ultimately, to Spain.

For neither of these two groups has it been easy to adapt to a new environment. The Anglo-American arrived in the Valley strongly motivated by pioneering values. He was firm in his belief that the region and the people who inhabited it were subject to improvement: They represented a challenge to these twentieth-century frontiersmen, one which was met head on. Since the arrival of large numbers of Anglos to the lower Rio Grande Valley, the delta lands have been successfully cleared of useless brush, the Rio Grande has been tamed, communications have been opened with such marketing centers as St. Louis, Chicago, and New York, and pleasant, clean towns and cities dot the region where only cattle and sheep had ranged.

With the same well-intentioned motivation which led to their remarkable success in utilizing the natural resources, the Anglos set about to meet the challenge posed by the presence of the Spanish-speaking group of ranchers and workers with whom they did not share basic values. Efforts to change the way of life of the Mexican-Americans have proved in some instances to be a rewarding experience to the Anglos, whereas other efforts have met with a dismaying rejection.

For the Mexican-American the novelty of life in New Lots has been doubly difficult. His movement to this city was not prompted by a dream of improving anything other than the social and economic security of himself and his family. Since their arrival the Spanish-speaking countrymen have been required to adjust their customary beliefs and behavior, which had evolved in a familiar environment of dispersed family hamlets where everyone spoke Spanish, everyone was a Catholic, and neighbors were relatives. They have had to adapt themselves to the unfamiliar environment in which they presently reside: a densely settled urban neighborhood in which a family is surrounded by nonrelatives and in which the formal institutions—police, judiciary, politics, education, and health— are all premised on a logic which is alien to chicanos and, contrary-wise, familiar to their Anglo counterparts. Each of these novel situations—life in a city and life in association with a dominant Anglo group—has demanded some considerable readjustment on the part of the residents of Mexiquito.

After two generations in this new, urban environment, those of Mexiquito continue to treat with others in personal terms and, to a remarkable extent, they continue their primary orientation to their small family units, instead of becoming active participants in clubs, civic groups, parent-teacher associations, or other kinds of nonfamily organizations. Professor Lyle Saunders has commented that a Spanish-speaking villager who undertakes life in an urban setting, especially one in which Anglos constitute a dominant social and economic force, "cannot be expected immediately to shed his cultural ways and take on those of the city."[1] Such adjustments take time.

---

[1] Lyle Saunders, "The Spanish-Speaking Population of Texas," *Inter-American Education, Occasional Papers*, No. 5, p. 212. Cf., Julian Samora and Richard F. Larson, "Rural Families in an Urban Setting: A Study in Persistence and Change," *Journal of Human Relations*, 9, No. 4 (1961), 949–503.

On the other hand, there is every reason to suspect that even when the people of Mexiquito do become fully adjusted to city life and even after they have had significant opportunities to decide which of the Anglo attitudes and behaviors they wish to adopt for themselves, the social life of these Mexican-Americans will never be a mirror-image of that which is characteristic of their Anglo-American neighbors. Assuredly, the evidence from such long-established urban centers as San Antonio, Austin, Laredo, and Brownsville in Texas; Denver, Colorado; San Jose, California; as well as Mexico City, Buenos Aires, and Rio de Janeiro, suggests that, unlike others, Latin Americans sustain a very viable way of life in cities while at the same time emphasizing familial orientations and associations which are based on personal, rather than contractual, relationships.[2] Indeed, at least one prominent historian, Richard M. Morse, writes strongly to this point when he warns: "Wherever we pick our way in the study of the modern Latin American city, we must be careful not to trip over concealed premises that derive from familiarity with West European or North Atlantic cities."[3]

The above is not meant to imply that the residents of Mexiquito are not changing, for nothing could be further from the truth. They are changing in ways which are sometimes subtle and at other times very evident. But none of these changes which are occurring today, and none which will occur in the future, take place without due consideration of the consequences. A chicano woman who brings a crying, diarrheal child to an Anglo physician does so on the assumption that the latter may be of assistance. On the other hand, she continues to take account of the advice offered by relatives that a physician neither understands nor has competence in such conditions, and that the time spent in his office might better be used with a lay healer. She is willing to consider the physician an acceptable alternative to lay healers because of a factor which overrides other considerations:

[2] The evidence derives from unpublished field notes on social organization in the Texas cities. See Saunders, "Spanish-Speaking Population of Texas"; Margaret Clark, *Health in the Mexican-American Culture;* Oscar Lewis, *Five Families,* and *The Children of Sánchez;* Anthony Leeds, "Brazilian Careers and Social Structure: An Evolutionary Model and Case History," American Anthropologist, 66, No. 6 (December, 1964), 1321–1348; Tomás Roberto Fillol, *Social Factors in Economic Development: The Argentine Case,* Chap. 5.

[3] Richard M. Morse, "Latin American Cities: Aspects of Structure and Functions," *Comparative Studies in Society and History,* 4 (July, 1962), 488.

her concern for the well-being of her child, which demands that every possible means be exploited to heal the sickness.

Another illustration is presented when a young man decides to foresake the use of Spanish and to use only English, even among his friends in Mexiquito. Such an action immediately brands him a "traitor," one who has "turned his back" on his traditional culture. An individual must reflect long and seriously the grave consequences of such a decision, yet a very few in Mexiquito have already taken such a course. They have done so on the basis of *their* understanding that chicanos would be better off if they were to become fully assimilated into the Anglo society. These are subtle changes; they represent decisions which are made individual by individual over the course of time, each decision affecting the process by which other persons choose between a traditional technique of an already well-understood mode of thinking or acting, and a way of coping with the world to which they have been newly introduced.

There are other, more apparent, changes which even now affect the people of Mexiquito. One of these is a universally felt need among young adults for English-language and literacy skills. No longer is the rejection of English extolled as it was among many of the older generation. Today, in the minds of youthful chicanos, English and literacy skills are closely linked with aspirations to leave the "stoop labor," which has customarily been the major source of income. Similarly, one does not encounter among younger people an orientation toward Mexico as opposed to the United States. They have relinquished the allegiance their parents felt toward the Republic to the south, and consider themselves to be integral parts of the social, economic, and political structure of Texas and the United States. Here is where they were raised, and here is their home. Those sentiments prevail despite the ambivalence of their social position, a condition which is so poignantly expressed by a Texas-born chicano youngster who asks of his Texas-born parents: "Am I an American citizen?"

The concern which these Spanish-speaking people of Mexiquito and elsewhere in the border region feel about their social status with respect to the larger society is shared by well-intentioned Anglos who find it difficult to understand why the chicanos think and behave as they do. It is worthy of note that the chicanos are just as puzzled by customary ways of the Anglo as the Anglos are by the chicano way of life. In New Lots each group has perceived the other through lenses peculiarly its own. A truly satisfactory resolution of the problem which derives from the settlement of two groups in the same city, each with distinctive traditions, will not be brought about by striving to make either group exactly like the other. Instead, this desired and necessary solution will be found when each attains understanding of the reasoning which lies behind the attitudes and conduct of the other. These pages are dedicated to that end.

BIBLIOGRAPHY

Abstract of Title of Lands of Llano Grande Plantation Company, Inc., (in the legal library of Mr. Gardner Smith and Associates).

Acta de Visita, 1767, Comargo, quoted in Betty Earle Dobkins, *The Spanish Element in Texas Water Law.*

Agricultural Geography of Latin America. Washington: Foreign Agricultural Service, U. S. Department of Agriculture, Miscellaneous Publication number 743, n.d.

Banfield, Edward C. (with the assistance of Laura Fasano Banfield). *The Moral Basis of a Backward Society.* Glencoe: The Free Press, 1958.

Barnes, J. A. "Class and Committees in a Norwegian Island Parish," *Human Relations,* 7, No. 1, (1954), 39–58.

Barnhart, Clarence L. (ed.). *The American College Dictionary.* New York: Harper and Brothers, 1960.

Barnouw, Victor. *Acculturation and Personality among the Wisconsin Chippewa.* Memoir 72, Menasha: American Anthropological Association, 1950.

———. "Chippewa Social Atomism," *American Anthropologist,* 63 (October, 1961), 1006–1013.

Beals, Ralph. "Acculturation," *Anthropology Today.* Edited by A. L. Kroeber. Chicago: University of Chicago Press, 1953.

Benedict, Ruth. *Patterns of Culture.* New York: Mentor Books, 1957.

Berlandier, Luis, and Rafael Chovell. *Diario de Viaje de la Comisión de Límites que Puso el Gobierno de la República.* Mexico City: Juan R. Navarro, 1850.

Blanksten, George I. "Political Groups in Latin America," *American Political Science Review,* LIII (March, 1959), 106–128.

Bolton, Herbert Eugene. *Texas in the Middle Eighteenth Century: Studies in Spanish Colonial History and Administration.* University of California Publications in History, Volume III. Berkeley: University of California Press, 1915.

Bott, Elizabeth. *Family and Social Network.* London: Tavistock Publications, 1957.

Broom, Leonard, and John I. Kitsuse. "The Validation of Acculturation: A Condition to Ethnic Assimilation," *American Anthropologist,* LVII (February, 1955), 44–49.

Browning, Harley L., and S. Dale McLemore. *A Statistical Profile of the Spanish-Surname Population of Texas.* Austin: Bureau of Business Research, 1964.

Cancian, Frank. "The Southern Italian Peasant: World View and Political Behavior," *Anthropological Quarterly*, XXXIV (January, 1961), 1–18.

Clark, Margaret. *Health in the Mexican-American Culture.* Berkeley and Los Angeles; University of California Press, 1959.

Cohen, Albert K. *Delinquent Boys: The Culture of the Gang.* Glencoe: The Free Press, 1955.

Corpus Christi Call. October 10, 1958.

Cumberland, Charles C. "The United States-Mexican Border: A Selective Guide to the Literature of the Region," *Rural Sociology*, Supplement to XXV (June, 1960), 90–102.

Curtin, L. S. M. *Healing Herbs of the Upper Rio Grande.* Santa Fe: Laboratory of Anthropology, 1947.

Dickinson, Robert E. *The Population Problem in Southern Italy: An Essay in Social Geography.* Maxwell School Series, II. Syracuse: Syracuse University Press, 1955.

Dobkins, Betty Eakle. *The Spanish Element in Texas Water Law.* Austin: University of Texas Press, 1959.

Doyon, Bernard, O. M. I. *The Cavalry of Christ on the Rio Grande.* Milwaukee: Bruce Press, 1956.

Eggan, Fred. "Social Anthropology: Methods and Results," *Social Anthropology of North American Tribes.* Edited by Fred Eggan, enlarged edition. Chicago: University of Chicago Press, 1955.

Erasmus, Charles J. *Man Takes Control.* Minneapolis: University of Minnesota Press, 1961.

Fillol, Tomás Roberto. *Social Factors in Economic Development: The Argentine Case.* Cambridge: M.I.T. Press, 1961.

Foscue, Edwin J. "Agricultural History of the Lower Rio Grande Valley Region," *Agricultural History*, VIII (March, 1934), 124–138.

Foster, George M. "Relationships between Spanish and Spanish-American Folk Medicine," *Journal of American Folklore*, 66 (1953), 201–247.

———. "Interpersonal Relations in Peasant Society," *Human Organization*, 19, No. 4 (Winter, 1960–1961), 174–178.

———. "The Dyadic Contract: A Model for the Social Structure of a Mexican Peasant Village," *American Anthropologist*, LXIII (December, 1961), 1173–1193.

———. "The Dyadic Contract in Tzintzuntzan, II: Patron-Client Relationship," *American Anthropologist*, 65, No. 6 (December, 1963), 1280–1294.

Freidson, Eliot. *Patients' Views of Medical Practice*. New York: Russell Sage Foundation, 1961.

Friedmann, F. G. "The World of 'La Miseria'," *Partisan Review*, XX (March–April, 1953), 218–231.

Giddings, Luther. *Sketches of the Campaign in Northern Mexico in Eighteen Hundred Forty Six and Seven*. New York: George P. Putnam and Company, 1853.

Gillin, John. "Ethos and Cultural Aspects of Personality," *Heritage of Conquest*. Edited by Sol Tax. Glencoe: The Free Press, 1952.

————. "Ethos Components in Modern Latin American Culture." *American Anthropologist*, LVII (June, 1955), 488–500.

Glasscock vs. *Parr*, Supplement to Texas Senate Journal, 36th Session (Austin, 1919).

Graf, Leroy P. "Colonizing Projects in Texas South of the Nueces, 1820–1845," *Southwestern Historical Quarterly*, L (April, 1947), 431–449.

————. "The Economic History of the Lower Rio Grande Valley: 1820–1875." Unpublished Ph.D. dissertation, Department of History, Harvard University, 1942.

Hallowell, A. Irving. *Culture and Experience*. Philadelphia: University of Pennsylvania Press, 1955.

Hawker, H. W., M. W. Beck, and R. E. Devereux. *Soil Survey of Hidalgo County, Texas*. Washington: U. S. Department of Agriculture, Bureau of Chemistry, 1925.

Honigmann, John J. *Culture and Ethos of Kaska Society*. Yale University Publications in Anthropology, XL. New Haven: 1949.

————. *The World of Man*. New York: Harper and Brothers, 1959.

Honigmann, John J., and Irma Honigmann. "Notes on Great Whale River Ethos," *Anthropologica*, n.s., 1 (1959), 1–16.

Hudson, Wilson M. (Ed.). *The Healer of Los Olmos and Other Mexican Lore*. Dallas: Texas Folklore Society, XXIV, 1951.

Ianni, Francis A. J. "The Italo-American Teen-Ager," *Teen-Age Culture*. Edited by Jesse Bernard. The Annals of the American Academy of Political and Social Science, CCCXXXVIII (1961), 70–78.

James, Bernard J. "Some Critical Observations concerning Analyses of Chippewa 'Atomism' and Chippewa Personality," *American Anthropologist*, LVI (April, 1954), 283–286.

Kelly, Isabel. *Folk Practices in North Mexico*. Austin: University of Texas Press, 1965.

Kenly, John R. *Memoirs of a Maryland Volunteer*. Philadelphia: J. B. Lippincott and Company, 1873.

Kluckhohn, Clyde. *Navaho Witchcraft*. Papers of the Peabody Museum of American Archaeology and Ethnology, Volume XXII, Cambridge: 1944.

————. "Values and Value Orientation," *Toward a General Theory of Action*. Edited by Talcott Parsons and Edward A. Shils. Cambridge: Harvard University Press, 1954.

Kluckhohn, Florence R., and Fred L. Strodtbeck. *Variations in Value Orientations*. Evanston: Row, Peterson & Co., 1961.

Kroeber, Alfred L. *Cultural and Natural Areas of Native North America*. University of California Publications in American Archeology and Ethnology. Berkeley: University of California Press, 1939.

————. *Anthropology*. New York: Harcourt, Brace and Company, 1948.

Kupferer, Harriet J. Unpublished Field Notes.

Landes, Ruth. *The Ojibwa Woman*. New York: Columbia University Press, 1938.

————. "The Personality of the Ojibwa," *Character and Personality*, VI, No. 1 (1937–1938), 51–60.

Leeds, Anthony. "Brazilian Careers and Social Structure: An Evolutionary Model and Case History," *American Anthropologist*, 66, No. 6 (December, 1964), 1321–1348.

Lewis, Oscar. *Five Families*. New York: Basic Books, 1959.

————. *The Children of Sánchez*. New York: Random House, 1961.

————. "Review of *Now We Are Civilized*, by Charles Leslie," *Rural Sociology*, XXVI (September, 1961), 309–310.

————. "Urbanization Without Breakdown: A Case Study," *The Scientific Monthly*, LXXV (July, 1952), 31–41.

Lieban, Richard W. "Sorcery, Illness, and Social Control in a Philippine Municipality," *Southwestern Journal of Anthropology*, XVI (Summer, 1960), 127–143.

Lin, Paul Ming-Chang. "Voluntary Kinship and Voluntary Association in a Mexican-American Community," Unpublished Master of Arts thesis, University of Kansas, 1963.

Linton, Ralph. *The Study of Man*. New York: D. Appleton-Century Company, 1936.

Lopreata, Joseph. "Interpersonal Relations: The Peasant's View," *Human Organization*, 21, No. 1 (1962), 21–24.

Lowie, Robert H. *An Introduction to Cultural Anthropology* (Revised Edition). New York: Farrar and Rhinehart, 1940.

Macklin, June. "The Curandera and Structural Stability in Mexican-American Culture: A Case Study." A paper presented to the American Anthropological Association, Chicago, 1962.

Madsen, William. "Shamanism in Mexico," *Southwestern Journal of Anthropology*, 11, No. 1 (1955), 48–57.

————. "Hot and Cold in the Universe of San Francisco Tecospa, Valley of Mexico," *Journal of American Folklore*, 68 (April–June, 1955), 123–139.

————. *The Mexican-Americans of South Texas*. New York: Holt, Rinehart, and Winston, 1964.

Metraux, Rhoda, and Margaret Mead. *Themes in French Culture: A Preface to a Study of French Community*. Hoover Institute Studies, Series D: Communities, Number 1. Stanford: Stanford University Press, 1954.

Metzler, William H., and Frederic O. Sargent. *Incomes of Migratory Agricultural Workers, Bulletin 950*. College Station: Texas Agricultural Experiment Station, March, 1960.

Mintz, Sidney, and Eric R. Wolf. "An Analysis of Ritual Co-Parenthood (Compadrazgo)" *Southwestern Journal of Anthropology*, 6, No. 4 (Winter, 1950), 341–369.

Mireles, Jovita González. "Social Life in Cameron, Starr, and Zapata Counties." Unpublished Master's thesis, University of Texas, 1930.

Morse, Richard M. "Latin American Cities: Aspects of Structure and Functions," *Comparative Studies in Society and History*, No. 4 (July, 1962), pp. 473–493.

Moss, Leonard W. "Review of: *Moral Basis of a Backward Society*, by Edward C. Banfield," *American Sociological Review*, XXIII (December, 1958), 760.

Moss, Leonard W., and Stephen C. Cappannari. "Patterns of Kinship, Comparaggio and Community in a South Italian Village," *Anthropological Quarterly*, XXXIIII (January, 1960), 24–32.

Moss, Leonard W., and W. H. Thomson. "The South Italian Peasant: Literature and Observation," *Human Organization*, XVIII (Spring, 1959), 35–42.

Murdock, George P. *Social Structure*. New York: The Macmillan Company, 1949.

Naroll, Raoul, and Roy G. D'Andrade. "Two Further Solutions to Galton's Problem," *American Anthropologist*, 65 (October, 1963), 1053–1067.

Parisot, P. F., O.M.I. *The Reminiscences of a Texas Missionary*. San Antonio: Johnson Brothers Printing Company, 1899.

Paul, Benjamin. "Ritual Kinship with Special Reference to Godparenthood in Middle America." Unpublished Ph.D. Dissertation, University of Chicago, 1942.

Pitkin, Donald S. "A Consideration of Asymmetry in the Peasant-City Relationship," *Anthropological Quarterly*, XXXII (October, 1959), 164.

Pitt-Rivers, Julian. *The People of the Sierra*. London: Nicholson and Weidenreich, 1954.

————. Paper delivered at the Annual Meeting of the American Anthropological Association, November, 1961.

Pitts, Jesse R. "The Bourgeois Family and French Economic Retardation," Unpublished Ph.D. dissertation, Harvard University, 1957.

————. "The Family and Peer Groups," *A Modern Introduction to the Family*. Edited by Norman Bell and Ezra Vogel. Glencoe: The Free Press, 1960.

Radcliffe-Brown, A. R. *Structure and Function in Primitive Society*. London: Cohen and West, 1952.

Rankin, Melinda. *Twenty Years among the Mexicans: A Narrative of Missionary Labor*. Cincinnati: Chase and Hall, Publishers, 1875.

Redfield, Robert. *The Folk Culture of Yucatán*. Chicago: The University of Chicago Press, 1941.

————. *The Little Community*. Chicago: University of Chicago Press, 1955.

————. *Peasant Society and Culture*. Chicago: University of Chicago Press, 1956.

Reichel-Dolmatoff, Gerardo, and Alicia Reichel-Dolmatoff. *The People of Aritama*. Chicago: University of Chicago Press, 1961.

Reissman, Leonard. *Class in American Society*. Glencoe: The Free Press, 1959.

Report on the World Social Situation. New York: United Nations, 1957.

Romano, Ignacio Octavio V. "Donship in a Mexican-American Community in Texas," *American Anthropologist*, LXII (December, 1960), 966–976.

Rubel, Arthur J. "Concepts of Disease in Mexican-American Culture," *American Anthropologist*, 62, No. 5 (October, 1960), 795–814.

————. "The Epidemiology of a Folk Illness: Susto in Hispanic America," *Ethnology*, III, No. 3 (July, 1964), 268–283.

————. "The Mexican-American Palomilla," *Anthropological Linguistics*, 7, No. 4 (April, 1965), 92–97.

Rubel, Arthur J., and Harriet J. Kupferer. "The Atomistic-Type Society." Paper presented to the American Anthropological Association, San Francisco, 1963.

Samora, Julian, *et. al.* "Medical Vocabulary Knowledge among Hospital Patients," *Journal of Health and Human Behavior*, No. 2 (1961), 83–92.

Samora, Julian, and Richard F. Larson. "Rural Families in an Urban Setting: A Study in Persistence and Change," *Journal of Human Relations*, 9, No. 4 (1961), 494–503.

Sánchez, José María, "A Trip to Texas in 1828," *The Southwestern Historical Quarterly*, XXIX (April, 1926), 249–289. Translated by Carlos R. Castañeda.

Saunders, Lyle. "The Spanish-Speaking Population of Texas," *Inter-American Education; Occasional Papers*, No. 5. Austin: University of Texas Press, 1949.

————. *Cultural Difference and Medical Care: The Case of the Spanish-*

Speaking People of the Southwest. New York: Russell Sage Foundation, 1954.

Schoolcraft, Henry R. *Information Respecting the History, Conditions and Prospects of the Indian Tribes of the United States,* quoted in A. I. Hallowell, *Culture and Experience,* p. 143.

Schulman, Sam. "Rural Health Ways in New Mexico." In *Culture, Society and Health, Vera Rubin* (Editor). Annals of the New York Academy of Sciences, 84 (December, 1960), 950–959.

Scott, Florence Johnson. "Customs and Superstitions among Texas Mexicans," *Publications of the Texas Folk-Lore Society,* II (1923), 75–85.

———. *Historical Heritage of the Lower Rio Grande.* San Antonio: The Naylor Company, 1937.

Silone, Ignacio. *Fontamara.* Revised edition. New York: Dell Laurel, 1961.

Simmons, Ozzie G. "Anglo-Americans and Mexican-Americans in South Texas." Unpublished Ph.D. dissertation, Department of Social Relations, Harvard University, 1952.

———. "The Mutual Images and Expectations of Anglo-Americans and Mexican-Americans," *Daedalus* (Spring, 1961), pp. 286–299.

Sjoberg, Gideon. "Comparative Urban Sociology," *Sociology Today: Problems and Prospects.* Edited by Robert K. Merton, Leonard Broom, Leonard S. Cottrell, Jr. New York: Basic Books, Inc., 1959.

Stambaugh, J. Lee, and Lillian J. Stambaugh. *The Lower Rio Grande Valley of Texas.* San Antonio: The Naylor Company, 1954.

Steward, Julian H. *Theory of Culture Change.* Urbana: University of Illinois Press, 1955.

Strickon, Arnold. "Class and Kinship in Argentina," *Ethnology,* I, No. 4 (October, 1962), 500–515.

Strong, Donald S. "The Rise of Negro Voting in Texas," *The American Political Science Review,* XXIV, No. 3 (August, 1930), 510–522.

Taylor, Paul S. "Note on Streams of Mexican Migration," *American Journal of Sociology,* XXXVI, No. 2 (September, 1930), 287–288.

Tienda de Cuervo's Inspection of Nuevo Santander, 1757, quoted in Betty Earle Dobkins: *The Spanish Element in Texas Water Law.*

Tylor, E. B. "On a Method of Investigating the Development of Institutions Applied to the Laws of Marriage and Descent," *Journal of the Royal Anthropological Institute,* 18 (1889), 243–272.

Vailland, Roger. *The Law.* New York: Alfred A. Knopf, 1958.

Verga, Giuseppe. *The House by the Medlar Tree.* New York: Doubleday and Company, 1955.

Vielé, Mrs. [Egbert L.]. *Following the Drums: A Glimpse of Frontier Life.* New York: Rudd and Carlton, 1858.

Wagley, Charles, and Marvin Harris. "A Typology of Latin American Sub-Cultures," *American Anthropologist,* LVII (June, 1955), 428–451.

Weatherford, Willis. *Geographical Differentials of Agricultural Wages in the United States*. Harvard Studies of Labor in Agriculture. Cambridge: Harvard University Press, 1957.

Weeks, O. Douglas. "The League of United Latin-American Citizens: A Texas-Mexican Civic Organization," *The Southwestern Political and Social Science Quarterly*, X (December, 1929), 257–279.

————. "The Texas-Mexican and the Politics of South Texas," *American Political Science Review*, XXIV, No. 3 (August, 1930), 583–627.

Wheat, James D. "A Study of the Midwife Problem in Cameron and Hidalgo Counties," Unpublished typescript in the author's possession.

Whetten, Nathan. *Rural Mexico*. Chicago: The University of Chicago Press, 1948.

Whiteford, Andrew H. *Two Cities of Latin America: A Comparative Description of Social Classes*. Publications in Anthropology, Bulletin Number Nine. Beloit: Logan Museum of Anthropology, 1960.

Whiting, Beatrice B. "Paiute Sorcery," *Viking Fund Publications in Anthropology*, No. 15. New York: 1950.

Whyte, William Foote. "A Challenge to Political Scientists," *The American Political Science Review*, XXXVII (August, 1943), 692–697.

————. *Street Corner Society: The Social Structure of An Italian Slum*. Chicago: The University of Chicago Press, 1955.

Williamson, Rene. *Culture and Policy*. Knoxville: University of Tennessee Press, 1949.

Wilson, Godfrey, and Monica Wilson. *The Analysis of Social Change*. Cambridge: University Press, 1945.

GLOSSARY

(Unless otherwise noted, all words and phrases in this list are Spanish.)

abuelita: an endearing form of "grandmother." Sometimes used to distinguish a maternal grandmother from a paternal grandmother.

a cada cabeza un mundo: each head is a world unto itself.

a falta de padres, padrinos: when parents are lacking, then godparents.

ahijado: a godchild.

amigo de confianza: an especially close friend who serves as one's confidante.

angel de guarda: a guardian angel.

animalitos: the dimunitive of "animal"; refers to any small animal as well as to insects and micro-organisms.

asustado: the condition of a person who suffers from a *susto*.

ataque de corazón: a heart attack.

autoritá (Italian): one who controls the power to command others to do his bidding.

ayudar a la gente: to be of assistance to the people of *la raza*.

barrios: sections or neighborhoods in a town or village of Mexico.

bolillos: a slang term referring to Anglo-Americans.

brujería: witchcraft.

cabellos: human hairs.

cabrones: literally, male goats, but usually used to refer to distasteful people; cuckolds.

caída de la mollera: an illness presumed caused by the fall of the fontanel; only young children are susceptible.

campanalismo (Italian): village parochialism in Italy.

cantinas: beer halls.

capo (Italian): a noncommissioned officer.

castigo de Díos: a punishment from God.

chicanazgo: the entire territory inhabited by the *chicanos*.

chicanos: from the Spanish *Mexicano*; it has reference to the Spanish-speaking people of Texas, differentiating them from the *manos* or *manitos* of New Mexico.

chiflando: whistling.

chupar: to suck or sip.

civile (Italian): to be polite or amiable.

clase obrero: the working class.

colonia parziaria (Italian): the practice of renting or sharecropping a plot of land.

comandante (Italian): an authoritative figure.

compradrazgo: a system by which people enter into kinlike relationships with one another; for example, the relationship between godparents and their god-children.

compadre: the reciprocal term used between the parent and godfather of a child.

compadres de casamiento: a man and woman who together have sponsored the wedding of one's child.

compadres de pila: a man and woman who together have sponsored the baptism of one's child.

compartecipazione (Italian):   the practice of renting or share cropping a plot of land.

compartimento (Italian):   region, a political unit.

conuños: the husbands of sisters.

cuñada: a sister-in-law.

cuñado: a brother-in-law.

curandero: a lay healer who practices by virtue of a gift from God.

diario: a custom whereby the prospective groom gives the bride's parents a sum of money intended to demonstrate his ability to maintain her.

Don; don: a title awarded a respected man, thus, Don Pedro; a gift from God.

¿donde andas?:   where are you?

duce (Italian):   a dictator.

echó algo: literally, "he threw something," but in context, "he caused something to be intruded into the body of the victim."

egoísta y rencorista: egotistical and malicious.

el centro: downtown.

el deber de los hijos: the obligation of the children to care for their parents when the latter are no longer able to care for themselves. This concept carries with it strong overtones of expected repayment for the earlier effort expended by the parents in bringing up their children.

el lado americano: in New Lots, the south side of the tracks, where the Anglo segment of the population lives.

el mero palomilla: those male friends with whom one most often associates, as distinguished from those acquaintances with whom one sometimes associates.

el oso: the bear.

el perdido se va a todo: he who is lost tries anything.

el problema: a stressful period for a girl, the time when she indicates a desire to marry and thus to leave the household of her parents.

el pueblo americano: in New Lots, the south side of the tracks, where the Anglo segment of the population lives.

el pueblo mexicano: in New Lots, the north side of the tracks, where the chicano segment of the population lives.

empacho: an illness presumably brought on by the sticking of a piece of food to the intestinal tract.

enerine: an herbal potion.

ensalme: a prayer which is said for the ill.

envidia: envy for the goods or well-being of another. *Envidia* is often assumed to take the form of witchcraft.

espíritu: the soul.

fiscal y juez: prosecutor and judge.

fratello-cugino (Italian):   a first cousin.

fregados: a noun which refers to people who annoy one.

gavachos: a slang term used to refer to Anglos.

gringo: a slang term used to refer to Anglos.

gritos: loud, triumphant cries peculiar to males; a huzza.

hábito: the replica of a gown worn by one of the images in church. It is blessed by a priest and worn by a gravely ill person. The *hábito* may also be worn by someone who is very close to the patient.

haciendo la cruz: a reference to a single individual's sponsoring the baptisms of three brothers and/or sisters.

haciendo movida, hay mucha movida: the act of stirring up activity, often used in reference to activating the presumably dormant chicano group to participate in political affairs.

hay voy: colloquial for "I am coming."

hermana: a sister.

hermano: a brother.

hiel: bile or gall.

hijas: female children (daughters).

hijos: an individual's male children or the collectivity of his children, both male and female.

hizo cuerpo: [he] moved his bowels.

il nucleo central (Italian):   the nuclear family.

intercambio: an exchange [of services].

interesse (Italian):   advantage, usually used in terms of advantage for one's nuclear family.

jefe de la casa: head of the household.

jefe de la família: head of the family.

la famiglia (Italian):   one's kin, including those to whom one is related by marriage.

la gente: literally, "the people," but usually has reference only to chicanos.

la greta: lead protoxite.

la lux mexicana: one of the traffic lights located on the north side of the tracks. At one time, it was the only traffic light located in *el pueblo mexicano*.

la raza: the Spanish-speaking people of the world.

la sociedad para ti es la suciedad para mi: that which is sociability for you is filth for me.

liga: a charm which binds one person or animal to another.

los agraciados: the recipients of land grants and their descendants.

los fierros: literally, "the irons," but more specifically the forceps.

los medianos: those of modest income.

los rinches: colloquial reference to the Texas Rangers.

los tuvos: a scornful allusion to chicanos who once were rich and powerful by virtue of being landowners, but who are no longer better socially or economically than others.

los vecinos: the neighbors, referring to those who live immediately next door as well as to those who reside in the same general neighborhood.

lumbre: fire or bright light of any kind.

madrina de hábito: a woman who is a ritual kin by virtue of having purchased and sponsored the blessing of an *hábito* to be worn by a patient.

madrugaron: reference to two or more people who remained awake together until dawn.

mal artificial: a class of illness presumedly caused by the malevolent intent of others, in contrast to illness caused by natural means.

mal de ojo: a natural illness presumedly caused unwittingly by the covetous gaze of another.

mal natural: a class of illness presumedly caused by natural means, in contrast to *mal artificial*.

mal puesto: illness which is caused by witchcraft or sorcery, usually used synonymously with *mal artificial*.

mamá grande: a grandmother; sometimes used to distinguish a paternal grandmother from a maternal grandmother.

mamar: to suckle.

media molestia: a little annoyance.

medicinas caseras: household remedies.

mediero: a sharecropper whose portion is half the proceeds of a harvest.

mero amigo de confianza: a very close friend.

Mezzogiorno (Italian): Southern Italy, inclusive of the regions of Abruzzi e Molise, Campania, Apulia, Basilicata (Lucania), Calabria.

molestia: an annoyance.

molino: a mill for grinding corn and other grains.

mollera: the fontanel.

mortificaciónes: the vexations or torments which afflict an individual.

mosca: a verbal thrust made at the expense of another.

muy feo: embarrassment.

muy recto: very correct.

nixtamal: corn dough used in the preparation of tortillas.

norteños: the people who trace their cultural heritage to northern Mexico. In Mexiquito it refers particularly to those from the northeastern regions of Mexico.

nuestro lado: our side [of the tracks].

ojo: colloquial for "mal de ojo."

pachuco: a term which refers to young Mexican-Americans who dress in a distinctive fashion and speak an argot, which distinguishes them from their elders and from Anglos as well.

padeciendo: suffering.

padrino: a godfather.

padrinos de bautismo: those who have sponsored a child's baptism.

padrinos de pila: those who have sponsored a child's baptism.

paesano (Italian): one's fellow villager.

palo blanco: a tree found in South Texas.

paloma: a dove.

palomilla: a covey of doves and, by extension, those youths and young men with whom one regularly associates.

pandillas: a term used elsewhere to refer to the same association described by palomilla in Mexiquito.

paño: a handkerchief.

parientes: kinsmen.

parteras: midwives.

pecho a pecho: literally, "chest-to-chest," a confrontation.

pelóns: bald-headed individuals.

peóns: agricultural workers who, prior to the Mexican Revolution, were commonly kept in bondage by debts owed to the landowner.

perra fina: a thoroughbred dog; a lap dog.

pescar brujos: a technique for catching witches.

pirul: a bush used for medicinal purposes.

podere (Italian): the isolated family farm of Central Italy.

pogroms (Russian): an organized massacre, especially of Jews.

poner mal: to cause illness by the intrusion of an object into the victim's body or by other deliberate activities.

portador: a respected person who assumes responsibility to represent the suit of a young man to the parents of his intended bride.

pozos: wells or holes dug in the ground.

preoccupazione (Italian): a state of mingled worry, fear, anxiety, and foreboding.

presión: high blood pressure.

primos: cousins.

primos hermanos: first cousins.

pulmonía: pneumonia.

puro palomilla: a reference to acquaintances or friends, separating them from strangers.

que vívas: wishes of well-being.

quinceaños: a fifteenth birthday; a particularly important milestone in the life of a girl, but not in that of a young man.

ranchero: the inhabitant of a ranch or isolated hamlet; a shy or timid person.

recto: correct.

remedios: remedies.

respaldado: supported; literally, backed [up].

robamientos: elopements.

robando la nóvia: the act of elopement, phrased as if the girl were only a passive participant.

robar [la novia]: literally, "to rob," but in context it refers to stealing (eloping with) one's sweetheart.

Santos no puede si Díos no quiere: [even] saints cannot heal if God is not willing.

sarampión: measles.

se volvía loca: she showed signs of insanity.

sobrina: niece.

sobrino: nephew.

susto: an illness associated with the loss of one's soul.

susto complicado: an illness associated with multiple instances of soul loss.

susto nuevo: a traumatic experience occasioning a loss of soul in a person whose previous illness has not yet been completely healed.

susto pasado: a soul loss which is still unhealed.

tis: tuberculosis.

tomateros: a colloquial expression which refers to persons who earn their
  living by working in the fields.

tumor: a tumor.

vara: a measurement of approximately three feet; also a small branch.

vela: a candle or a suppository.

velório: a vigil or wake over the corpse.

vivía asustado: I lived in fear.

INDEX

Abel: 120, 122, 126, 130, 133
Abelardo: 149–150
Abrám: 83, 133, 134, 152
Abruzzi e Molise, Italy: 220, 221
agraciados. SEE gentry
agriculture: 27, 221. SEE ALSO migratory workers
ahijado: 81–82
American Legion: 153
amigo de confianza: 112, 209
Anglo-American–Mexican-American relations: general, 3–7, 44–48, 91, 122–123, 204; in education, 11, 44; discrimination in, 19, 20; socially, 20, 22, 79, 206; in business, 22; historically, 37–41, 51, 242; politically, 49–50, 123–133 *passim*; in medicine, 193–198; outside New Lots, 209, 211–213; mentioned, 24, 25, 171
Antonio: 74
anxiety and disaffection: avoidance of, 80–81; reasons for, 80, 126, 149, 153, 203, 206–207, 214, 239; manifestations of, 89, 90, 126, 129, 141–145, 149–155 *passim*, 168, 210, 255; existence of, 154, 204, 207, 232; in South Italy, 224, 230, 231; lack of, 237–238; and atomistic society, 237, 239
Apache Indians: 26
Apulia, Italy: 220
Aritama, Colombia: social relations in, 217–220
Arkansas: 92, 150
atomistic-type society: definition of, 207, 239; in different cultures, 216, 234–235; and anxiety and disaffection, 237, 239; mentioned, 118, 207
Arturo: 163, 165
Austin, Texas: 243
Avellino, Italy: social relations in, 220, 226–227
Azogue (quicksilver): 167

Bagnoli del Trigno, Italy: social relations in, 227–228

Báldemar: 57, 112, 122
Banfield, Edward C.: 220–232 *passim*
baptism: 81–82
Baptists: 7, 32
Barnouw, Victor: 234
Basilicata. SEE Lucania
Beef Trust: 20
Benítez, Mrs.: 163–165
Benjamín: 121
bereavement: and *palomilla*, 114–118
Bexar County: 128
Bible-Study Class: 20
Block (family): 37
bolillos: 7
Border City, Texas: social relations in, 210–215
Brethren of the Sacred Heart: 218
Brown, Mrs.: 159
Brownsville, Texas: 31, 35, 43, 193, 243

Cadereyta, Mexico: 26
Caída de la mollera: 182
Calabria, Italy: 220, 229–232
Calderón: 104
Caldo: 106
Calvo: 151
Campania, Italy: 220
Cancian, Frank: 226–227
Carranza, Venustiano: 43
Catholic War Veterans: 152
Catholic parochial school: 10, 23
Catholics. SEE Roman Catholicism
Cerralvo, Mexico: 26
Chamber of Commerce: 20
chicanazgo: 213
chicanos: definition of, 7
Chico: 122
Chippewa. SEE Ojibwa Indians
chiropractor: 175
Christians: 7
Christian Science: 7
church. SEE religion; individual denominations
citizenship: 8, 48, 244